The
Dragon's
Eye

Envisioning
Women's Wisdom

Herta Payson

Matrix Press

Grateful acknowledgement is made to: Dylan Thomas: "Poems of Dylan Thomas" © 1945, The Trustees for the © of Dylan Thomas. Reprinted by permission of New Directions Pub. Co.; to Yale University Press for permission to quote from Olga Broumas "Begining With O" © 1977; to Routledge for permission to quote from "A Dictionary of Symbols, 2nd.ed, "Mandorla", pub. 1971; to the American College Dictionary, ed. .C.L. Barnhart, © 1968 for permission to quote the definition of "wisdom"; to HarperCollins for permission to quote from Barbara Walker's "Dictionary of Symbols and Sacred Objects" © 1988, Barbara Walker's "The Women's Encyclopedia of Myths and Secrets" © 1983, and from "Truth or Dare" by Starhawk © 1988;. Excerpts from FOUR QUARTETS, © 1943 by T.S. Eliot and renewed 1971 by Esme Valerie Eliot, reprinted by permission of Harcourt Brace & Company.

Publisher's Cataloging-in-Publication Data
Payson, Herta, 1933-
The dragon's eye: envisioning women's wisdom / by Herta Payson
272p. : :ill.; 21cm.
Includes bibliographical references and index
ISBN 0-9659389-2-1
1. Women--Psychology. 2. Intuition. 3. Wisdom. 4. Women--Mythology. 5. Self-actualization(Psychology)
HQ1206.P3394 1998
Library of Congress Catalog Card Number: 97-94239

Matrix Press
Box 119
Groton, CT, 06340

Printed in the United States of America on recycled, acid free paper

First Edition

10 9 8 7 6 5 4 3 2

THE CHARGE

FROM THE GODDESS, MOTHER OF US ALL

I stand on the edge of the world. My head brushes into the clouds, my feet grow roots into the earth. I made this world, and you within it, and I am angry that it has been so damaged. My eyes, so tender with your love, shoot lightning bolts into the black and gathering clouds. How dare they so destroy my beauty?

You, little one, and all your sisters, near and far, join hands however you may, keep strong in your resolve to find your true way of knowing. Within your Heart, Herta, Earth may find the way to heal. Turn the letters of your name, respelling on your fingers, dance the e, the a, the h, watch them shift and slide to form the new, familiar word. The earth needs heart, to make the turn, Herta must bring her weaving to join with Kathleen's poems, Jennifer's sight, Patricia's words, Karen's art. Priestesses all, artists all, passionate followers and makers of truth, search and find each other, meet and mingle, share and grow. Creating the Mysteries anew, return to your inherent knowing, shredding the veils of illusion, doubt and fear. It is your right, your destiny, and your delight. The time for hiding has past. The time for emerging is NOW.

Blessed Be.

For the Goddess,

Immanent and Manifest

and for Betty

CONTENTS

∞ **Preface** ∞   i

∞ **A** ∞   1

Flight
View from Above

∞ **B** ∞   19

Living in Cycles
The Process

∞ **C** ∞   29

Beginning
First Circle: Virgin, Child

∞ **D** ∞   41

Holding the Wonder
First Intersection: Child into Woman

∞ **E** ∞   53

What Is a Woman?
Second Circle: Woman, Mother

∞ **F** ∞   65

Unwinding the Spell
Second Intersection: Woman into Elder

∞ **G** ∞   81

Remembering Wisdom
Third Circle: Sophia, Wise Woman

∞ **H** ∞   **93**

Tell Me a Story
Third Intersection: WOW to child

∞ **I** ∞   **105**

The Dragon's Eye

∞ **J** ∞   **123**

Medusa: The Myth Unfolded

∞ **K** ∞   **139**

Wise Body
Third Circle: Second Cycle

∞ **L** ∞   **153**

Magical Woman
Second Circle: Second Cycle

∞ **M** ∞   **165**

Can You Imagine...?
First Circle: Second Cycle

∞ **N** ∞   **177**

Ancient Connections
Overlap: Three Mandorlas

∞ **O** ∞   **191**

In My End Is My Beginning

∞ **Appendix** ∞   **211**

∞ **Endnotes** ∞   **217**

∞ **Selected Bibliography** ∞   **245**

∞ **Index** ∞   **253**

∞Preface∞

I am interested in the inner knowing of women, the wisdom which rises intuitively from deep within and is felt in our bones. This is the ancient knowledge, knowledge of healing, of earth cycles, of the mysteries of birth and death, of the language of the animals.

We seem to have lost connection with this knowledge. Centuries of repression, of denial, of fear, as well as actual elimination of wise women who were carriers of the wisdom, have removed even the memory of knowing. Both men and women have suffered from this disconnection and men, too, are becoming aware of the need for attention to their inner knowing. In this book I focus on the experience of women, for this is what I can know intimately, and it is woman who has been denied, both in her physical being and in the inner Feminine. It is time for reclamation. There is a new awareness surfacing among many women as we seek to recover our true selves.

I believe that one way to facilitate this recovery is to attend to the small, secret memories of childhood. When we were young children, we often did not know things were impossible. A child hears angels talking or sees a beautiful sky woman or practices jumping down stairs quietly until she can float over a number of steps without touching them. Some see auras around people, some have clear communication with animals. Adults tell them they must be imagining it, they dreamed it, adults make children afraid to tell these wonders by mocking, ignoring, or punishing.

The child often does not know anything is unusual until the adult reacts. These things that happen, these abilities, are so natural that the child thinks everyone must be able to do what she can do, see what she sees. Once she finds out that her family, her friends, her teachers, do not understand, she represses her knowledge and ability and conforms to the expected pattern of being human.

I believe that if we women can remember and reclaim these memories, these gifts which we had as children we will be able to access our long lost knowledge. Sometimes the memory is so deeply hidden we may not realize it is there until something reminds us. Sometimes it is the secret we never told because we knew, somehow, we wouldn't be believed. Sometimes it is an ability or knowledge we use in our present lives but don't understand. For a fortunate few, the ability has been nourished and accepted.

Our world is in a disastrous state for we have lost touch with the rhythms of this planet Earth and are rushing towards ecological catastrophe.[1] We are at war with each other on every level of human interaction. Changing these patterns into which we seem locked will demand a change of the basic paradigm. We all must allow our basic assumptions and expectations to expand into other realms of understanding if we are to survive. Women can lead the way in this recovery; the world needs our perceptions and understandings in order to right the imbalance from which we suffer. We must rebalance our presence on this planet. I believe the reclamation and development of our natural abilities and ancient knowledge has the potential to make possible humanity's continued existence.

These pages chronicle a journey of exploration and discovery, a search for woman's deep knowing, lost for centuries, and only now beginning to emerge. It is my personal journey, with support from many women who shared their gifts with me. Men also have a journey to undertake, to discover themselves and the Feminine complement to their Masculine. Each of us undertakes the process in ways unique to the individual, yet the experiences of us all intermingle, supporting, informing, developing, growing at last into a cohesive whole. We each came into this life with our own gifts. Our struggle is to know these gifts and to make them part of our lives.

There is a spiral rhythm to the chapters which invites the reader to journey along with me and the women who have contributed their stories and their energies. Beginning in the first two chapters with an introduction to the content, intent, and process, we enter the circling at childhood, continue to middle age and mothering, coming then to the wisdom of the wise older woman. Each of these three circles overlaps another, and within each overlap is time for reflection on the energies the interface contains. Thus between child and mother we look for ways to keep the wisdom of the child intact in the transition to adulthood; between mother and elder the subject of women identified with evil is explored, while the connection between the wise older woman and child is the telling of stories.

Moving within the three circles image, we enter the labyrinth, circling into another dimension, to discover the truth of the body of woman. The Dragon's Eye leads us into the realm of Medusa, enabling an exploration into another aspect of the Triple Goddess and an opportunity to retrieve the myth of the fearful snake-haired woman. Within this story we reclaim our right to our passion, our bodies, and our woman selves.

The visit with Medusa is completed within the wise woman circle and we return to the heart of the labyrinth. With our new-found connection with body and center, we cycle again into the Earth, exploring magic and relationship from the perspective of the second circle. Coming then to the place from which we began, we imagine a world where as children our special gifts are recognized, encouraged, and developed, a place where all our stories are honored.

In the center of the three overlapping circles is a place where all three merge. Here we see the necessity for interconnection and explore a way of being in the world which engages our woman selves. Finally, recognizing the end is also the beginning, a story emerges which bodies forth this energy and brings this journey to conclusion.

The chapters are identified by letter rather than number for two reasons. First, I wished to stay as much as possible within an alternative form, ever more conscious of the subtleties of the hierarchical system within which we live. Second, it seemed appropriate to begin with A and end with O, Alpha and Omega, for the end and the beginning are always present, as T. S. Eliot has so skillfully told us,[2] and as the cycle of the seasons makes clear.

*   *   *

It has been wonderful to work with the women who responded to my inquiries. I am deeply grateful to them and for the opportunity to share in their stories. Their names are listed in the appendix, as well as a compilation of their experiences. I received a great deal of support from many people. I am grateful to William McKelvie, Bethe Hagens and The Union Institute which fosters creative and innovative work. Nettie Tamler, Rhea White, Linda Herr and Judith Aubrecht helped me in many essential ways. I thank Edith Sullwold for her gracious presence, Lori Weinstock Wynters and Jean Troy-Smith for their love and sharing of their expertise, and Kathy Medbury, Pat Stamm, Bettie Chu, Mary Mangano, Joyce Chandler, Lucy Eddinger, Kathleen DesMaisons, and Myles Laffey for their consistent encouragement. Gail Gavert provided editorial expertise and cheerful nurturing. Demaris Wehr gave me wonderful enthusiasm at just the right time. I thank Christine Downing whose living example has often nudged me to the edge.

This has been a family endeavor: my son, Allen Joslin, has been incredibly patient as he guided me through my endless struggles to understand my computer while son David Joslin brought his talent as an artist to the cover design. My daughter, Rachel Whitehouse, gave of her skill in public relations, and Betty's faith and patience has been unending. I am grateful, too, to my clients, many of whose journeys take them on paths similar to mine. This has been a labour of love, and I have felt the Presence in countless ways. I give deep thanks.

∞ A ∞

Flight

View from Above

Tiberon, May, 1994.
Sitting on a hill that edges out over the bay, I watch the swallows catch the downdraft. Wind comes in high and blue today, after the spring rain. Hang gliders float in imitation of the birds, suspended beneath their multi-colored wings like giant butterfly bodies, cocooned against the breeze.

We humans long to soar the heights, following the flight of the black-winged feathers. "Understand," we are told when we are very young, "gravity is a fact of life. You will always fall down, never up." And children grow up to invent new ways to make bird-like wings, believing this is the only way to fly. Paper airplanes float to the school room floor, rubber-banded balsa wings catch in the playground trees or land on the inaccessible roof. "Don't climb up there, you'll fall." Again and again we hear the message, over and over the cells in our bodies learn this truth. Gravity reigns, falling hurts, humans can't fly.

But consider for a moment. How many children secretly remember knowledge of flight? Why must we be told so many times we cannot fly? When I was little, I jumped, one, two, down the steps from the attic apartment. "Sssh" said my parents, "don't disturb the neighbors." They didn't say "Don't fly." So I breathed in light air and floated, one, two, over the steps. When I grew older, I forgot how to do it. Did I let the air inside my lungs seep between my bones? Or was it an energy that shifted gears to take me into flight? I do not know — but I have heard that other children also flew. None of us can do it now.

In the earth beside me is a swelling, small green shoots emerge beside brown bulbous stumps. Some growing thing lived its summer life and then, dying, was cut back to wait till spring would bring rebirth. Now memory stirs and promises return. Forgotten is the rock which lay across the path last year, forcing the stalks to bend themselves around to grow in curious, crooked shapes. This year the stone is kicked aside, and new growth moves directly upward.

Must I be cut back to birth, once more, to regain my own remembrance? Or might I, remembering night dreams of flying, think again of day-time childhood exploration. Might I re-teach my cells, returning them to simpler times, knowing I am not endowed with feathered wings but human consciousness?

Because — consider this. If dreams revisit memories, re-weaving pieces of our lived lives, why then do we so often dream of wingless flight? Where is the archetype which this embodies? Even our angels carry wings upon their backs — yet seldom do we wear them in our dreams. What is the secret?

If you find out, tell me.

* * *

When I was about three or four, we lived in an attic apartment with an enclosed stairwell down which we went about ten steps to a landing, turned left, down a few more steps, and opened the door into the second floor hall. An only child, I was sometimes alone in the apartment while my parents were elsewhere in the house. To entertain myself, I began to experiment with jumping silently over the stairs. With practice, I found I could float over three, then four, then five steps. Eventually I was able to sustain the flight sufficiently to turn the corner at the landing and alight, carefully, on the small oriental rug which rested on the polished hardwood floor of the hall. I was delighted with my accomplishment, but never told anyone, somehow knowing I would be stopped if I were seen. We lived in this place for a few months. In subsequent homes it did not occur to me to try again.

Although I never told anyone about my flying, I always remembered. When I heard that the human brain is largely unused, I was fascinated. What are we supposed to do with those unused parts? The logical answer for me has been that we might use them to do things which seem to have no place in our normal lives.[1] Why, I wondered, cannot everyone know what someone else is thinking, as mind readers and psychics can? If telekinesis is possible for a few, why not me? Why cannot I travel from here to there as easily as I can think about it? Somehow I always knew that while my brain could do these things, my brain also stopped me, telling me they were impossible. But then, I reasoned, I once flew, so the information that I cannot leave the ground in sustained flight is a result of conditioning.

I was born in 1933, into a very different world from the one in which I live today. My parents were interested in occult and mystical matters, but we all knew we had to be careful to whom we talked about such things. Now the world is changing rapidly, and the Age of Aquarius has ushered in a new climate of exploration in which there is a hunger for knowledge of realities which previously were feared and scorned.

Many people are aware, by now, that a change is coming, that the millennium is just around the corner. Morris Berman says: "Western life seems to be drifting toward increasing entropy, economic and technological chaos, ecological disaster, and ultimately, psychic dismemberment and disintegration..." [2] There are many predictions of what form the change will take: earthquakes, floods, famine — these are already upon us. Some say the earth will shift, a tidal wave will wipe out the east coast, the west coast will fall away into the water, and there will be such massive changes in the ecology of the planet that life as we know it can no longer be sustained. Others acknowledge the inevitability of change but feel it will be an evolutionary step into the next level of consciousness. Perhaps we are about to have the modern equivalent of the great flood of biblical times, only this time the ones who will survive to move into the next epoch will be the ones who can develop their extraordinary abilities. I hope for the latter choice, for I love this planet dearly. It has given me from its abundance since I was a small girl, in love with a southern pine.

The writers of fantasy and science fiction have been wondering what such a world would be like. Today we are catching up with some of those ideas; television, computers, fax machines, all would seem like magic boxes to someone from even a hundred years ago yet children today take them for granted, understand how to use them, and rapidly outstrip their parents in that knowledge. Something is missing however, and that something is crucial to our survival and continuance on this planet. We do not seem to be able to stop the headlong slide into disaster by the methods we presently possess.

Psychotherapists and spiritual leaders have been understanding, each in their own way, that the world is lacking in heart, in soul, in spirit.[3] Violence rises in our cities, spreads to our suburbs, infiltrates the farthest reaches of the lonely country roads. Respect and consideration for human life all too often are lacking entirely. It seems most people are intent on getting what they can for themselves, often at the expense of someone else, whether that be a neighbor, a co-worker, or an underpaid laborer in a mill in Taiwan. It matters not. Pain and misery are everywhere, and most of us now suspect that money will not make us happy, although it certainly buys lots of possessions.

I believe that what is missing is a body of knowledge which originates in women. The absence of this knowledge dates back to the matriarchal era, when the rise of the invader overwhelmed the cultural and spiritual practices of the Goddess, sending Her people into hiding and eventually into oblivion during the widespread witchhunts of the 14th and 15th centuries.[4] The knowledge which was hunted down and destroyed at that time was knowledge of healing, of cycles and rhythms of the earth, of simple magic which helped people. When that was gone, finishing off the last remaining pockets of remembrance, woman was completely at the mercy of the patriarchy, the priests and the medical profession; out of touch with the way her body functioned, she came to believe the men truly knew what was best for her. If she had some herbal knowledge, or magical awareness, she was wise if she kept it hidden.[5]

It is not an easy task to reconnect to the wisdom of women. There are so many ways in which this knowledge is suppressed, its energy and power discouraged. Women have a deep fear that to be truly connected with one's self, to have access to the inner truth, to allow the voice to sing and the spirit to shout, is intensely dangerous. When the Greeks created the myth of

Medusa, who could turn men to stone with her glance, they made a lasting statement about what happens to strong women who embody their power. Medusa's crime was to lie with Poseidon in the temple of Athena, thus bringing spirit and body together. Her punishment was transformation into the fearful monster. To reconnect with the simple magic of cycles is to move again into relationship with body and earth, but the fear is there that the power thus released brings rejection and death.

The search for wisdom leads into dark corners where old abilities lie, forgotten. For years parapsychologists have been studying people who have experiences which are out of the ordinary. Books are full of these experiences, files stuffed to overflowing in countless offices. People can do unusual things: in such numbers, in fact, that if these abilities were not still considered unusual, they would enter into the mainstream of knowledge and be accepted as normal. With the advent of the Aquarian Age, more psychics, channellers, seers and shamans are appearing and there is an entire sub-culture with numerous magazines of every description, shelves of books in every store. Respected medical doctors and scientists are moving towards a mind, body and spirit integration. Conferences and workshops proliferate with an ever increasing number of attendees. It is clear that the general public is interested, active, and participating in the new paradigm.

Curiously, with all the interest in growth and inner knowledge, something is missing. The particular knowledge of women is still being suppressed. It is returning, gradually, but there is also widespread opposition, witchhunts are still happening in many ways,[6] and there is a lack of full understanding of what this body of knowledge contains. The fearful Medusa is repeatedly created and destroyed. There are mysteries here with which individual women and groups of women are in touch, but the main swell of energy eludes us. We reach too short; we do not allow our minds and souls to believe the writers of fantasy. We think that magic happens on another planet, in another time, and do not consider that it can happen now.

Yet it must. We must reach beyond ourselves, into the other

parts of our brain, access the abilities, uncover the knowledge, remove the repressions which have bound us for centuries. It is not only women who contain this knowledge for it is available to all humans, but it resides in and arises from the Feminine, the Goddess and thus is particularly available to women.[7] This deep Feminine knowing has been systematically wiped out in ways which we are still experiencing, in ways which we do not even know. The search is on for the old knowledge, and we must do everything we can to help recover it, expand it, and incorporate it into our lives.[8]

The method of proceeding is also important, for a purely intellectual approach will not open the doors into the sought-for regions of the mind and soul. C. G. Jung has helped us to understand that humans organize incoming information in a variety of ways. Some are thinkers. Some understand the kinesthetics of our world and are called sensation types. Feeling types comprehend the value of our connections with the stream of history, see events and objects in relationship to others. Some of us receive the majority of our information subjectively, intuiting the next step, reaching into hidden areas for the pieces which we put together to reach conclusions.[9]

To this search I bring an ability to move within each of these areas, but my primary and favorite mode is that of the intuitive, one who places the inner authority in a dominant role. Being also an introvert, I am in a good position to search in the subjective realms of knowledge. My intent here is to map the journey in a variety of modes which are designed to stimulate subjective awareness, and to allow the images to speak. For it is through images that subjective learning largely takes place, and we must become comfortable with the language of the soul if we are to travel in that land.

The dimensionality of the process is elusive. How do you write words in linear fashion which are describing a multidimensional process which is primarily circular, or a spiral ever turning upon itself, as those geometric designs turn on a computer that is waiting for you to request a function? It is that sort of complexity that will allow the emergence and recreation of the body of knowledge. Therefore this writing, which you must read in a consecutive fashion, will offer you images which may echo in your awareness and overlap with others, producing an awareness of still another image which can only be seen by the combination of the two. Cathedrals were often built with the intent of letting just such a thing happen with music; the echo of one musical phrase could linger in the vast height and combine with the next sequence of notes, creating in the listener a sensation of resonating with another dimension entirely, transporting one to the realms of glory. Listen, as you read, watch the images intertwine, let yourself be carried along as my words move through your intelligent mind until they reach your memories, your body's response, the reverberations of your unconscious.

What do you know that you don't know you know?

Think about it.

"What do you know that you don't know you know?"

When I propose this question to a woman, the same thing always happens. The look on her face changes, she shifts to an inner questioning, a listening, there is a pause, and then she nods in understanding. What is it that responds? Where does that question go? Somewhere, hidden behind layers of repression, is knowledge; somewhere there is an answer, as if someone was hiding deep inside, saying "Yes, there is knowing, you have sensed it all along, it is the stirring that has contributed to the groundswell of feminism, of women coming out from a diminished status and requesting, demanding, equality." The origin of the stirring has no name, but it is felt by women as a vague longing, a sense of searching for who knows what, and when the question reaches that origin, it responds affirmatively, "Yes, there is knowledge here, thanks for asking."

A woman has a unique relationship to this knowledge. It is connected to her cycles, to the pull of the moon and the tides that she feels each month. Within the body of a woman a child is conceived, formed, nurtured. Her body shifts its function and labors to bring the child through the birth process; this same body continues to feed and nurture the new being after birth. Woman carries within her a space where this miracle can happen, and she is connected to it, whether or not she ever actually gives birth.   Through connection to her own cycles, woman is attuned to the ways the earth changes, to seeds bursting in the moist darkness, pushing up their green leaves to seek the sun.   She can open her awareness and know the thoughts of the animals who are her friends.   She can touch another body and sense the blockage of energies; her hand can smooth the tension, untangle the knots, and bring a healing.

When a woman is free within herself, she can look at a man and see him as he is: another being, different from herself in body and perspective, with his own particular and unique wisdom.   Harmony between man and woman is a result of recognition and respect for their separate and unique ways of being, knowing and expressing themselves.

When a woman is free within herself, she can look at another woman and see her uniqueness while recognizing the commonality of experience.   Whatever the relationship, be it mother, daughter, lover, friend, women can partner each other with delight in their individuality.

Women's wisdom has been systematically suppressed in so many ways for such a long time that it is difficult to reach through the layers of years to come upon the pure essence which lies within.   It will, however, rise to meet inquiry, it can be invited, and we each have our own portion, a special gift, a certain way we listen, see, and know.

What is this body of knowledge, once familiar, now shrouded and obscure, which we define as women's wisdom?   Because the essence and practice of it was lost, it is hard to know the complete definition.   Clues are surfacing daily, written in books, dreamed, intuited, kept alive in the heart.[10]   As women regain their bodies, possessing once again that which is rightfully theirs, new understandings appear, as a plant emerges in newly tilled soil which previously seemed to be barren.   Seeds will wait until conditions are right; some desert grasses can sprout after a seven-year dormancy.   So the seeds of our knowing lie deep within us, waiting until the shifting of the earth leaves only a thin layer above them and they can push new green shoots into the sun.

There are other clues. We can look to what is suppressed,

notice those things we know we are not supposed to see or do. What have we been told is bad? I work with many people in the exploration of their dreams. Animals are frequent visitors in the night journeys, sometimes frightening, sometimes friendly. After discussion, we sometimes turn to the books of traditional meanings for various symbols, looking for how a particular creature has been understood by means of mythology, tradition, and spiritual connections.[11] It is surprising to discover how many animals, such as the bear, the goat, the spider, are connected with the Devil in Christian traditions, animals which are not related to evil at all in any other culture. Research into Pagan practices and beliefs, however, reveals that these same animals were sacred to the Goddess and important in her rituals of worship and celebration.[12] Knowing the Christian tradition of overlaying Pagan shrines with churches and replacing Pagan statues with images of Jesus, it is not difficult to realize that if an animal is connected with the Devil, it was probably previously related to the Goddess, the connection deliberately shifted to sever the link with the nature-centered religions.

This brings us to a reconnection with Nature, which includes honoring Her as a living being. And we must reach still further, ask our minds to stretch beyond the familiar limits of our world, into a way of being where the Feminine is the Queen. Many women know they are missing some inner connection. Judy Grahn writes of discovering "a terrible gap in myself and in the world, the missing Greater Feminine, missing in public life, and missing in the origin stories of history, science, art, religion, and literature." [13]

What do you know that you don't know you know?

* * *

When you were a child, was there something you could do that you later found out others could not, did you see things that your parents did not, could you hear sounds that no one else seemed to hear? How many of you remember that you could tell what other people were thinking? Which of you had conversations with trees? Did any of you have a playmate only you could see? And who among you learned how to fly?

Each child comes into this world an individual self. I believe we carry with us our own connection with the inner wisdom, and that this manifests in a special ability, a gift, something that can contribute to the understanding of the whole of life. All too often this gift is not appreciated and not accepted. I think we might recover much of the wisdom which we know but don't know we know by attending to these small gifts.

Children usually keep such things hidden, for they soon find out that it is not considered to be acceptable behavior, that they will be laughed at, not believed, or even punished. Soon the gift is shrouded in silence, layered under denial, slid into a dark corner of memory, yet never completely forgotten, lying ready to be called up if there is ever a safe time to remember. What if each of these things, these special gifts, was a piece of the puzzle we humans need to recover our sense of humanity, to renew the earth, to transcend our self-imposed limitations? What might we discover, were we to begin to invite these gifts to emerge? In sharing them with each other, might we begin to reweave our wisdom, bringing the shining threads through from the source, to blend together into a new multidimensioned whole?

Some of you may still be connected to these abilities. Some of you may have other things you have discovered or that life's experiences have developed. But I wonder if the earliest thing we remember is not truly the most important, that gift which came into the world with us, and which we have cherished, somehow, all these years.

There is the story of the two-year-old girl whose baby brother has been recently born. As the parents bring the baby home from the hospital and settle him into his crib, the little girl asks to be left alone with him. The parents demur, explain she is too little, she can see him with them present, but the girl is very insistent, she must be with him alone. Eventually they withdraw, leaving the baby monitor on, ready to return at the first sign of trouble. They hear their daughter go up to the baby and ask him, urgently, "Tell me what God looks like, I'm forgetting!"

A lovely story, and one which may make you smile. But when Bettie tells it, she always cries. She has repeated it many times, and she is always deeply moved.   What does she, perhaps, not remember?

Usually we do not talk about these things, even with close friends. Last year I told Sheila, whom I have known for a very long time, about my childhood flying experience.. She looked at me in complete amazement and said she too flew, but in her bed, out the window onto the summer fields around her home in England. I was the first person she ever told.

This is my second question to you.

What is the secret you have carried all these years?

* * *

My third question is more of a concept, a way to understand the shape our future might take. Most of us believe that in order to learn about a new subject, we must take a class, read books, go to lectures, build up the body of knowledge piece by piece. It is a very linear style of learning which we have been thoroughly trained to believe is the only way. How else could we know a fact unless we heard it or read it?

And yet—have you ever had the experience of finding out something and realizing you already knew it but didn't see how you could have because you don't remember ever learning it? Have you ever explained something to someone and found yourself saying something you didn't know you knew? Sometimes as familiarity with a subject grows, more knowledge seems to appear. And how do people come to new conclusions, understandings, how do they make leaps to previously unknown discoveries?

The new field of quantum physics gives us an explanation, one which is mirrored in psychology by Jung's concepts of the collective unconscious and archetypes, and in spiritual teachings by the disciplines which lead to oneness with All. This explanation says that we are all part of the whole, that each of us carries a part of the whole, and that the whole has within it fields of knowledge, formed by all the people who participate in that knowledge, and that each of us can tap into any field. [14] Therefore my oldest son, when he was 13, encountered his first computer in school, and in a very short time was using languages found on the college computers in the lab into which he talked his way. Once within that field, he moved rapidly, absorbing knowledge far beyond the offering of the beginning high school class.

Biologist Rupert Sheldrake[15] suggests that we think of the brain as a receiver for transmissions, as the TV set is the medium through which we receive the broadcasts. Without the TV we do not see the program, yet the program does not originate in the set. Understanding the function of the brain in this manner opens up consciousness to see how the concept of the fields of knowledge makes perfect sense. Each time a new piece of information is understood, and it slips into its place, as a puzzle piece slides so easily into its matching curves, the picture becomes more visible. If we think knowledge is stored in the brain, the image is that of a vast storehouse containing everything we ever imagined or experienced. When we shift the image to that of a complex receptor, the world opens up around us, immediately becoming interactive in an entirely different fashion.

I frequently have the experience, in the midst of a discussion, of needing to explain something about which I have just gotten an idea, and as the words come out of my mouth, part of me is watching, amazed, wondering how the paragraph will end. And as it ends, and I conclude the thought, I know without a doubt that what I have said is valid, could be verified with an expert in the field, and is new information to me. I have tapped into that particular field of knowledge and thus have access to all its information.[16]

This correlates with the discoveries made by Jung when he realized humans have not only a personal unconscious in which resides all the memories of the present life, but also a collective unconscious through which an individual can access the stream of human experience through the ages.[17] Seekers within many spiritual disciplines come, through meditation and prayer, to a similar understanding, although the manifestation is of a different nature. The state of oneness with the Divine is sought for with great intensity and effort, for it is truly a miraculous state, and one in which the seeker knows completely that All is One, and One is All.

If we acknowledge the quantum physics comprehension of the holographic nature of the universe,[18] we then realize that the All can conceptually lead us into an understanding of fields of knowledge, for if we can experience the state of All, then our minds can leap to the concept of a place without location where all the ideas and information about any given subject gathers, and to which we can tune our receptors, thereby entering into synchronous knowledge.

Add to this the idea, as Sheldrake suggests, that our minds are receivers rather than storage facilities, and we begin to grasp the magnitude of the concept.[19] What this means to the recovery of Woman's Wisdom is that the Wisdom is never lost, but only shielded from our receptors, wrapped around with lead, as it were, so that when we have discovered and removed the shields which were placed to keep us from access, we will begin to tune ourselves to receive that knowledge. Indeed, in many ways, the shields are beginning to slip already.

Each of us has our own thread, a conduit through which our own particular piece of the knowing travels. It also links us to the whole, and allows us to travel inward to the source. Quantum physics has brought scientific validity to this image with the concept of fields of knowledge. It is not a new idea for mediators, practitioners of spiritual disciplines, artists and other creators who have known and used this connection to the center for centuries. What is new is the acknowledgement by scientists that there is reality within the intangible, and that it can be known and used. They lead us back to the source, legitimizing the unseeable facts, and allowing us to leap through the weight of three dimensions into the wider understanding.

*   *   *

These, then, are the three parts to my inquiry: first, the search for access to a specific field of knowledge which was known to women in the past; second, an awareness that each child has a piece of that knowledge; third, the understanding that entrance into a field can give access to the entire field. These parts form a pattern which will lead us in a spiral journey. The quest reminds me of the series of Chinese pictures known as the Ox-Herding Pictures. In them the first circle portrays the unawakened man. Soon he discovers the tail of the ox, and chases it through the trees. Catching it, he struggles to bring it to him. Then he rides, and in time the reins are forgotten; he plays his flute, comfortably in harmony. Eventually the ox disappears and the man, entering into contemplation of the universe, experiences the oneness with all which is known as enlightenment. At the end, he returns to the world, recognizing all beings as part of the whole.

I have always heard that the ox represents the ego, with which a man must struggle before it can be released. I find a reinterpretation possible from a woman's viewpoint; now the ox is that which I seek, the part of myself whose presence I sense, unseeing. Once the ox becomes visible through the trees I can ride her, learning her ways. She becomes the vehicle for a shift of being from person alone to person in unity with Nature.[20]

We are in the Age of Aquarius, when expansion of vision is possible in ways that were not available in the previous centuries. Astrologers explain this by noting the shift of planetary influences on the houses, thereby releasing the mind and its domain from the restrictive energies of Saturn which held it prisoner in a low-ceilinged room. Now that Aquarius is the ruler of that house, the sky is open for the mind to range far and wide. For me this shift feels like coming home, and each new piece of information, each new piece of the puzzle, once it has turned itself so the hooks and curves fit exactly where it belongs, feels like an old friend who has been absent, and I welcome it back saying, "Where have you been? I am so glad you are here, you make me feel so much more alive." And I wonder how I ever could have been otherwise, for once we have stepped outside that narrow low room, we then know what is outside, as Eve knew wisdom when she ate the apple. There is no turning back.

Apples. I pick up an apple from the green glass dish and consider it. What have we been missing about the apple? Biting into its smooth red skin, chewing the juicy white sweetness, I wonder if it is perhaps a link which could bring me into awareness. Is this little piece of fruit, which we all take so much for granted, a coded entry into the wisdom which I seek? [21] What if food links us to energies in the universe, like the micro-chip in the TV carries the electrical impulse. The image expands with this idea, shifting the concept from food containing energies to food being a connecting link into energies.

These are the clues which I seek. "An apple a day keeps the doctor away." Bring the apple to the teacher. An apple is standard fare in lunches. It keeps well, nourishes, is well liked. And how many millions of computer users, myself included, now connect daily with it symbolically? Indeed, it is a symbol for knowledge as well as health. It is impossible to kill knowledge, one can only contain it, kill the practitioners, submerge the memories. The knowledge remains. When we have access to the field, we are once again able to discover the wisdom. The clues are often right under our noses.

Consider the recent unfolding events in the field of physics. Small anomalies which had been ignored as inconsequential by researchers have now been recognized as important, and the discovery of the patterns of Chaos and Complexity have emerged.[22] The signs were there all along, but the vision was too narrow.

We are, indeed, discovering that there is a great deal more in our world than we previously believed. We have been imprisoned in a pattern of thought which eliminates everything which does not fit the model, as physicists eliminated the unexplained anomalies, as archaeologists ignored the complexities of the fossils of the Burgess Shale.[23] Jung helped us to understand that the polarities of our gendered existence formed themselves into two perspectives, the Masculine and the Feminine. Building on the ancient Chinese concepts of Yin and Yang, our understanding of these polarities defines the Masculine as linear in its thinking, responsible for form, focus, and structure. Feminine is diffuse, circular, germinative, nurturing. Masculine is bright, sunny, Feminine is dark, mysterious. In the Judeo-Christian world, Masculine is good, Feminine is bad. The only possible model for progress and popularity, therefore, is Masculine, and the patriarchal perspective has held the throne for centuries, setting the Feminine in an inferior position, defining her, subtly, as Evil, not to be trusted.

Eve ate the apple and then shared her wisdom with Adam.

One could see this act as the desire of the earth-centered spirituality to connect with the patriarchal system, Goddess offering this wisdom of the earth and the body to the new God. The tree of knowledge and the wise serpent are familiar symbols from the Pagan practice. But He will have none of it. Desiring to be in control He rejects this union as Adam rejected the first woman, Lilith, because she would not lie beneath him. [24] Adam and God apparently thought Eve would be more compliant, but she turned out to be another uppity woman so she was punished for eternity. The serpent became an evil creature as well, blamed with Eve for the Expulsion from the Garden.

The difficulty with the patriarchal system is also its strength. We must have focus and clarity in order to act. Structure is important for form. But exclusive intent on the goal excludes everything around the path, and the necessity of achieving the goal demands elimination of all distractions. It becomes crucial to control everything which might come onto the path to the desired end, and this need for control often becomes an end in itself, an obsession which sweeps everything aside in a rigid determination to make the physical and psychic environment conform to desire.

This has left the Feminine in the position of an intruder, a distraction, a foolish woman who does not understand the need for a goal, and who must be kept in her less important place lest she hinder the forward march of progress. Repeatedly diminished, often violently, the last remaining practitioners of the earth wisdom were attacked throughout the fifteenth and sixteenth centuries. With the wise women and witches eliminated, the medical profession and the church were able to institute their reforms and their disciplines which had as a hidden agenda the continuation of the barriers to the Feminine. It is these barriers that we are now encountering, and it is these barriers which we must discover, name, and re-name so their energies can be freed to join with the growing gathering of Feminine wisdom and the knowledge which they conceal is once again able to take its place in the grand design.

We define, therefore, that which we seek by its absence as well as its presence, as the missing piece in the puzzle leaves a hole of a certain shape for which we then search. There is a body of knowledge which we define by the term "women's wisdom" or "women's knowing" which transcends our current awareness, yet is intuited by women because there is a recognized resonance to the concept. And women want this knowledge, not simply because it will provide a sense of personal power, ability, and self-esteem, but because there is a clear perception that it may be what the world and all who inhabit it need to survive.

When I ask the question "What do we know that we do not know we know?" a whisper of an answer flits through the inner space, ghost-like, unformed yet called into response. Some of this answering is generated by awareness that there is something once known, long forgotten. Another part of the answering comes from a more recent memory, within this lifetime, something known or perceived when the woman was a child. Within this memory lies our clearest key, for this is our own individual and unique way of understanding the mystery which we seek.

Thus our task becomes more clear, as we understand the possibilities inherent in the search. And again we attend to the method of proceeding. We must discover the magic word that unlocks the gates and frays the spell into mist that blows away on the wind. The prince comes to the wall of briars and must penetrate to the center where the sleeping princess lies. Fairy tales are full of clues. Poets point the way, artists and musicians meet the center point daily. Slip into meditation and "way will open."[25]   We begin.

∞ B ∞

Living in Cycles

The Process

The moon travels nightly across the heavens, repeating in sequence her phases; new, full, dark. Women watch the moon: watching her cycles we learn our own rhythms. Whether we be wimmin, womyn,[1] witch or sybil, young or old, the breath-indrawn moment as night falls: "Look! The Moon!" catches us all. Her beauty comes upon us unexpectedly, at a different time than the last night we noticed, in a different place from last month. She is constantly changing. The dedicated observer learns her pattern, understands her rhythm, knows what she will do. Yet no one can predict the beauty she creates with clouds and moisture. Some nights she shines cleanly across the darkened sky, sailing among the stars, dancing with the planets. Other times she wraps herself serenely in a fluff of white, creating illusion with the patterns of the shifting clouds. I have seen her encircled with a rainbow, magical in its unexpectedness, or floating within the large white ring which proclaims the advent of snow.

The moon links us to our deeper women selves, her cycles drawing our blood to follow. Within the night, mysteries unfold, secrets are told, wisdom is born. Within the night, terror stalks. The moon-wise woman knows both sides of joy. She understands beauty and despair, fear and delight. The light of the moon creates strange shadows as it falls to earth, and many humans are caught in the distortions lurking within those shadows. To be moon-wise is to know this truth, and to know also the particular brilliance of the white light which demands a different sight.

Searching for the deep wisdom, we cry, "Who will teach us? The wise women are all gone." Always the answer comes, "Look within. Learn to listen to the small stirrings of your own soul."

When I first heard the call of the Goddess, an awakening wonder deep within my being, I had no idea how to proceed. At that time, the present richness of writings in the field of Women's Spirituality and the research into the ancient eras of the Goddess had not begun to grace our shelves. I had a book by Esther Harding called *Women's Mysteries*, a grounding in the works of C. G. Jung which included a good deal of exploration into the archetypal Feminine, an enlightenment from the innovative work of Jungian James Hillman, and my own life experience with some wonderful friends in the Friends Conference on Religion and Psychology, an annual gathering of Jungians and Quakers.

I lived, then, on a farm in Connecticut with my husband, three teenage children, a horse, some cows, chickens, ducks, cats and dogs. I had no idea how to connect with the Goddess. So I began, moved by some sense of rightness, to walk out into the light of the moon each night. Our farm was on a hill which allowed me to see most of the horizon, and I became familiar with the places where the moon appeared. Nightly I simply stood, raising my arms to the white light, marvelling within the beauty, touched deeply without words. Nightly I went back inside, to the struggles of marriage and children.

Gradually, as I walked the land, planted and harvested my garden, read books, connected with special friends, and sat in silence in Quaker meeting, I began to understand the deeper impulses of the Goddess. I learned to recognize her Presence by the responses of my body. I found that She seemed to come from below and to my left side, in marked contrast to the appearance of the familiar Light of the Spirit which now seemed more masculine. The Light entered my head from above, splitting me open, permeating my being with brilliance. The Lady comes in as a quiet flood, gently spreading Her awareness throughout my body.

It is a curious thing, to move back and forth through time, remembering twenty years ago while writing this re-creation on a computer which did not exist then. In those days I wrote by hand, with pencil on unlined paper, words falling and tumbling from my fingers as the intent of the piece took shape. Later I transferred the words to typewritten form. Now the sentences flow easily from my fingers to the computer keys and once again the looked-for moment arrives when suddenly the emerging phrases write themselves, following the inner stream of image and thought. One evening during my early dance with the Goddess, rain began to fall as I hurried to finish planting beans in the late spring dusk. I felt the stirrings of inspiration and, the row completed, went inside to my desk and paper. I felt myself moving into a quiet space where earth and water meet within the gathering dark. The words fell from my pencil.

Birth

The rain beats on the window. Outside, in the dark of the spring moon, new witches dance in the garden, dance on the beans, the peas, the cabbages. This is the night of the turning, when the old, magical moon of last month ends, and the unknown begins.

New seeds grow in old compost. Yestermoon remembers friends ringing a circle, naming each other, looking, loving, each touching the other into being. Fertile soil for spring planting.

The witches dance behind my eyes. A long passage opens, dark, wondering, listening through my body. Single file the witches tread on tendrils of silk, drawn fine in a breath, spun by spiders of fate who wait, fat and watchful, as the passage turns anew. Dark threads ravel about their heads, patterning the maze for the witches' dance.

Shape and turn. Hand to hand, hair streaming black on black, dark women reach deep within, searching the measure, questioning the shadow for the secret known only to itself. The passage turns and twists. Outside I wait and watch, tracing the course of the dance by the movement in my throat, my chest, my ribs. The pregnant belly seethes, full blown with motion; wilder grows the dance as naked feet tread deeply into flesh and fancy - but this is real - and my new-milked breasts pour forth as the women move deeply, descending to my pelvis, treading, treading, working the ground of my body with their feet until they knead and beat and shape the being into birth.

Then the passage opens into light, and the cocooned body slips gently past the watching shapes. It falls on lustered milkweed floss, shining in starlight, watered with rainfall, new as new to grow, with the ground-hugged seeds, until the moon comes once again into her fullness.

I do not know how these images and words appear; they are simply there, creating the picture and the experience. In the years since I began to court the Goddess and the Moon, I have had many such openings into another way of knowing. Always I feel awe as the phrases shape themselves, always I welcome the sense of altered time and space which I enter or am swept into, always I honor and am grateful for the gifts given.   The experience comes when I give over my need to control, and make the connection to the timeless space of Universal Being, touching the sensations lightly, letting the words emerge, dancing within the rhythm. Then I enter the flow and the flow is within me, and the sentences shape themselves.

Looking back, I realize I was always in touch with the "Unseen World" as I learned to call it when I read Marion Weinstein's book on Wicca and Magic.[2] Yet "unseen" is the true term only when we are firmly within our three-dimensional existence. I grew up the only child of parents for whom connections with other realities were as real as breathing. Long before I was born they had set aside or satisfactorily answered any doubts they may have had about the truth of communication with those who had died, about the reality of fairies and angels, and about the power of prayer. Our home had a sense of unseen presences which was unremarkable because it was so totally accepted, so much so that until this moment of writing I never realized how completely this acceptance has influenced my life. I have never had to question the other realities.

I do not see fairies with my physical eyes, nor do I see auras, I cannot foretell the future. Rather there is a knowing of existence, of something more than the usual. I notice it when I am in Nature, looking at a tree, a river, the ocean.   There is a vibrancy, an aliveness which seems entirely natural. A certain combination of colors, the movement of wind in leaves, or the way light catches the edge of rock, can generate excitement throughout my being. It surprises me when a companion does not respond in the same way.

We have the ability to create our world. I can walk in the woods and create for myself a pair of wings with which to fly to the highest tree. Or I can place myself in the hollow of its trunk, open a chamber, and imagine myself moving down a tunnel into the earth. My mind can imagine anything I choose, and the power of the imagery attests to its reality, for my perception is changed by the world I create.

How can we know what we do not know? How can I move between the worlds of fantasy and everyday awareness, shifting through multiple realities, giving voice and honor to all, even those I do not know are present?

I begin with a desire to move into the field. There is a stilling of my ego self, a loosening of structure within, and an entering into a different place. It is very familiar to me, a state which I might describe as the place between the letting out of breath, before the new air is drawn into the lungs. If you slip into the meditative breathing, which is a conscious watching of your breath moving in and out of your lungs, you will find things slowing in the familiar way. If, then, you pause between the going out and the coming in of your breath, waiting for a moment when all is still, you will find the other world opening up, as a door slips silently open. You enter.

Once you are in, by a simple shift of desire, you can stay. Within this place breath continues in your body, but there is a sense that it happens outside, for in here you are in another place. Yet you are also aware of being within both worlds. Time changes, becomes another form. Breath moves in and out, continuing the sequence. Attention expands to include both levels of knowing. Look—we are at the ocean, the waves wash the shore, swell, splash, slip back along the gleaming sands as sandpipers run in tiny rapid steps seeking their morning food. Water swells, falls, retreats, repeating the rhythm of your body's breath until they merge, flowing together, in, out, in, out. Now your mind is free to walk the shell strewn sands. Listen. Your body and the ocean are attuned. You are your body, and your body is the ocean. You walk the sands, stepping carefully so as not to cut your feet on the sharp edges of the shells.

Here we move within a world which becomes as real as any beach on which our physical bodies ever walked. And stay, for a moment, in this world, let the ocean's breath carry you out on the wave, and in the space between the exhalation of the wave and its return, slip again into another time. World within world within world, the shapes of each place mirroring themselves endlessly, as your image in repeating mirrors trails off into the distance ever smaller and fainter. Here each new world is the brightest, and the reality of your meditating body fades, receding into time to be recovered with a thought, when you eventually decide to return. Now we move suspended in the air, a brightness surrounds us. This is the realm of pure intention, where all things begin. Here breath hangs in the balance; here we need no breath. Somewhere behind us the ocean splashes silently on the shore, and further back our body breathes quietly and slowly. Here awareness spreads, as the water in the ocean spreads, slowly, touching and enclosing each mote of brightness, absorbing the interstices of the pattern until soul and spirit are one. Here is where the universal pattern begins, unseen, simply known. Here is the place where our intent merges with the universal mind, moving at last in harmony, free of fears and expectations.

Now the universal knowing shapes our being, one and together with all that is. A moment here is an eternity, and forever but a fraction of one breath. Resting here, we reach a finger of awareness into the world of daily familiarity. And holding fully to our dual knowing, we can see with greater clarity the pattern of our days, the questions we might ask, the actions we might take.

Quietly we remember our breathing. Slipping through the ocean's wave, stepping once again on the shore where the sandpipers search, we return to our patient body. The renewing breath holds memory of salty moisture, fresh sea air, and an indescribably delightful brightness.   And now the moments coalesce, our bodies rise, refreshed, and time begins again.

* * *

Part of the powerful link which women have with Goddess is Her multiplicity of images and manifestations. Recognizing the wide variety of roles and energies which are part of being a woman, the figure of the Triple Goddess emerged and has been repeated time and time again, throughout many cultures and ages.[3] Linked to the phases of the moon, these Goddesses embody the three main phases of a woman's life. The first is the young maiden, daughter, Virgin; Hebe, Artemis, Parvati, Ana, are some of her names. Second is the Mother, the nurturer, called Durga, Hera, Juno, Matri. The third is the Old Woman, the Crone, Sophia, Kali, Hecate, Minerva.[4] Watching the moon, meditating on the three phases, feeling the pull to turn inward, connects us with our triple selves. Regular awareness of the monthly cycle of the moon, linking us to our own blood cycle, brings the overlapping phases together. Now we realize the appropriateness of the ancient statues which portray a column composed of three women joined at their backs, each facing a different direction. We are daughter all our lives, mother in countless ways, and often in touch with wisdom long before we reach the age associated with the wise old woman.

My exploration into the knowing of women also falls into three parts, three phases of understanding which link and interconnect with the circles of the Triple Goddess. When I first gathered the pieces of this journey together, my head was awash with the chaos of multiple ideas. My desire to bring together the Feminine, the historical misuse of woman, the energy of the Goddess, the Essential Self of the child, fantasy, quantum physics, parapsychology, and psychotherapy, thereby creating an environment within which it would be possible to reconnect with the inherent knowledge of woman, made sense as long as my mind could circle and spiral around the components in a multidimensional manner. It was, however, impossible to force this sense into a formal outline, for to remain true to the integrity of the interrelation of the subjects I also had to think in a spiral fashion. To hold all things in equal relationship, resisting the drive to impose an order upon them, is an ability which I recognize as arising from the Feminine aspect of Self and which is antithetical to the Masculine desire for form and goal.

The mix of possibilities contained within the Feminine is delightfully varied. Because of its cyclical nature it is endlessly forming and reforming potentials. Change is completely natural to the Feminine and is recognized as necessary as the cycle for growth and decay upon which all living things is embarked. Within the mystery of the Feminine lies new life, begun before we are aware, as well as the darkness of depression and the deep journey down into the roots of being. To the outside, masculine, eye the Feminine is inconsistent, whimsical, erratic, irrational. From the inside, however, the Feminine knows itself to be rich, potent, fluid, and creative.

My need to hold the pregnant mix of energies and information in its fluid state until it was able to spin itself out into the necessary phrases was opposed by the need to write in the linear fashion of one word following another, line after line, a condition which can stifle the moving image and freeze it into boring immobility. I needed a form, but it could not be a traditional outline.

Jung recognized that we possess an ability which he termed the Transcendent Function, whereby the unconscious is able to create a solution to seemingly intractable problems.[5] In order to access this function, it is necessary to hold the opposites in equal balance without forcing a decision, thus allowing a tension to develop which becomes unbearable to the unconscious self. This situation then induces the Self to produce a creative solution which satisfies all needs and resolves all difficulties.

Edith Sullwold tells a story about Jung which demonstrates the activity of the Transcendent Function and is also an example of the struggle between the Masculine and the Feminine. Jung and Laurens VanderPost were having lunch at the chocolate shop in Zurich. They ate upstairs in the tea room which was very much a ladies' place, but they shared a passion for the wonderful chocolate desserts. The two men had their lunch, ordered dessert, and were waiting when Jung suddenly said, "I have to leave. I cannot stand listening to them." They were sitting next to a circular table around which six women were having their lunch. "Why?" asked VanderPost. "One says a few words, another says something totally unrelated, another says a few more words," Jung complained. "They make no sense, there is no order to their conversation. They are making me crazy. I have to leave." VanderPost protested. "Wait! We came here particularly to have our chocolate treat. We can't leave now, before we eat it." "All right," said Jung, "I will try to bear it." A few minutes later he suddenly said "Oh! I understand. Now I see. Under the table they are weaving a beautiful piece of lace!" and he happily ate his dessert, no longer troubled.

The creative solution which my unconscious produced was a diagram, a model which became the form through which I can write and from which direction can flow. Once it appeared, it was easy to set the various components of my interest into their appropriate locations. Three circles cluster together, overlapping one another. Each circle contains one of the three aspects of woman; Virgin, Mother, Crone, though these words are but one way of naming them. The overlaps naturally become the locations of the transitions which occur as a woman passes from one aspect into another. The center, where all parts join, becomes the empty place, the One which is the All, the All in One.

Cycles and thoughts overlap when the linear model of words following one after another is released. Attached to this circle of exploration and understanding are a number of other circles, spinning out on their own course, related, separate, all clamoring for definition. They must fall onto the printed page one at a time, unless I draw a picture to help the mind leap ahead, to create the concept of multiple realities. Thus, one circle intersects with another and another, each intersection creating another world between the two, and all overlapping within the shared center. Move the circles into three dimensionality and realities become stacked; the more circles intersect, the more realities inhabit the same vertical column.

Thus it is necessary to keep the ideas of one reality in mind as another is spinning out its tale.[6] The mind can do this easily, with the cooperation of the body, for sensations and memories are stored in all our cells in infinite complexity.[7] Expanding our dimensionally-oriented mind into a release from the necessity of naming before knowing, we open ourselves to the overlap and move to previously unreachable spaces. In this way it becomes possible to come into contact with wisdom and with specific knowledge which was seemingly inaccessible.

This model allows me to spiral through the various aspects of woman and permits me to explore one while the awareness of the overlap with another is present. It also communicates my process to you. It provides us with a means of understanding, acknowledging that the standard outline and list of chapters is not the only dimension in which we are proceeding. Thus we honor and respect the potential for a different way of understanding, an alternate method of living within this world, and a possible state of being in which the deep wisdom of the feminine can be an integral part of all our lives.

Listening, sensing, seeing within, allowing the overlapping realities, weaving through the circles, watching the changing colors, holding, waiting, moving: this is the way I enter the Unseen World. Sometimes it is complex, other times the shift is instantaneous. It reminds me of stories about a window in time, an opening into another world which is there under certain circumstances and gone in an instant. Bilbo the Hobbit understood, at the last moment, what was meant by the instruction: "Stand by the gray stone where the thrush knocks and the setting sun with the last light of Durin's Day will shine upon the keyhole." [8] The stone flaked off, the key was turned, the sun set and the magic stopped. But he had understood; he and the dwarves were inside the mountain, and their journey could continue.[9]

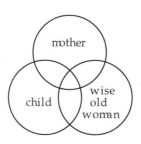

∞ C ∞

Beginning

First Circle: Virgin, Child

She is a small girl sitting in the long grass. The sun shines on her back, her blond hair escapes from braided patterns. She plucks a strand of grass, carefully pulling the stem free from its sheath, and chews the tender end. She delights in the taste, and in remembering she discovered this by herself.

Discovery means to gain knowledge or sight of something previously unknown or unseen. A blade of grass, a hidden path, a tree, a bird. If I have never seen it, I can discover it. If someone else shows me something, I will be glad to know this new thing, but if I can find it out for myself, my excitement and satisfaction is far greater.

I remember moving to an old house in Mobile, Alabama when I was nine. I loved Nancy Drew mysteries because Nancy always discovered things which solved the crime. I started looking around our house, and realized there must be a basement because there were basement windows. But there was no sign of a door anywhere. I searched and searched, and my father helped me; finally we discovered the door behind a tall bookcase which appeared to be built into the wall but was actually moveable. I remember the thrill when we opened that door and found the stairs leading to the unfinished cellar. It became my special place, and my father helped me set up a board across orange crates for a desk where I could read and write.

If we are lucky, we never stop discovering new things, but the thrill is seldom as complete as it is when we are children. I suspect that my father knew where the door must be from the beginning, but he let me figure it out for myself, thus giving me the gift of deduction and discovery.

I am grateful I grew up in a world without television. I had many opportunities to explore and discover. I was the only child of two loving parents who each had interests which preoccupied them, leaving me to entertain myself most of the time. I felt secure within myself as I was fortunate to be recognized by my parents with delight and appreciation for my individual self. Before we moved to Mobile, we lived in the country outside Fairhope, a small Southern town, and I spent most of my time outdoors. The world was a wonderful place. Our land was uncultivated, full of wild things, trees, bushes, flowers, grasses. There had once been a house there, long ago burned down, and Nature had reclaimed the land, sending vines and weeds through the cement foundation and driveway. My father built a little one story house under two huge mulberry trees. There was a large bamboo clump in the yard, crepe myrtle, yucca plants, magnolia, pecan and persimmon trees. I name them like a mantra, a ritual to bring me into their presence. They were my friends, and I gradually discovered all their secrets.

Childhood for me was a safe and happy time. For many little girls it is not; abuse and neglect are all too common. The unfailing presence of Nature, of trees, ponds, rivers, fields, hills and valleys, provides an escape, a place of retreat and safety, which many grown women remember with relief and gratitude.

I remember the trees more vividly than my friends or my animals. I say the name, Azalea, and it appears instantly in that place within which memory resides. I am again small. It is a hot summer day and I have crept under the low-bending branches loaded with pink blossoms and am crouched on the cool moist ground which is covered with fallen flowers. I pick a perfect petal from the bush and lay its cool sweetness on my tongue. It feels smooth. The intense color permeates my tongue, as though I can taste it. I have no desire to eat, only to experience the sensations. I hold the petal lightly within my closed mouth, savoring the beauty.

Within this moment of discovery, I am connected through the flower into a deeper knowing. I have awakened my taste for color. Even today, many years later, my tongue responds when I see strong color, salivating and experiencing the vibrant intensity. I followed my instincts in my exploration, and did not eat the flower. I did not know azalea flowers were toxic, but I knew not to eat these petals.

Each of the trees and plants had its own story, each provided moments of discovery as the seasons turned. I lived within the ease and wonder, "happy as the grass was green",[1] playing and exploring, intimately connected. This time of my childhood has always been a warm and glowing memory. Recently I have understood another aspect.

I have had, since before I remember, a family of three white porcelain penguins, once belonging to my mother's sister and passed on to me. The mother stands about two and a half inches tall, and is robust and strong. The babies are an inch high, and one imitates the stance of his mother, head up, beak pointed out, flippers slightly extended. He is ready for the world.

The other baby has her beak down and flippers resting at her sides. She turns her head to the left. When I was a child, I was always careful to arrange this family in the right way; the shy one had to be in a position of safety, closer to mother, a little held back. This was very important, and through all the times of rearrangement in different spaces, little penguin was placed just so with great care.

Recently I chose this little figure to bring to a sharing which was held by a women's group, and I used it to demonstrate an aspect of myself which is not usually apparent. I never know what to say in social situations, don't like parties, and have always felt I was basically very shy. I have learned the "social graces", but they feel unnatural. As I talked about my shyness, I realized that this was not the right word, and that there was something else which made me hold back in conversations, which made me uncomfortable at parties, and left me bereft of anything to say. Returning home with my penguin in my pocket, I let the question drift into memory and my unconscious. What is this feeling, if it is not shyness?

One of my early childhood memories is of riding in the back seat of our car, listening to my parents talking in the front. We were going to visit friends, people my mother and father knew. As an only child, I went everywhere with them. From the back seat I listened very carefully to their conversation, trying hard to memorize it so that I would have something to say when we got to the friends' house.

This has always seemed an amusing example of my shyness and introversion. But as I allowed the question to expand into my memory, this incident came back to me. Suddenly I was in that car, listening to my parents have a discussion, trying to memorize it. Then I realized that this shy inner self does not communicate in spoken language and she is, therefore, at a complete loss when she has to interact with someone. Even now, after sixty-plus years, I still react. I sat, on a recent Thursday, in the faculty dining room by myself by choice, hoping, as always, no one would want to sit with me. A woman at the next table, when her companions left, asked if she could join me. What could I say? I said yes. And immediately my mind thought: "I can say how good the soup is. That is something to say."

The implication that the spoken word is not the most natural language for me is incredible. One part of my mind is astonished at the concept, another part is grateful to have a better explanation for the life-long problem, and yet a third part, which is more than a part and is rather the whole, the soul, knows this has always been true, that I have always known it, and have lived my life in accordance with this reality. I must acknowledge all these reactions, for one by itself is not the whole truth.

I understand, now, that my early intimate connection with the trees and grasses was my natural and first language, and that English will always be the second. Humans are born with the innate ability to learn whatever language is first presented to their young minds. Growing up more or less alone, outdoors a great deal of the time, with parents who were connected with the symbolic and metaphysical realms, it was natural that I would learn first the language of image. When I was three, we left the wonderful beach house in Florida where we had lived for a few months. I was in love with the pine tree in our yard, and apparently I grieved to leave my friend. I remember my wise mother telling me to go talk with it, to tell it I was leaving and would always love it. I vividly recall the feel of its rough bark on my cheek and arms as I hugged my tree in a tearful farewell.

I remember, I remember. As I speak, you remember long walks in the woods. Solace entered your soul as you discovered the new green shoots of the skunk cabbage. May apples followed, then lilies of the valley. Sitting beside the emerging green, your heart uncurls, the tears dry on your face. Sunlight slips sideways through the trees to fall across your feet. A soft wind stirs your hair. Gently the muscles in your back unfold, your teeth unclench, your eyes relax. Peace.

Silently, silently, the moment arrives. Flowing, you merge with the plants, the trees, the ground. Difference vanishes. At the center, you are one, the many parts connected, soul and heart are green and growing. You feel the sap rising, the myriad cells filling with juice and life.

You were miserable when you ran from the house, seeking the comfort of the trees. Now you remember the peace that comes when the earth enfolds you in Her embrace. And we both know deeply that as long as there is one small plant or branch or flower that we can touch, see, remember, our connection will not be broken. Nature is always waiting for us, we have but to arrive.

So many women remember their deep connection with the trees. "100%," says Sage, one of the women responding to my research inquiry. "We were one. There was no need for *talk*. It was the only place I felt safe, secure, loved, taken care of, connected or peaceful." When there is no human person who will protect or nourish the small girl, Nature is there.

> I learned who I was, fitting the woods into
> a protective ring containing all the elements I
> needed to own. Trees became homes; pine-
> needles; soft piled rugs, puff balls and fungi;
> acorns, and moss, all had a numinosity greater than their
> own..
> I thought of the secret path into
> the woods as an entry into a place which was totally mine,
>   where I was a welcome scout. I needed to be very quiet
> I was left alone. . Here the others never came.

> It was my own birthing place.
> World.

Lee's words are echoed again and again by all the women I spoke with who grew up deprived of the essential nurturing every child requires. If this care is not forthcoming from the adults around her, she seeks it in Nature, and Nature does not disappoint her.

There is a sequence of events which unfolds naturally after birth which is designed to awaken the senses of the new born infant and complete the transition from the fluid environment of the womb into the unfamiliar air. In a miraculously simple exchange, the mother holds her child close to her left breast and the child nurses. By this act, the complex range of sensations which we enjoy is set in motion. Sight and recognition of the mother's face results in a smile; thus learning has begun. Taste, touch, smell and sound follow as mother holds her child, talking, crooning, stroking, and the beat of her heart soothes and comforts. People who study the development of the child have realized the extent of damage done to the child when such stimuli are not given immediately after birth and continuously thereafter. We are damaged as a nation by our traditional birthing practices which separate mother and baby, and each one of us cannot help but feel the need to search for that primary nourishment and care.[2]

I am saddened and frightened as I read the results of these studies. I remember my own children who were born by the method we called natural childbirth.   I did not know then that cutting the umbilical cord immediately after birth deprives the child of an important transition process, and that if left intact, the cord will complete the transfer of blood and oxygen in about five minutes. It can then be severed appropriately.[3]   The cord is long enough that the infant can be at the mother's breast immediately. I nursed my children, but all three were taken to the nursery after birth and brought to me later. I did not know. I had lost my connection with that knowing, as had we all, including the doctors.

The heart to heart connection of nursing also awakens an ancient nurturing instinct in the mother, if she is able to allow it, so that she knows intuitively what is needed by her beloved child. "This is the intelligence of the heart, a non-verbal, ancient knowing. She has, in bonding to her infant, bonded to her own heart and has come into her own power,unlocking the insights on which our species has depended for millennia."[4]   How easy it seems! Simply by the connection, the necessary wisdom is called forth. When it is there, the child knows she is safe, loved, cared for, attended to. To whatever degree we are fortunate enough to have had this essential attention, to that degree we will know ourselves to be secure.

Nourishment is needed in many ways by the growing child. I was nurtured and loved by my parents, but I craved the connection with the outdoors. There is an essential energy that can only be experienced in contact with the earth. In the warm long summers of Alabama, I rose early, dressed in panties and a loose cotton dress pulled on over my head, and I was ready for the day. I never wore shoes from one end of the summer to the other, except to go to church on Sunday, or occasional visits to the city of Mobile. My feet communicate with the earth. In the New England winters I must wear shoes, but they come off as soon as I am in the house, and I look forward eagerly to the warmer days when my toes can wriggle through the earth and the soles of my feet can connect with rich texture and energy.

This is how I reconnect with my native language. The bond with mother activates our innate abilities, the bond with Nature reaches deeply into our souls, connecting us with the Eternal

Mother as well as the wonder of the land. The relationship with Nature is dependable. Where human mothers fail, through ignorance and destructive desires, Nature is always there, the tree stands, year after year, the flowers come up in the same place each spring, the rocks speak of stability and of the solidity gained by standing one's ground. Nature teaches us, supports us, feeds us, an unfailing source of energy, comforting, challenging, always renewing.

Through the earth, my feet receive messages which have no words, no form. My cells respond, sensations flow. I become, when I think about it, centered. Mostly I don't think. It is easier to simply be, to breathe in the heat or the cold, smelling the changes in the weather. January days in New England often bring me a whiff of spring to come. The moon gleams in her fullness through my office window and I gasp with delight. On my knees in the spring garden, my hands full of plants, I give them to the ground to nurture with tenderness and grace. Summer's heat, dusty, breathless, bakes my bones as they store warmth for the winter to come.

I learned my language from the trees and the animals, as did all of you who are nodding in agreement. How many of you have said, or would say, that your cat or dog understands you, and you know what the animal, who is your best friend, is thinking and feeling? So many people have this experience that it is almost an acceptable thing to talk about, even though it is not scientifically provable. Rupert Sheldrake is currently conducting experiments to show that pets know when their owners are coming home, even though no one in the house is aware of the fact.[5] His intent with this and other simple experiments is to transform our view of reality, to go "far beyond the current frontiers of research, and...reveal much more of the world than science has yet dared to conceive".[6] Isn't it strange, that something which is so natural needs studies to bring it to our attention, to permit us to accept it as real?

Fitting the knowledge we have as children into the adult world is often a problem. Most of us don't tell our parents that our cat is talking to us, because they only laugh, or humor us; we know they don't believe what we say. Jeanne didn't tell about the little people she saw in the woods. Ashley didn't tell anyone she could lift rocks without touching them. I didn't tell about the petal on my tongue and tasting color. I heard a story about a girl who was able to find a valuable piece of jewelry which had been lost at school by a classmate. She just knew where to look. She was punished, because it was bad to know things like that. We soon find out that some of the things we know are not acceptable, and we had better keep them hidden.

There is a fascinating study concerning the way children learn the names of things. The natural method, once a child learns the concept of names, is to point to something, hear the name the adult provides, such as "car", "horse", "Mommy", and move on to the next. Blurton Jones observed this activity, but he also noticed that frequently the child pointed to seemingly empty space. When no name was forthcoming, the child moved on. This happened with sufficient frequency that it seemed children actually were seeing things which were not there for adults. Since no confirming response was received, whatever the child saw was soon erased from the named world and became invisible once again.[7]

How many things are we missing? My cat sits by the sliding glass doors that look out into the back yard. During the day she can see the birds flying back and forth to the feeder. Her ears twitch, she sometimes emits small miauws of excitement, her head turns to follow their movements. She also watches at night, intently, her eyes and head making the same movements. I look out. Even on clear nights when the full moon illuminates the yard, I see no moving thing. The birds are asleep in their trees. Last night she was joined by the other cat. They both stared intently, heads moving in unison. I stared. I saw nothing but shrubs, plants, trees. What do they see? Was there a time, when I was very small, that I might have seen what they so clearly observe? What potential for the future of humans are we ignoring? What are the gifts we came with as children? How can we know what we don't know we know?

We can remember. We can reach back to the early memories of childhood and be there once again. Let your mind drift back with the question. Look for the small thing you never told anyone. What was special about your growing up? Let the question lead the way, searching and sifting through the memories, till something rises to the top of the pile and stays there. Till one moment seems to shine more golden than the rest, till you say "I don't know if this is what you are looking for, but I ......"

Was there something you could do that others couldn't, and you never understood why not? Sometimes the gift is so natural you might not notice it. Jill could tell what others were thinking, but she didn't realize it was unusual until she got married and her husband objected. He didn't like having his mind read. Bettie had an "imaginary" playmate who lived in Salem in the 16th century. She speaks about the wonderful conversations the two of them had, sharing information about their lives and times. She thought everyone had such a playmate.

Do you remember a guardian angel or presence? Many people do. What do you think might have been in those "empty" places in the room that you pointed to, perhaps, when you were very little, learning names?

The haunting slip of memory, the wisp of sensation gently tugging at the corner of your ear, a feeling in your body, strange, yet always familiar; these are clues which point the way to the hidden treasure. Stories contain clues; were you moved by the baby in Mary Poppins who could understand the speech of birds on the window sill, before she grew older and forgot?[8] Maybe you, too, could hear that wonderful language. What story do you remember? Maybe you used your gift to protect yourself. Pat also could tell what people were thinking; in her family, her gift helped her avoid some painful situations.

I always knew when it was going to rain. I could tell because I would get the urge to crawl under something, to get cozy. I used to make close little spaces by draping a blanket over a couple of chairs; curled up in this tiny sanctuary, I would listen to the rain when it came, feeling incredibly safe and secure. I have just remembered this, as I write the words to invite you to reach back into your younger days. It rose into my mind as a fish rises to the bait, rose from deep within the waters of my unconscious. How many years since I thought of that ability, called now into consciousness by this exploration. If you think there is nothing there, keep fishing.

Remember, she says, that once you were in Nature and Nature was in you. Remember when you knew the tree loved you.

In the deep part of my being, the answer stirs. Blond hair tossing, the child climbs up from the bottom of the sand gully. It is a steep climb. At the top, where the grass grows sparsely in the dry soil, she rests a moment. Then she backs up, to get a running start. "Let's go!" she shouts, launching herself forward. At the edge she takes a wild leap. Gasping with delight, she sails through the air to land, tumbling, in piles of soft sand. Does she remember flying down stairs when she was three? It does not matter. It is the air, the flight, the edge of danger, it is laughing at gravity, it is being one with the world, the sand, the warm breeze, the dark red earth. It is daily discovery of wonders that are magical. It is knowing with her whole being that this is her earth, her trees, her flowers, her world.

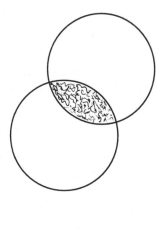

∞ D ∞

Holding the Wonder

First Intersection: Child into Woman

Mandorla: The union of two worlds, or the zone of intersection and interpenetration...is represented by the mandorla, an almond-shaped figure formed by two intersecting circles.[1]

Circles. They overlap, revealing a deeper dimension. The Mandorla opens, the cave beckons. Where is my guide? I beseech her: *Please, open my eyes, my heart. Give me the images, the words, the path, the forest within which to create the poem for you.*

Slowly the seed unfolds. Slowly the child turns within the womb. Patiently the watcher waits. My voice is here—why does it not speak? Listen to the wind. Within my ears the silence swells, roaring like the sea. I drink tea and wait. Women wait. It is part of what we understand.

This is my child and the child of the world into which I was born and in which I now live, struggling to express itself, to convey the images of my dreams, struggling to speak the language without words. Listening to my womanself, my wise woman child mother, shadowed by the triple Goddess within, unwilling and unable to speak anything which is not of the truth of woman, I wait. The threads of the warp lie spread out in my hand, wound waiting on their cones, and I wonder which color will lie beside what other.[2] How shall I resolve the chaos, how will the question unfold?

The truth of the woman permeates my body; hands and feet tingle, a flush of heat spreads through the roots of my hair, into the centers of my cells. Little green shoots begin to emerge, my body is growing. I am a garden. I can enter willingly into the state known as altered, but this is not altered, this is the true home condition; here I can connect cleanly with my self, the woman I am, the body I inhabit, the mind I enjoy. Sink within this place, being cautious to stay alert, connected to the surroundings and myself. It is easy here to step into the dark waters of Lethe, the river of oblivion, a stagnant swamp with fog and miasma, for in this place it is common. Woman has been swept away into that fog, thrust into the forgetfulness of Lethe, the waters close over our heads, our lives are lost. It is with an effort of will that the sun emerges, and the wind begins to blow.

Moving within this state, this place, this condition of being, I come to the center, a place I frequent. Through years of meditation, Meeting for Worship, contemplation and prayer, I am familiar with this eternal moment of suspended animation, the pause within breathing which expands to fill the world.

Holding lightly within this moment, loving the Presence which fills me, enwrapped in the silence, I reach for the elusive awareness that I am a woman within this place. A Woman. This means something else; this is a new yet familiar sense. I am a woman. I have a woman's body. I have a woman's soul. Reach. I am woman.

Scales fall from my eyes. Old plates of armor crack, shedding flakes of metal and concrete. Wisps of voices, whispering "Thou Shalt Not..." flee into the wind.

A fresh wind blows. My body comes alive, deep

murmurings fill my soul. I hear the voices of women echoing down through the ages, joining each to each, swelling, expanding, filling my awareness. My center stretches, shakes, begins to dance. A slow, measured tread at first, as women, young and old, mothers and babies, move into the circles which overlap, turning, lifting, falling. Hands joined, arms around each other, hair flying, feet treading deeply into the earth, the joy expands.

How could I not have known? How could I have spent so many years in search of the Center of Being and not have understood that I was missing the experience of being a woman?

When a child is severely abused, she isolates her essential self, walling it off to protect it from destruction. She also isolates the memory of the abuse, separating it from conscious recollection. She may split so completely that she cannot remember either the experience or the self. Knowing the abuse which women have endured for centuries, much of it life threatening, I can better understand how this separation could occur at the root of my being.

Yet now, at the core, I find the truth. We are all alive, vibrant, ready to enter into the fabric of life. Here in the place of the core of silence, the center of being, here where connectedness becomes the whole and the part, here where we can, with a thought, step within any field of knowing, here is where the wall of fog has lain, centuries old, nearly impermeable because we have not known it was there, or perhaps knowing, not being able to find where it lay. A good hiding puts the hidden in plain view, only camouflaged so as to never notice it is there, as a valuable diamond replaces the cheap crystal in a little dragon statuette.

Spells are strange things; I never knew this was where the fog originated. Familiar with this place, this center, I always felt the ground was firm, that here I could stand, knowing myself. Now, to find the subterranean chambers, the other world, opens my understanding into realms never before visited. What we once knew as the end of the world is now a beginning. The blind alley in the maze is the way into understanding.

What does it mean to be a woman in this place, this wider

understanding, this expanded consciousness?   Can we, now, enter into our birthright, returning to ourselves to know and remember our truth?   How can we discover something which has been hidden away from us for centuries?   It is difficult. The search is elusive for we hold the truth in our hands and it slips through our fingers like shining sand. The fog and sleep settle over us quickly; we forget what we just noticed.

> *The way is often dark. Listen.   There is a way to reach the inner circle, the place below the rock where we sit in council, slowly calling you all to us.   Mothers of the earth, we grow, Power gathering.   Come, sit, we will speak with you, you have much to learn, and you have learned much, to have arrived here.   Structures shadow the walls. This is the cavern of the Wise.*

The dwarves and the Hobbit had the key to Smaug's mountain for a long time before Bilbo recognized the meaning behind the runes on the ancient map.   It is a familiar theme in fairy tales, echoed by the discoveries we make in our own inward journeys, that the treasure we so ardently seek is already residing within our heart. To embark, therefore, on a journey to re-discover and re-create connections with wisdom once known and now forgotten, we need to remember that the key is probably in our possession, tucked away somewhere, small and insignificant, yet ready to be released when the moment is right.[3] We can climb many mountains, swim in strange waters, struggle through narrow passage-ways and endure long journeys across desolate plains.   All these are a part of the search; yet we may find as we rest, discouraged and exhausted, that the truth is there within us and we simply have not been able to see.

Tales of wonder and transformation are full of magic.   Both the old and the new stories contain the moments when something shifts, through design or accident, and people who were doing everyday activities find suddenly a door opening into another world, a wizard appears in their midst, an old woman reveals herself as more than she seems.   Perhaps a girl realizes she can understand the language of the animals, or a boy finds his words have power to make changes.   It is fine when the Elves turn up to save the day, or a friendly witch provides a meal for hungry travellers, but the best stories are those in which the characters are people like you and me and learn to do magical things such as becoming a tree, as Morgan did in *Riddlemaster of Hed*, or learning they can Lift themselves as the People do in Zenna Henderson's stories. Raderle learns to weave fire, in another volume of Patricia McKillip's Riddlemaster series, and Segnbora finds she must make room inside herself for a dying dragon in Diane Duane's *The Door into Shadow*. The Youngest Camel learns to make wise choices within the magic which offers itself to him in Kay Boyle's charming tale of the same name, Irene discovers she must find her own way while following her grandmother's thread in *The Princess and the Goblin*, the classic by George MacDonald, and Will takes council from the wisdom of his guide, Merriman, to release the land from the shadow in Susan Cooper's *The Dark is Rising*.[4]

All these are people who have a gift which circumstance demands they exercise. Ordinary people, going about their business, not asking for magic or wonderful things to happen, they find themselves unexpectedly and often unwillingly participating in a serious event, the outcome of which will affect the kingdom, the country, the world.

The continual appeal of such stories lies not only in the imaginative and vivid portrayal of the dangers and delights of living in a world where the boundaries of expected behavior are continually crossed. Reading tales of magic can be deeply satisfying to that part of ourselves that, in spite of all obstacles, believes such things are true. Crossing through the interface between the accepted collective reality and the individually intuited possibility, imagination is freed to reach into unexpected places, revealing doors we never knew existed. All great discoveries come to us through this interface, and many of the miracles we take for granted today would surely have been possible only through magical intervention fifty years ago. Present-day technological developments continually challenge the borders in many areas of our lives.

Brian Attebery says: "Though the fantasy may contain verisimilarly conceived characters, events, and settings, it is not intended to be judged primarily on its faithfulness to experience but rather on its effectiveness in conveying a sense of a radically altered or augmented world."[5]   Fantasy stretches our minds, pleases our souls, awakens longings in our hearts.   It reminds us that there is more to the world than we think.   It also nourishes our childhood memories.   When I found the stories of the People which Zenna Henderson gave to us in the 1950's, I felt I had discovered a precious treasure.   Here were people who could fly, lifting off the ground, playing with sunbeams.   I had always remembered my own flying, knowing it wasn't a dream.   These stories told of men and women who fled to this world when their Home Planet was destroyed, choosing Earth because of the similar environment, but who had abilities far beyond those of humans.   Persecuted for these differences, they learned to conceal themselves while at the same time making substantial contributions to the welfare of their neighbors.   The stories chronicled the search for other survivors of the Crossing and told of the terror and subsequent delight experienced by the People as they discovered and mastered their Gifts.[6]   I was entranced.

Searching for the truth of woman, knowing the exploration will take me beyond the boundaries which I currently recognize, I find comfort and encouragement in the possibilities inherent in the radically augmented world of fantasy.   These stories remind me to believe in magic, in something which seems impossible until we know how to do it.   Through these stories, I am able to hold the wonder of child and step through the intersecting space into woman.

> When we walk to the edge
> of all the light we have
> And
> take
> that
> step
> into the darkness
> of the unknown,
> We must believe
> that
> one
> of two things
> will happen;
> There will be

```
       something
       solid
                           for us
                           to stand on,
                 or
       we will
       learn
           how to fly.7
```

Flying allows us to make a leap beyond the expected. Creative imagination takes wing, leads us into worlds beyond worlds. Intuition sees around the corner, puts odd things together, comes up with a new perspective. These are ways we may come upon the hidden door and remember the shape of the key.

In the 1960's, I read stories by Anne McCaffrey about gifted people who were able to know the future, teleport themselves and objects, and read minds. Outcasts within their time, they banded together to prove themselves and to help solve some of the world's problems. They were good stories, but for me they were more than tall tales, because I knew people could really do these things, if only they could find clear recognition and skillful training. It seemed to me McCaffrey concurred.8

Fifteen years later a woman whose name I don't remember told me she flew, just like I did, when she was a child. It was a wonderful validation of my reality, to have my memory mirrored by another person. This encounter stirred my interest at a still deeper level.

Among other things, I am a weaver. I love to take tangled threads and follow each strand to its end, winding and straightening as I go. I then can thread the loom, weaving patterns with many colors. As I untangle and weave, gather and sort, a lifetime of small events and stories and memories shift, making a new pattern. I find myself wondering how many women remember something special. I begin to ask. Cathy tells me of the way the sun shone when her swing swept her into its center. Karen saw a beautiful sky woman, who came often as she played in the field. Each one I ask has a little something. I am excited. I begin to think: what if we all had held onto these gifts, been encouraged to develop them? I have known for years there are

parts of our brain which are largely unused, and it has seemed
logical that they wait for us to stretch into them. Could it be that
we have already received the gift?

Brooke Medicine Eagle speaks of the ancient recognition of
this gift in many cultures, saying : "At the time of birth, there is
a tremendous opening of the wings of spirit" as the special gifts
of the newborn emerge. These gifts then lie hidden until around
the age of five. The elders watch for the reemergence of the
wings, the gifts, which are then carefully nurtured, the wise of
the tribe teaching the young.[9], Kim a young woman graduating
from college and a talented actress and director, told me she was
able to know what others were thinking, and in fact still does. I
asked her, "What would it have been like, if this ability had
been recognized as a gift when you were little, and you had
received training in its use?" She was stunned, at first thinking
this was not possible; then, realizing the implications, she was
overwhelmed. The idea had never occurred to her.

We do not have such a system in place. We can, however,
learn to recognize our individual gifts and begin to realize how
they might be useful within our daily lives. So I asked a number
of women to remember their stories, the special memories they
have kept safely though the years.[10] We have come to realize, as
we talk together, the intense delight we experience as we are
freed to share, often for the very first time, something that is a
basic truth for each of us. This validation becomes a permission
to experience the feelings once again. Kathleen, who flew down
the halls of her parent's home at night, says "no more hiding -
down halls of fear." We no longer have to keep the secret and
can, instead, move forward toward integration.

The archetype of the Feminine, as described by Jung, is
associated with Eros, the principle of relationship. Women, and
those men who are fortunate to have a positive connection with
their inner Feminine, hold a special ability to connect with
themselves, with others, and with Nature. The Feminine is
interested in rhythms, feelings, interactions, the deep meaning of
life, germination, holding, receiving; it moves in cycles, knows
that in the Great Round all things will come again. It knows,
intuitively, that each is connected to the All, that each action and

thought affects the whole of life in some way.[11]

We have lived for centuries under the Masculine mode of thought which provides focus, direction and structure, ingredients which are essential for any manifestation but devastating in their impact when they are allowed to exist unbalanced by the Feminine influence. Hierarchies of government, schools, science and other institutions, intent on moving ahead into excellence, become sterile, forgetting their origins, unable to relate to or provide for the needs of the people they are intended to serve. Individuals within those structures struggle to maintain a connection, but no matter how hard they try, they are defeated by the system. The result of all these centuries of repression of the Feminine is a collision course with disaster, along which we are rushing headlong.

Within the search to reclaim women's wisdom and power lies the inherent necessity to approach the journey from the Feminine realm. We cannot hope to understand the inner workings of something simply by observing it from the outside. Women researchers have discovered this as they talk with women about their problems. When Lyn Mikel Brown and Carol Gilligan were embarking upon their research at Laurel School, looking at the time of transition which is the crossroad from girl into woman, they discovered that the traditional forms of inquiry were interfering with the progress of their work. They realized they needed to "create a practice of psychology that was something more like a practice of relationship,"[12] and that they needed to develop a more responsive and listening mode of questioning. They became vividly aware of their own reactions and growth as they listened and remembered. By paying attention to the relationships between themselves and the young women they were interviewing, by being willing to set aside their training in traditional research methods, they found themselves moving into new forms of interactions which were previously considered unacceptable to the scientific community because of the personal involvement of the researchers. They write:

> Our work gained a clarity we had not experienced before. Out
> of what could be seen as a collapse in form—a letting go of our

planned research design for the messiness and unpredictability
and vulnerability of ongoing relationship—a way of working
emerged which felt more genuine and mutual, precarious at first,
disruptive, unsettling to those of us used to our authority and
control in professional situations and in the conduct of
psychological research.[13]

I am fortunate that others such as Gilligan and Brown have
done their work well and that the methods of feminist research
have gained a measure of acceptance.[14]

As I continue to immerse myself within the mysteries of
woman, I gradually come to knowledge which it seems I have
always known.   I recognize that the way to this knowledge is
through paths which are not recognized within the system of my
culture, that the methods acceptable to the traditional institutions
of learning will not serve my search, for they were formulated to
keep hidden that which I seek.[15] Desiring to feel my way into
the deeply Feminine energy in women, I must allow my body to
participate. This is not an exploration to be made entirely within
the mind; rather there needs to be a relationship which flows
throughout my whole being, spirit, mind, body, and soul,
intertwining, intuitive, flexible.   Woman's wisdom has been
denied and repressed for so long it would be impossible to plan a
formulated outline which could adequately develop an approach
to this knowing.   Traditional research has been carefully struc-
tured to eliminate variables which might confuse the outcome. It
is this structure which effectively eliminates the fluid, often
messy, immersion in the process of deep searching which results
from following one's intuition.

As I shift from child into woman, it is crucial that I find the
way to hold to the wonder of fresh discovery. It is all too easy to
lose connection with the upsurge of delight at the sight of the
morning sun, pale through the wintry trees. The first flower of
spring, light and blue amid the fresh snowfall, should be the
occasion for a song of joy.   Maintaining faith that I could fly
keeps alive the part of me that knows magic is possible. I must
search and read and write and dream, living always with the
expectation that the next step will appear when it is ready.
Holding the wonder, attending to the process, keeping faith with

truth, these are things I can do while I wait.

The importance of this creative searching finds resonance in heuristic research, a system of inquiry developed by Clark Moustakas in the early 1960's. It employs a methodology which allows for the subjective exploration so necessary to any study undertaken from the Feminine perspective. *Heuristic* "refers to a process of internal search through which one discovers the nature and meaning of experience and develops methods and procedures for further investigation and analysis."[16] Building on works from Maslow, Polanyi, Gendlin, and Rogers, among others, Moustakas and his students have allowed research to acknowledge a deeply human dimension. He says,

> The heuristic process is a way of being informed, a way of knowing. Whatever presents itself in the consciousness of the investigator as perception, sense, intuition, or knowledge represents an invitation for further elucidation. What appears, what shows itself as itself, casts a light that enables one to come to know more fully what something is and means. In such a process not only is knowledge extended but the self of the researcher is illuminated.[17]

One must come to heuristic research through a personal encounter with that which is being explored and a passion to discover the deeper dimensions of the question. Through a process known as Indwelling, this passion is carried into the heart of the researcher, seeking to remain with the many aspects of the question until there is a creative synthesis.

> The indwelling process is conscious and deliberate, yet it is not lineal or logical. It follows clues wherever they appear; one dwells inside them and expands their meanings and associations until a fundamental insight is achieved.[18]

It is wonderful to repeat the six phases of heuristic inquiry: *initial engagement, immersion, incubation, illumination, explication, creative synthesis.*[19] Each calls up memories of the unfolding process, deeply engaging, completely satisfying, richly rewarding. Within this method my woman self can unfold and flourish, for it allows her free rein to grow where she will.

We must remember our bodies, our woman selves, when we walk forward into the field, knowing it is our body. Under our feet, the grass continues to grow . Mind must rest. Wrap, instead, the body in soft silk, feel the hair on your head lift gently, rise up on tiptoes to honor the dance and begin.

Surrounded by others who are pushing past the barriers, I search on this path alone, understanding that the way is within me. Religions of the East, esoteric teachings, true teachers, all recognize that real learning must come from within, that if the student does not make self-generated connections, knowledge is only a repeat of the statements of others and has no life within the individual. I seek, as do countless others, for the true knowing that arises from clear connections and profoundly affects my life.

There are three circles of wisdom, ancient and modern. Three circles, three faces, three aspects of the Goddess. First is the new moon, the beginning, the child, the daughter. In the second we grow into fullness, ripening with birth, mothering ourselves, nurturing the earth, feeling the maturity of relationship with another, be it self, man, or woman. Third, as the cycle turns to completion, Sophia the woman of wisdom unfolds the teachings of a lived life, the secrets of the dark, a meeting with death. Three circles, three cycles, three conditions of life.

Our dance leads us through them all, overlapping, intertwining, circle intersecting circle intersecting circle. Mandorlas open; they are windows in time and space. Entering them we move through multiple dimensions. From child into woman, if we remember the overlap, we will not lose the wonder.

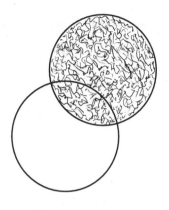

∞ E ∞

What Is a Woman?

Second Circle: Woman, Mother

Growing up is usually a confusing process, with mixed messages about behavior coming from all sides. As I matured physically into a young woman I began to feel a distinct lack of direction. I had good role models for developing myself into an intelligent, conscious, spiritual person but something was missing. I had no idea what it was, nor how to go about finding it, nor did I know it was related to being a woman. It is only now, in retrospect, that I can identify the searching for the truth of myself which occupied more than thirty years of my life as a longing for connection to my deep woman self.

My mother was a product of the Victorian Age, born before the turn of the century to a woman who never taught her anything about her female body. The two stories she always told me were that she thought, until she was in high school, that if she sat on a man's lap she would "get a baby," and that when she first began menstruating, her mother was so embarrassed she could not bring herself to explain what was happening and persuaded a woman friend to take Mother for a walk. In this way, my mother learned what the bleeding was, and what to expect.

I appreciate my mother's independent spirit which determined that her daughter would know these facts long before she needed them. As a result, I always knew where babies came from and how they were made. My first memory about the subject, at six or seven, was of being fascinated by the information that at conception the egg is ten times smaller than the tiniest dot you can make with the sharpest pencil you can find. I repeated this experiment many times, marvelling at the miracle.

Other aspects of being a woman were, unfortunately, beyond my mother's perception. I think she regarded her body as a necessary encumbrance, the same way she regarded sex, and always referred to "down there" if she had to speak about anything relating to the parts of her body which lay between her legs. My initiation into womanhood was the purchase of a sanitary belt and napkins, which I hated. I disliked the feeling, the encumbrance, the weird sensations, but there were no words to describe these reactions. I probably didn't even try to voice my feelings, for it was clear that I was to tolerate this unpleasantness, and that this was a necessary part of being a female. I think being a woman was, for my mother, a burden she had to bear, and she directed her attention to her Self, her Soul, and her Spirit, looking for the essence of Being, searching for the truth of her personhood. I have spent most of my life doing the same, with great rewards. It is only recently that I have begun to understand how my culture has denied me access to my Woman self.

What does it mean to be a woman? A heavy silence continues to surround the question which my soul yearns to answer. Deep inside, I KNOW. Between me and my truth lie centuries of misinformation, deliberate repression, denial, and death. I can list our history, the litany of depression, recognize the multitude of mutilations, hear the many subtle encouragements to remain in ignorance. I see the cycles through which women lift themselves into a small degree of independence and consciousness, only to be slapped down or undercut once again. In spite of recent advances for women this cycle is continuing, manifesting in today's society as the reaction to the Women's Liberation movement. In this context Susan Faludi points out a major obstacle to our full comprehension of our woman selves.

> A backlash against women's rights succeeds to the degree that it appears *not* to be political, that it appears not to be a struggle at all. It is most powerful when it goes private, when it lodges inside a woman's mind and turns her vision inward, until she imagines the pressure is all in her head, until she begins to enforce the backlash, too—on herself.[1]

Thus the search to discover the truth of Woman gets very confused, often lost in the spirals of society's demands, internalized until we think we believe our "place is in the home," that being feminine means being frilly. And then our own backlash comes into play, and we reject all the lace and pleasure in beauty as being a symbol of slavery.

We also experience a deep and confusing fear of truly fulfilling ourselves. Unreasonably, yet totally logically, we fear that if we really stepped into the potential we intuit for ourselves, individually, as powerful women, we would be destroyed. Our partners would cease to love us, society would reject us, and more than that, many of us feel intense terror that we would be killed, annihilated, mutilated, just as we grasp the shining truth of our being.

It is crucial to our continued exploration of ourselves as women that we understand the power of the centuries of oppression. We cannot release ourselves into the future until we can clearly see the intent and purpose of the restrictive patterns in which we have participated, believing them to be real. We read, daily, of abuses perpetrated against women; of rape, murder, battering; of genital mutilation and forced pregnancies.[2] We see everywhere the struggle for equality, for salaries based on performance, not gender, for women to be admitted into the priesthood and into active combat.

What is not so clear is the way through the questioning about the Feminine, about what makes us, as women, unique. We are unlike men; we do not need to think as they do to have equality. What we do need is clear awareness of ourselves as women who are persons organized differently from men.

C.G. Jung provided some insight and tools to help women and men begin to understand their differences when he defined the essential energies which organize our lives as archetypes, and explored their power to dominate or assist us.[3] Consideration of that aspect of woman which is the essential or archetypal Feminine has been of interest to many who have entered through the doors which he opened. Jung had remarkable vision and was able to point the way towards discovery and acceptance of the richness of the Feminine.

M. Esther Harding, a Jungian analyst, was an early explorer of the individual perceptions of women in her work *The Way of All Women*, followed in 1971 with the deeper dimension in *Women's Mysteries, Ancient and Modern*. Through myth and story, this book invites an approach to the archetype of the Feminine as manifested in various Goddesses associated with the Moon in her phases. Reading this before the current multitude of books concerning the reemergence of the Goddess were available, I responded strongly to Harding's assertion about the modern woman:

> For while the stirrings within, which require a field of activity
> in the outer objective world, are accepted by herself and others
> as legitimate, other longings, which also have their origin deep
> within her being, and which seek for a spiritual and subjective
> fulfillment, are not so generally acknowledged." [4]

Understanding through this book and other readings about the Feminine[5] that this was an area that was not fully explored, I realized the only way to discover my own truths was to make my own journey. At forty-six, married, with three teenage children, I felt this was my entry into womanhood. All my years of searching had been focused towards Spirit and Soul, valuable searching indeed, rich with wisdom from the East and the West. Through it all, however, while I felt I had maturity as a person, I could not come to a sense of myself as a mature woman. I remember wondering, when I was forty-three, when I would begin to feel like an "older woman." I had women friends whom I considered wise and mature. I perceived that they seemed to regard me in similar fashion; yet I continued to feel, inside, like a young girl. I did not understand what was missing until I began to move more deeply into the realm of the Goddess.

Depression is a common disorder among women, causing great pain and disruption. While there are some for whom this state is a true clinical depression, treatable with medication, many women find the underlying dismay at the life in which they find themselves trapped is a primary cause. Marriage or partnership, commitment, children, home, job, all grab the available time and energy, leaving her with nothing. Whatever the demands of the world may be, no matter how much she may love her family and her activities, she is left bereft spiritually, disconnected from her soul. Even God, in the patriarchal tradition, requires from her an unswerving obedience and devotion to His word and leaves little room for her own intuitive connection to Spirit.

In this situation, from far within, the deep self of the woman shifts, restlessly. Where is the attention she requires for survival? When is there time for her? How shall she be nourished? The deep self longs to shine, but she cannot rise beyond the layers of denial, neglect, and repression. And so the deep voice cries out, demanding consideration, and her demand rises, insistent, drawing the woman down. In an attempt to bring focus to the problem, the deep self begins to shut down outer desire, drawing the attention ever within. This demand is powerful, a bid for survival; thus any attempt on the part of the woman to pull herself out of the pit within which she feels she has fallen is only temporarily successful. The only solution is to turn her attention inward to herself.[6]

It can be a murky journey on a lonesome road. It is somewhat brighter if the way is lit by the clear peace of the Goddess. This is woman's work, an exploration of the inner Feminine Self. How much more supported one feels if the Presence which guides and nurtures is also female.

When I entered this journey, I continued the work of growth

begun by my mother, picking up where she was unable to continue. I had learned how to mother my children through the usual struggles, and had learned something about mothering myself. With three children born within four years, I had experienced the complete draining of energy that happens when there is a continual outpouring of nurturing for others, and I had found out the importance of taking time for my own needs. I had spent many years in a search for soul and spirit, entering into deep relationship with myself at a number of levels. What was missing, strangely but predictably, was my connection with the woman self. I was not fully conscious of this, I only knew there was some part of myself that was never satisfied. Centuries of repression had done their work and I did not know something had been systematically deleted. Carol Christ is eloquent on this point saying "Women have lived in the interstices between inchoate experiences and the shapings given to experience by the stories of men. In a very real sense, women have not experienced their own experience."[7]

In that farmland where we lived, I began the nightly connection with the Moon. In the warm summer months, hidden in the tall grasses of the field, I lay naked to the Sun whenever I could. I thought of my woman's body moving in imagined ways through intricate dances of ceremony and magic. I planted and harvested our vegetables, delighting in the partnership with the earth, deeply satisfied to be growing the food we ate. My family and I cared for my mother through her two-year struggle with the bone-disintegrating condition of osteoporosis until her death. I wrote my Master's thesis. And I met the Deep Feminine.

Dark caverns, wet with water trickling over the walls. Deeply I search. The gleam of silver, cold, shining, beckons me into the shadows. Journey down, alone, no one can come here. All must stay behind, and love stays with them, here is a different sort of love. Love for children, animals, land, partners, these all remain connected to them, living on the surface of the earth. Each step I take in this land of permanent shadows draws me ever further from such emotions. Here I am only with myself, moving with clear purpose, towards the dark, cold shining. Innana took just

*such a journey, and Psyche, so too did fair Persephone, albeit
unwillingly, travelling into the Underworld. Here there is
no story. Only myself and the dark.[8]*

Silence. Days pass. I search through volumes, papers, read
journals, write letters. Daily life goes on, but I never leave the
cave. I cook, clean, give advice, solve problems. Inside, I finger
the silver, feeling the intense cold, wondering. Rough walls enclose me, a vast dry desert lies in the heart of the cave, all journeys cease.

I learn about the absence of love for others. I accept the
demand of this deep calling. I feel the connection of the nightly
Moon and the deep silver. I wear silver bracelets, buy myself a
silver ring wrought with flowers curving around blue lapis
marked with silver. I read Linda Fierz-David

> Here she is pushed beyond any need of her own, or the needs of
> her nearest and dearest. Here she does not recognize outer time
> and its demands but only the unmistakable signs of an inner ebb
> and flow. Quite unconsciously and involuntarily this deepest
> part of her is concerned only with the growth and maturing of
> life which demands its rights, must demand its rights, whether
> she wishes it or not.9

Here my intensity is matched. The rights of the Deep
Feminine demand my recognition, and I have no choice. The
silver potentiates in the light of the moon and becomes silver fish
in deep dark water. The stars shine in the night sky and fall
reflected into the lake. One must pass through death to receive
life.

* * *

Fourteen years later as I write, remembering this time in my
life, I have difficulty returning to the present. The March wind
chases the clouds across the blue sky and I must step outside to
let the fresh breeze clear my thoughts. The pull of the Deep is
very strong, and I am reluctant to leave. This is a place of such
intense reality, such true knowing of myself, that I wonder how it
could ever have become lost. Only violent tearing could part me
from this connection. I weep for the loss of my woman self
through all the years, for the intricate interweavings of negation,

fear, denial, degradation and omission which keep us all continually away from this rich source of life.

All of us, mothers, grandmothers, daughters, are kept from our own bodies throughout our lives, encouraged to deliver them into the keeping of others. Our peers tell us how to dress; our parents tell us what is appropriate behavior. Our lovers, husbands, priests, and doctors dictate our relationship to our bodies; we birth our children by the rules of the medical profession unless we work hard to circumvent them. Within the last hundred years there have been a series of opinions, issued by men, about the relationship of women to body and mind which are stunning in their variety, and amazing in their contradictions.[10]   Many women doctors are now working to change some of these preconceptions; notable among them is Dr. Christine Northrup, who works to free the natural phases of women's life, such as menopause, from the "disease" mentality.[11]

There are so many layers of repression and denial that it is often difficult to listen to one's body. While I have moved a long way past my mother's inability to discuss her feminine parts, I am continually aware of the need to move ever more deeply into connection with my own body, and aware also of the intense opposition I encounter within myself. This opposition occurs in a variety of ways; I get distracted and think about something else, I get sleepy, I feel I am surrounded by fog and that my brain will simply not work. Or I get frightened by an intensity of feeling which is more than I am used to, and shut down. Gradually, I work through all of these obstructions. Gradually I begin to understand the nature of the necessity which has kept us separate from our woman bodies all these centuries. For I believe it is not only the desire of men to subjugate woman which keeps the door firmly closed.[12] I think there is also a serious fear, felt by both men and women, of allowing the power and wisdom of the Feminine its freedom of expression. I think this is a collective fear, stemming from the many years of the witch hunts, a memory in the cells of our bodies of the life-threatening danger of possessing this wisdom. Its power is sacred; it has the potential to make enormous changes in our personal and collective world. Our fear is real; it exists in our present moment and in our ancestral memory.

Gerda Lerner notes, as she reviews her extensive research into the history of women under the Patriarchy, "But the most important thing I learned was the significance to women of their relationship to the Divine and the profound impact the severing of that relationship had on the history of women."[13] The depth of spiritual connection which many women experience is so intense and so complete that it threatens to upset the established male order and thus must be subjugated. When we look at the lives of the women mystics who lived in earlier centuries, at Julian of Norwich or Mechthild of Magdeburg, it is clear their encounters with the Divine were experienced with their whole being: body, soul, and spirit. Their writings are full of the rapture they experience in union with the Beloved. They physically held Christ, fed him, made love with him.[14] J.Giles Milhaven says this complete bodily experience was difficult for the men of the Church to comprehend:

> It is not the intimacy of the women's union with God that repels the theologians. The theologians affirm with awe the intimacy of soul and God which God makes possible on the mystical heights and in the immediate vision of God which all the faithful have after death. It is the degree of physicality of the women's experience that make it unintelligible and often repugnant to mystical theologians of the tradition, even modern ones.[15]

Apparently it suited the male theologians to discredit that which they could not understand, and this contributed to the incredibly widespread persecution of women who were simply following their own truth of connection with the Divine. Incited by the publication of *Malleus Maleficarum: The Hammer of Witches*, the work of two German monks, Kramer and Sprenger, which said, among many inflammatory statements, "It were a thousand times better for the land if all Witches, but especially the blessing Witch, might suffer death,"[16] many women who were simply following the guidance they received from the Spirit met their horrible deaths.

As modern women exploring their connections with the Goddess and the feminine aspect of the Divine have been discovering, an intimate relationship with the spiritual aspect of life brings with it a sense of security, of independence, and of great joy. For the women in the fourteenth and fifteenth centuries, this independence was life threatening. Mary Daly comments:

> ...the witchcraze focused predominantly upon women who had rejected marriage (Spinsters) and women who had survived it (widows). The witch-hunters sought to purify their society (The Mystical Body) of these 'indigestible' elements—women whose physical, intellectual, economic, moral, and spiritual independence and activity profoundly threatened the male monopoly in every sphere.[17]

We carry the burden of this persecution today, not only in the many areas of woman's life which are not allowed full expression, but in our collective unconscious, where the whispered messages of caution and terror keep the sense of the Sacred Power hidden and repressed.

Aware of the denial of woman on so many levels, I listen once more to my body. My mother could not speak of her female parts. Many women, myself included, carry this taboo: do not name your vagina, your clitoris, your uterus. To do so is "not nice." Yet as I continue my journey into the Deep Feminine, I cannot help but notice sensations arising here, in my secret and private places. Acknowledging their presence I realize that I also know, with the clarity of truth, that these feelings are sacred.

Once again the journey draws me down, knowing as I go that I join with many women as we find ourselves on the journey into our own womanself depths. Venturing or plunging, these depths draw us as we encounter our own intensity, feeling the sharp shards of our personality splinter off to dissolve in the bleak richness of inner awareness. There is a sharp pain at the center of this world, sensed within our woman's body as the place below the navel, known as Hara, Omphalos, an egg of comprehension nestled within our being. Only woman can bring this particular egg to birth. Within us modern women the egg has grown a hard shell, a protection needed to endure throughout the centuries. Our wisdom will now allow us to dissolve this shell, sending the calcium and proteins which it contains out into the system for redistribution. And what then, as we sense the softening of the shell, and the Feminine within stirs, awakening after a long sleep? We bring our own woman kiss to her, touching her lovingly, welcoming her emergence into our lives. Tenderly touching the hard shell which surrounds our womanhood, we are woman touching woman. We know, now, that our bodies are sacred to us. The wisdom of the body recognizes that physical sensations are a language which can speak clearly to us if we will pay attention. Through the deep mysteries of the female body we come to know our unity with the divine Feminine. It is a unity of body and spirit which my mother was unable to realize, for while she moved far beyond her Victorian upbringing, she could never completely shed the repression imposed on her sexuality.

Mother died at home, her care shared by my husband and our three teenaged children. The following year I was staring out the kitchen window one day:

It is August. My mother has been dead for nearly a year. I am thinking of her, grieving for the missed connection, the last part of Self and Soul which we could never connect. We both felt it, knew it, acknowledged it verbally, yet never knew what it was. For me it felt like a thin wall between us, We loved each other deeply, liked the same things, shared many experiences. We should have been able to meet, the wall should have dissolved, disintegrated, never existed.

Now I know, in a flash of understanding. I have moved to the other side of the wall, in the intervening months. During that time I have come to cherish a deep love for a woman. Through that love, I have come to understand my woman self in a richly personal way. I have spiralled into connections with body, Goddess, and Soul. My Deep Feminine has led me to new knowledge of my woman self and the whole world looks changed. my energy and delight are boundless. I am in love with woman, personal and collective.

In this flash of comprehension I realized it was the absence of our deep woman selves that kept us apart, and I longed for

Mother to be alive again, so I could share my new insight with her. Yet I knew then, and also now, that it was not enough for me to have crossed that line. She was kept inside that wall herself, by her own history, and though it would have helped if I could have brought this gift to her, it would not have been enough. So I told her that August day, and tell her again today, for now the rift can be healed through my own explorations and understanding. Now I can come to her, in memory and in her felt presence today, acknowledging our Feminine nature, our connected selves as mother, daughter, and as women together, once apart, now able to be joined in spirit through renewed energy.

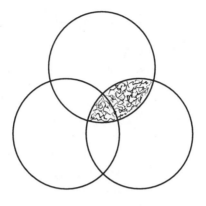

∞ F ∞

Unwinding the Spell

Second Intersection: Woman into Elder

At a conference for women in New Hampshire in the fall of 1993 I participated in a workshop on Trance Dancing. The basement room where we gathered grew dark as we began to listen to music designed to awaken our bodies and send us into rhythms of movement. Gradually I settled into moving comfortably, ceasing any attempt to interact with others. I came into contact with my own insides, and felt my movements were originating from my organs. I felt them shaking, shifting, propelling me into a dance which was entirely outside my own volition. If there had been more space and familiarity, I believe I would have released completely any hold I had on consciousness. I was truly on the edge of trance.

That ended, and there was a period of uncertainty, during

which I kept moving, unsure of what would come next. Then, suddenly, I was swept into an awareness of a deep darkness. Urgently I was impelled to let myself sink as deeply as I could. Within this intense dark was a vivid awareness of present and past. As if on a screen, I saw the fields of crosses at Verdun, the site of the battle in France during World War I. Row upon row of identical white crosses, marking many deaths of many men. And below that, in the darkness, as I moved under that picture of identified death, I knew I was in the place of many other deaths, those of women burned at the stake as witches, women stoned to death, women drowned on the dunking stool, women tortured endlessly to wring false confessions of union with the Devil from their dying lips. There are no graves for these women, no rows of white crosses marking the battlefield of their small villages where the hysteria of fear created a war against those who could heal, and women who were wise threatened the establishment of power controlled by the church and society. Within this place there was only silence and memory.

As I stood within the darkness made deeper by the weight of years I saw, of a sudden, a tiny yellow candle lit. I remembered we had been given little yellow candles to carry with us during the conference, and that there was a ceremony planned to honor the wise women who were destroyed during the many years of planned persecution. And as I watched, I saw more thin yellow candles lit, each one lifting the darkness from the spot in which it burned. As the lights continued to increase, patches of grey appeared and the darkness was less intense. And then the yellow candles and their lights began to rise, lifting upwards, and my arms lifted with them and I felt my spirit soar with them, for I feel I, too, was one of those women, long, long ago. I watched them rise and expected they would all soar into the sky to disappear into the heavens. Instead they turned, and as I stood there with my arms outstretched, all the yellow candles came together and descended into my open hands, entering into my care.

I weep again, remembering. I am charged to do this work. I must follow this trail wherever it leads, my hands full of candles. Untangling the skein, coming upon the tensely

wrapped knots, I search through the crossings and bindings,
realizing I must know the origin of each thread before the
spell can be unsaid.

Margaret Atwood, in her novel *The Handmaid's Tale*,[1]
postulates a time, not too far into the future, when the repression
of woman has reached horrifying proportions. The woman who
tells the tale has one purpose in her life; to bear a child for the
high ranking couple to whom she is assigned. The grotesque
details of her submission, her ritualized monthly impregnation,
the narrowness of her life without reading, music, or
conversation, create an intense portrait of the denial of woman's
spirit. It is particularly frightening placed within the context of
today's climate of increasing freedom and opportunities for
modern women, for it reminds us that power can be seized at
any time by those who are willing to kill to gain and maintain
their position. We have only to open the morning newspaper to
recognize the truth of this statement. Across the world forces
battle for supremacy, the struggles fueled by desire for land and
food, by religious fervor and hate, and at root, by desire for
power. Any minority suffers during such struggles, the word
defining, in an instant, anyone whom the majority hates. Jews,
African Americans, homosexuals, persons of Asian descent and
Native Americans are the usual targets for hate in this country;
other minorities bear the brunt in other parts of the world. The
repression and hatred of women, however, is universal, and in
any war rape becomes a tool of power and violence.

When there is an emotional experience which is shared by
many people across time, it can be defined as an archetype. This
archetype, which has universal characteristics, can then take up
residence in the psyche of anyone who has some connection with
that experience. Thus one can become possessed by despair, by
an overwhelming need to mother, by a desire for power, or, if
one is fortunate, a perpetual sense of delight, for archetypes can
be positive, though we usually concern ourselves with them in
their negative aspect.[2]

Archetypes can also possess a group of people, a country, or
an era. Jung recognized just such a national archetype when
Hitler was coming into power in Germany, identifying it as that

of Wotan, the wanderer and the aggressor.[3] He accurately predicted that wide scale disaster would occur, should this archetype gain the upper hand. Hate and fear are powerful archetypes that enter into the equation of the widespread possession.

When hatred and fear focus on a particular group of people, there is no reasonable argument which will combat or change the prejudice, and it can continue for generations, as witness the African American position in the United States. No matter how intelligent, educated, well dressed, wealthy, or highly positioned a person descended from those who once were slaves might be, there is always an undercurrent among those who experience the prejudice, a small voice which remembers these were once "niggers", and this small voice can swell incredibly quickly when the right stimulus is applied.

Prejudice is an archetype which runs beneath all our consciousness, lurking in the basement, hairy and grotesque, waiting for an eruption of the unconscious to bring it to the surface. Conflict, struggles for power, war, fear, all can create conditions which allow the monster to become manifest. Pero Popovic, a Bosnian Serb, has told of his experience as a guard in a concentration camp for Muslims. He said: "The worst part of it was knowing the prisoners. I had grown up with these Muslims, as had all the guards. And yet we beat them with pieces of timber and iron rods. How could anyone imagine such things before they started?"[4] Such tales are commonplace during wartime. What is not often reported is the prevalence of rape, for it only shows up when the children appear. One can only speculate how many women are raped and abused during any war, for it is seldom talked about. Yet it seems to be an accepted privilege of the invading soldiers.

We understand, today, that rape is an act of violence. How strange that the sexual act, which is clearly designed to be a pleasurable, unifying, even sacred experience can be used to degrade and humiliate. The juxtaposition seems unthinkable, and yet it happens every day in multiplicity. How quickly the archetype turns, and she who was revered is now the object of hatred.

The archetype of Woman as evil has settled into the

unconscious of the world's inhabitants to such an extent, for so many generations, that most never notice the countless ways in which they are ruled and guided by this insidious and powerful energy. Wolfgang Lederer, MD, in his book aptly titled *The Fear of Women*, says in the introduction that he will see, in his consulting room, "...strong men fret, and hear them talk of women with dread and horror and awe, as if women, far from being timid creatures to be patronized, were powerful as the sea and inescapable as fate."[5]

It is a strange and mysterious thing, this power which men seem to sense and fear, and which they seek always to keep under control. The majority of women are not aware of these shadowed emotions and do not realize that their very independence can arouse a man's subconscious fear of domination and destruction.

The association of woman with dark and evil, sin and dissolution, makes certain the necessity for men to retain the control in all things. The incredible savagery of the European witch hunts could not have happened without a general acceptance that woman is inherently evil, a belief fostered by the story of Adam and Eve and nourished by the *Malleus Maleficarum* which defines woman as the lesser sex, in league with the Devil.[6] The need to keep the dark force at bay infuses both men and women, thus repeating the supposition that everything would fall apart if the true Feminine were allowed to reign. And yet many of us are now realizing that the desire for control is destroying our planet. From control of people to control of environment, we see the enormous results of war, famine, destruction of forests and oceans, as well as the eroding of personal relationships.

It is important to understand the prevalence of the fear of women which lies within the collective unconscious, for without full acceptance of this knowledge, it will be impossible to bring about any significant shift of consciousness. As a woman, I seek to understand the extent to which this archetype pervades our lives, for this widespread prevalence clouds our vision and inhibits our abilities to know truth. Follow a woman's feeling of low self-esteem down into her inner memories, and the fact of her being a girl is usually part of the information she received as a child, a girl who was not as good as her brother, especially in the eyes of her mother, a girl who found things were not the same for her as for the boys with whom she played.

Recognizing this underlying information of being somehow not quite as good as boys, and living in a society which is based entirely on the superiority of men, the grown woman finds herself supporting and contributing to this belief in ways which are completely opposite to her knowledge of her basic self, and yet seemingly impossible to change. The infinite variety of the forms which inequality takes makes the task of discovery difficult, for many attitudes are so ingrained they seem completely natural. It may be helpful to remember the archetype of woman as evil, relating each instance of repression back to it to see how it fits. Whenever a woman is regarded as less than a man, not as good at some task as a man would be, there must be some basic dislike, distrust, or fear of that woman lurking in the unconscious, for why else would it be necessary to be so consistent in forcing her into the role of being controlled?

Anyone who grew up with the Old Testament of *The Holy Bible* knows that in the book of Genesis, Eve ate the forbidden fruit, tempted Adam so that he also ate, and was therefore the cause of their subsequent expulsion from Paradise. In this simple story, the role of woman as the evil temptress was indelibly set. Desiring to reverse the centuries-old patterns of a religion which honored the Goddess and the God and in which woman was revered as priestess and mother, the authors of this story choose some of the most sacred images from that time. The Tree of Wisdom, its fruit the apple, and the serpent who had, from ancient times, been connected with immortality, were recast in the tale of the garden of Eden and given a negative connotation. Eve was doomed, and we are left with the anger of a jealous God.

The sacred serpent reappears in a fearful role attached to the head of Medusa, and a woman, beautiful and powerful, is destroyed by jealousy, transformed into a hideous, death-dealing creature. The message works its way into our psyches: "Woman is evil, she turns man to stone with her glance, she must be killed." Medusa and Eve are powerful deterrents to full acceptance of our woman selves.

The roots of our remembering run deep, and the underground stream of our collective unconscious carries the awareness of our fear. There is a quiet voice speaking to many women which cautions "Don't be too powerful, don't speak too clearly about the things you really love. Don't be too different." The witch hunts are vivid in the minds of many modern women, both for the horrifying reality of whole villages left with but a few women alive and because there is a rising tide of remembrance. There are a number of women who either have memories of being alive in those times or have strong connections to the events, sometimes directly through their ancestresses.[7] I am one who senses a connection; I have an unreasoning horror of torture and mutilation of the body. As a small child I was terrified of a movie in which a man was being tortured on the rack. My fear was so great that my mother told me I could always leave any movie I didn't like. The next one which frightened me was *The Wizard of Oz*, and when the house fell on the wicked witch and her feet shriveled up, I left, my whole body vibrating with fear. Halfway home on that Saturday afternoon in the small southern town, I realized this movie probably wasn't all like that, and went back. I also remember, when I was maybe four, living for the summer next to a friendly man who began to read *Alice in Wonderland* to me. Early in the book there is a place where Alice finds a bottle which says "Drink me" and she promptly grows a very long neck. The accompanying picture sent me screaming home, and my mother came storming over to chastise the bewildered man for frightening me so. Explanations were forthcoming, and we continued the reading, but for years afterward I would not look at that page, for the sensations in my body were unbearable. Eventually I decided to overcome this fear and forced myself to look at the picture, quelling my urgent need to run, until it was bearable to see.

I never understood this terror, for my childhood was good, safe and peaceful. I knew not to see certain movies, read certain comics, I never go to horror films or watch them on TV. The images are unshakable. In recent years I have come to find the only explanation which makes any sense for this lifelong condition. Although I mercifully do not remember any specifics, I feel I must have been tortured, a victim of a witchhunt in an earlier time. In recent years I have met a number of women who also have had some sort of experience of memory which connects them to the "Burning Times," as the centuries of witchhunts are sometimes called.[8] Some feel it is a personal experience and have vivid memories; others are aware of the collective terror.

The intensity of these memories and experiences makes it easier to understand how difficult it is to regain the knowledge of woman's ways which these women possessed and practiced. I find the curtain between me and this knowledge is a thick fog, difficult to penetrate, in which I easily become lost and lose sight of the direction in which I was travelling. To explore and search, therefore, I must first encounter the fog, enter into it, and explore my reactions, my experience. As I do when I examine a dream, I begin with my associations, and allow the connections to emerge.

Fog. On summer days in New England coastal villages, the fog comes when you least expect it. One minute it is a beautiful sunny day, blue sky and high, white clouds, and you are gathering your towels for a trip to the beach. The next minute you feel a breath of cool air, look up the street, and see the fog rolling in. Inexorably it advances, seeping past the houses, wrapping around the branches of trees, moistening your hair, getting up your nose, and you retreat into the house, abandoning disgustedly the planned afternoon on the warm sand.

There are times when I cannot think clearly. It seems, then, as though a thick curtain has been pulled over my mind, blocking access to any ideas or understandings that might have been available to me a moment before. I also notice this happening with some of my clients. I ask a question, or a woman arrives at a thought; suddenly I notice she is staring into space, her eyes seemingly focused but beginning to glaze. I say something, and with a start she returns, saying she seemed to have lost track of my question, or forgot what she was saying. She says it is as if she has been lost in a fog.

It seems that just when we think we are trembling on the edge of knowing, when a thought pauses in its flight and we can, with a little reach, almost catch it, when we catch a glimpse of that for which we have long sought, that is when, like on the summer's day, the fog descends. It is particularly prevalent when we search after something which we know to be hidden. Memories of childhood long buried, intimations of something once known are particularly well wrapped in fog.

In the winter of '93, I set aside some weeks before the Solstice for inward searching and contemplation. The search for the understanding of the ancient knowledge, known to women of old, shared by those who honor the land and respect all life, occupied my thoughts, seeming always to be just beyond my reach. I was frequently overwhelmed by the fog. The following is an excerpt from my journal.

Notes from the Field Journal

This has been an incredibly difficult week. I am experiencing an intense resistance to entering into the work of reclaiming the ancient wisdom. My mind goes blank after a few minutes of reading. I cannot remember what I was just thinking; a fog settles thickly within my brain and there is no chance of any idea penetrating. I am struggling mightily against this, trying to wake up, trying to keep my mind on the project. I am beset by thoughts of inadequacy; I cannot keep up with all the other people in the program, I shouldn't be going for a PhD because I am more experientially oriented and cannot do the concentrated research required. I worry that I will not be able to find the money, that I do not have the time, that the energy I am putting into this is taking energy away from my practice and that I will never get any new clients. I see the disasters rampant in the world and realize there is no hope, we will all be dead soon anyway, so why put myself through all this. Why not just quit and go back to a quiet, private life; what an attractive thought.

When the fog lifts, as it occasionally does, I see signs of hope in everything I read. It seems that all sorts of people from all walks of life are realizing there is something more, that they do, after all, have a right brain, and are inviting it once again to have a place in their lives. Here the voices become active again, telling me that I could not possibly have anything new to offer, that I am not on the edge of tomorrow, stepping into the unknown.

All these people have already explored the territory and written books and I am simply trailing along behind, so why bother.

I shift, floating in the ocean of fog, steering towards the occasional glimpses of sunlight on the glistening water ahead, sometimes seeing the glint of green in the wave beneath me. Most of the time I have no sense of where I am. Something keeps me going; a commitment I made, a knowledge of purpose, an intensity for discovery. I struggle, determined to remember the question that started me on this journey. There is no thought in my head, but I keep going.

When I am in this condition, it feels as though a spell has been placed upon me. Not a personal spell, rather an injunction laid down long ago by many people. Do not remember, the voices without words whisper, do not remember these things; it is dangerous to remember, you will lose everything including, and at the end of much pain, your life. This information seeps into my brain and my body, altering my thinking in subtle ways, keeping me from matching words and actions to ideas. Don't be in the public view, don't show, keep this to yourself; I feel my mother's presence, and her mother, and who knows how many mothers before her. It is dangerous, they murmur, one never knows who is watching. And I keep quiet, speaking only to those I trust, those who I know are kindred souls, sometimes not even to them. It is safer to keep quiet. As long as I obey this injunction, I can think, feel, understand, I do not encounter the fog.

The minute I step beyond some unseen boundary, however, the other part of the spell moves in. This weaving is a great one, compounded of fog, of confusion, of forgetfulness, a miasma of vagueness. I wander in the swamp of Lethe, wondering where I am and where I was going. It doesn't matter any more because I can not keep my eyes open and my brain has shut down.

*   *   *

To address this amnesia and find the way into the clarity which I know is behind the veils, I must name and explore the fears, the disinterest, the reluctance, the forgetting, the loss of energy, the depression. All these are connected to the recovery of ourselves. Depression is how most women name this state.

Depression keeps us immobile. Depression leads us into terrible devaluing, to believing ourselves worthless, useless, inept, bad. And being all those things, and having no energy to combat that belief, keeps us stuck forever in not-knowing. We are safe, but we are also dead to life.

I realize that all my life I have been learning how to observe. Mother taught me, as a child, to observe nature around me. Louis Horst taught me to observe my body's least movement as I struggled in his choreography class, "Theme and Variations." Zen, meditation, and Quaker meeting taught me to observe my thoughts and silence. Gurdjieff and Nicoll taught me to observe the moment, the daily task, the emotion.[9] Teaching my clients to observe themselves teaches me again and again. I understand the power of observation. This training serves me well as I seek to learn the nature of the spells. As I name them, they turn, revealing another aspect. Each observation, each naming, uncovers the next thread, and the fog lightens.

Starhawk, in her book *Truth or Dare*, refers to fog as a sign of the Censor's presence, defining the Censor as an inner voice which stops us from knowing and speaking our truth. The Censor, she tells us, "stops us from revealing both our real pain and our power."[10] She writes that the Censor appears as fog, as boredom, as dullness and numbness, and to read her discussion of this state after I have experienced it myself is very affirming.

What I have noticed, and continue to watch for, is that there are many small ways in which we are distracted from connecting with our truth. By naming the fog and the boredom, I am encouraged to notice other signs of distraction. It is easy, for instance, to leave the main path and wander off in another direction, not noticing the shift until that path trails off, leaving the traveller wondering what to do next. Going back, picking up the thread, restating the intent, will facilitate the return.

When I work with someone on frightening images in dreams, or on life patterns which seem recalcitrant and resist any attempt to change them, it often happens that a reverse approach is more fruitful. When one accepts the threatening situation as real, and looks to discover what imperative drives it, the result is often surprising. The acceptance lets the image or pattern know it can relax, that no one is trying to eliminate it, and this allows it to shift and reveal itself. I remember this as I struggle with the spell; that I might try to embrace it instead of endlessly fighting. I imagine myself leaning backwards into the feeling of drowsiness, drawing it around my shoulders. When I can slip inside this cloak of sleep, before it takes me over completely, I am suddenly wide awake. Pulling the cloak about me, feeling its enveloping softness which is full of stars in a darkness I do not understand, I know that I am now inside a web of great density and age. There is wisdom in this cloak and I look to see the pattern, searching to understand a little so that I can reweave the spell.

When I am free, I can fly, move swiftly among ideas, write creatively, interface and entwine the words and images until they rest complete. Then I am released and the fog is a memory. But it lurks, sifting through the edges of my awareness, waiting. When I get too close to that which must be protected, it returns, again blotting out thought.

It is helpful to remember that this fog is not malicious. It came into being as protection against something harmful, insulating the true self from a real and present danger. We do not intentionally separate ourselves from our essential being unless there is good reason. Sometimes we know that reason, remembering a time when we were threatened, ridiculed, frightened, or confused. Other times it is not at all easy to understand the origin of the fog. We even have a phrase, "lost in the mists of time," which describes the situation in which we find ourselves when we try to recover something which has been absent for a long while. But there are ways to invite memory. One of these is to honor the creative imagination and intuition, allowing them to work together to produce something which, if it is not the absolute truth, may serve as a metaphor, the reality of which can tempt further revelations.

When I am inside the spell, and can see some of the threads of the weaving, I begin to believe it comes not only from the oppression but also from those who were persecuted and destroyed. I think of my own daughter. I think of her beauty, of the love we share. If I were in the middle of an immense persecution, if I could see that it was inevitable that all of us who had knowledge and power would die, if I could see that she, too, would die for her knowledge; then if I had any power of spell-making I would place a spell on her: that she would forget anything she ever knew of this so she could live and be somewhat happy. Even if I knew she would always have an undefinable longing, always feel as though she were searching for something unknown, even if I knew her daughters would inherit this same unrest, and her daughters' daughters, on and on for generations, I would choose that rather than the rack, the torture, the beatings, mutilation, and terrible deaths which I was witnessing all around me. I might choose death for myself and for her. Or I might choose forgetting for her, knowing I could not save myself.

As the daughter of countless daughters, I struggle with this spell. I forget, over and over again. Somehow the spell has worn thin, or it was intended to dissipate during our era. But the generations of amnesia have layered many veils over the truth, and they shift, blowing aside to tease me with a glimpse of clear knowing, and the next moment fall again into place, leaving me with the sense I saw something, but difficult to remember just what. I continually discover the same thing, over and over, each time remembering I knew that, why did I not remember?

Part of this journey, then, is to stay conscious of the spells which are upon me, to know that I have Goddess power, and that there are forces which are combining to keep me asleep. Through my struggle to recognize, name, and find transformation for these spells, I will free not only myself, but be able to offer the possibility to other women. Each one of us who finds her way through to knowledge can share it with another, and that other can then begin her own journey to freedom.

Here, then, is the story I imagine and intuit. I think there may be some grain of truth within it. Living with it, I am freed to search further, and this is another reason to give it to you.

Geas[11]

And their voices patter like rain in the back of my mind. Vast, empty space—absence—stretches itself between me and there. Cold wind blows relentlessly across the waste—do not go here. Voices return, pattering in with little insistent murmurs, overlapping, muttering, speaking, overlapping, telling, revealing, relating, no one completely distinguishable from her neighboring sounds. Telling, telling, across the centuries, blowing down the winds, whispering around the corners of history. Slip between the pages of the books, look out from the painted images, history becomes the faces of women, tortured, mutilated, silenced, their heads cut off, snaky locks twisted in some victorious man's bloody grasp as he holds her high, still fearing her power, knowing in his heart he can never truly kill her, a knowing which drives him out to rape and kill again, in ever more ingenious and brutal ways, hoping one day he will silence Her forever and knowing he never can; he returns home to his wife, his daughter and sees Her eyes looking out from their faces, and kills again.

Silence falls. The only safety is in our silence. Silently we continue on our lives, keeping our heads down, eyes turned aside, neither in nor out—to do either would be to betray power. Inside we feel the stirring, serpent restlessly coiling through our innards, seeking outlet, wanting to emerge, blinking, into the light of day. No, you cannot, we will die if you do, we say, and keep the doors to the within firmly shuttered. When serpent sleeps, the fog descends. Eyes glaze, cross, we sleep while moving through our tasks, bread baking, love making, touch the children gently for they hold the future locked behind their eyes, within their tongues. And we know, daughter, you must not be too forthright, do not make too much of yourself, do not be so proud of your developing body. The enemy is all around, he lies within your own brother, your father, the casual stranger who may take your beauty for his own and thereby deny forever your right to your own power.

We must remain quiescent. This is the legacy of history. Long ago a mother, desperate to save her daughter from the knife, the rack, the chains, the torch-lit dungeon far underground, wove a spell of Lethe. Forget, she murmured, forget forever, never remember the twisting words which turn into little mice who run to do your bidding, forget you ever knew how to turn smoke into shawls, never remember the passion of fire and the patterns you made as your baby hands played in the flames.   Forget the delight of flight, forget the birds who told you their mysteries as you played on the forest floor.   The panther who nuzzled you, begging for her belly to be scratched must now be your enemy, remember only fear as you look into her yellow eyes.   Your only safety, my daughter, is in your amnesia.   I lay the *geas* on you, to wander in the waters of Lethe, resting safe in her pillowed bosom, remembering nothing of all this, our life.   Thus she spoke, the mother, desperate to save her daughter, knowing that if she did not, there would be no more daughters.   And her spell was good, lasting down through the centuries, and the memory was gone, save for a faint shadow, visible only in the dark.   An unusual shadow, it fled completely in the light of day, for it was only safe to emerge in the company of many darkening trees, only to hint at its presence.   To see it, we darken the sun, bringing the moon to reveal, as heat reveals the invisible lemon writing on the seemingly blank page, waiting patiently with arms receptive and hearts fluttering, anticipating the longed for arrival of something we know we have always known and yet could never put entirely into words, for when we tried the words slipped away and confusion descended, twisting our tongues and rendering us silent in mind and spirit.   And now we wait, fragments turning within our soul, connections flashing, a sense of newness which is ancient permeating each cell within our body which is named woman, female, strange names which are derived from man, male, as though we have no name apart from him, another way to keep us separated from the power.   Perhaps we acquiesced in this, as in so many things, to keep the safety wrapped around us, a thick feather quilt, buffeting the wind and the rain, keeping the hail from destroying the tender growing shoot which seemed forever to be new.

Here, today, in the now within which we live, the green growing thing is turning, as the serpent turns, restless to be free.   Lethe looses her hold, the spell wears thin.   Or, perhaps, the wise woman who wove it turned a little loop over deep within, a little loop which held a promise of return when nothing else mattered, when we must have the knowledge because otherwise we would all die, or perhaps when the age turned in the heavens and somehow, against all hope, there would be hope. Now the loop has untied, the *geas* shifts, we peer around the corners at a shining thing, hold it gently within cupped palms, blow on the glowing embers, adding our soul to the life within. Wait, wait, listen softly, watch for the unexpected. It comes silently into the corners of our mind, waiting to see if we will notice, like a frightened child creeps past the doorway wondering if the bad man has gone away. Softly, do not rush to embrace, wait. Safety is all. Trust grows from inner certainty. Wait gently, hold the space softly open, prepare the place. She will come.

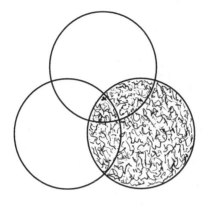

∞ G ∞

Remembering Wisdom

Third Circle: Sophia, Wise Woman

The third phase of the moon is the waning time, the time of harvest. It is the time of Sophia,[1] of the wise woman, for it connotes a gathering of life's experiences as the farmer gathers in the fruits of the fields. Not all old women are wise, and not all wise women are old. There is, however, a particular quality to the woman who has lived longer than most of us, who has survived decade after decade, and who can reach into a storehouse of layered experiences. She may have been partnered once, many times, or remained single all her life. She may have guided her children through the perilous paths of growing up or given birth instead to beautiful poetry or sculpture. She has a quiet wisdom which transcends experience, a special quality which defines itself.

A wise woman is significantly different from a wise man. One can be wise in the ways of humans without having the full dimension of Woman. A woman of wisdom embodies the full maturity which only comes after living through many cycles, tasting the depth of passion, sorrow, joy and loss. Wisdom implies the sort of knowing which comes after a wide variety of learning experiences. Wisdom gathers all the information into herself, synthesizing, exploring, expanding comprehension. The Wise One is always learning.

In the phases of woman's life we are child, often mother, and that which comes after the years devoted to children. In our culture, we do not have a good name for the last phase. Old age is neither respected nor cherished and is seen in these modern times as an illness, a disease, which requires that life be lived out in nursing and convalescent homes, places which are homes in name only and have generally little regard for the quality of life.

The English language does not have a word for this wise older woman. One of the old terms was Hag, which meant a holy one, from the Greek *hagia*,[2] but unfortunately it has been misused for several centuries. There is an attempt to revive the word Crone, which finds favor among some women, and ceremonies have sprung up celebrating a woman's entry into Cronehood. Others, however, are offended by this term's traditionally negative connotations, far too reminiscent of the ugly witch, and believe we cannot erase the introjected fear and disgust which the term engenders. Antiga, writing in "Crone Chronicles", reports that according to scholars at Oxford University, the etymology for crone "leads to a word which means carrion or dead meat."[3] This certainly reflects the prevailing attitude of the patriarchy which generally regards women as mothers, grandmothers, or burdens. The wise older woman is not entitled to her own word. Terms such as Grandmother and Matriarch imply motherhood, leaving no category for the woman without children. These words also connect a woman's wisdom to the bearing and raising of children, and while this certainly can make great contributions to mature knowing, it is far from the whole picture.

The truth is that our present day language doesn't have a

word for the woman who embodies wisdom because she hasn't been recognized as existing for as long as the language has been used. Virgin is acceptable as an innocent beginning, and refers to the young girl, (though another interpretation defines Virgin as "She who stands by herself," a woman who does not need a man for fulfillment[4]). She is expected to marry (an expectation which often creates deep problems for the woman who prefers to be partnered with another woman). When she marries, as most women do (for a wide variety of reasons many of which have nothing to do with love), she becomes wife and mother (though one can be a mother without marriage). After that, women just get older. If we become grandmothers we have another acknowledged role. A woman content with herself, in the fullness of experience and power, is so unacceptable to the underlying premise of our culture that we simply do not have a good word for it. In fact any woman who stays single, no matter what her age, is somehow suspect. The older woman who embodies the wisdom of age, who should be honored and revered as one who sees and knows, is instead mostly ignored. The beginning of the exploration of the wise older woman, therefore, is to recognize that our culture does not honor her with her own term. If we did that, we might find there are many more old women of wisdom than we suspect.

If we are fortunate to have one or more of these women in our lives, we recognize and value this presence. When I think of the older women I have known throughout my life, wonderful women, quietly wise, serene, radiating a clarity and sureness which declares their knowledge of their essential selves, I find myself smiling and growing warm with remembered love. Their presence weaves its way into all my life, providing gentle guidance, admonishment, hope. Their names make a mantra:

> *Henny, Dorothea, Eugenia;*
> *Laura, Lily, Anna.*
> *Winifred, Bettie, Eleanor;*
> *Margaret, Edith, Olga.*[5]

Women who have affected me deeply, and who live within me. More than half of them are no longer in this life, yet their presence is as real as if I saw them yesterday.

There is something very special about a woman who has lived a long and full life. Wisdom comes through many experiences, through struggle, compassion, sorrow and rage, joy and tenderness, all considered thoughtfully with the greater awareness which spiritual connectedness allows. Winifred Rawlins, one of my wise women, wrote, on the occasion of the death of another, Anna Cox Brinton,

> Something in the year's life
> Was waiting to be accomplished,
> A gathering up, a final ripening
> Toward a wholeness.

To understand death with this sort of peace, one must have lived very fully.

> By dying she completed herself.
> In leaving us she returns wholly to us.
> Wherever Friends meet she will be there in
>   the quiet.[6]

One of the names in my mantra is that of my mother, Lily Payson, who had a quiet wisdom recognized by her many friends as well as myself. I spoke before of the deep place where Mother and I could not connect but this difficulty did not interfere with the respect and admiration I had for her knowledge which spanned a wide range of fascinating subjects. She had a unique way of putting things together which brought gentle insight to any discussion of which she was a part. She never stopped learning, as is the way of the truly wise, was quick to acknowledge her mistakes, loved to share her understandings with others, and enjoyed a simple life. As I name these attributes of my mother, I realize they apply to all the women of my mantra. For each of them, truth is the essential necessity of existence, truth of their own heart, truth of the Spirit, truth of relationships. Their wisdom springs from their long commitment to the search for this essence, this center of their Being.

Some of these women were in my life when I was a child, some when a young woman, some as I grew older. Unfailingly, each of them met me exactly where I was, as do those who are in my life at this time. Each of them has accepted me for myself, valuing me, loving me. From them I have learned a wide variety of lessons. They have not hesitated, in their gentle way, to let me know when I have offended them or to offer advice when I have asked, for their sense of truth would allow them no alternative. Wisdom names truth, and we must expect to receive that for which we ask. The wise woman values the relationship between herself and the other, and knows it will flourish when truth is gently applied.

So from Henny Carioba, my wise and creative Jungian analyst, to Anna Brinton, strong matriarch of Pendle Hill who always seemed to value my thirteen-year-old self; from Winifred Rawlins, whose poetry speaks to me in secret places, to Olga Reigeluth, gentle friend in a year of pain, these women teach me of the beauty of friendship which spans the years. With Eugenia Friedman I read T.S. Eliot, James Wright, Theodore Roethke, wonderful poets whose imagery reached new depths under her guidance. Dorothea Blum created her life in a way which inspired me to reach for my own truth of existence. Laura Payson, mother of my gentle father, was my favorite grandmother. Bettie Chu's quiet wisdom is present in my life today, as is that of Edith Sullwold, advisor and friend, who models a blend of solitude and international teaching. Eleanor Perry combines strength of conviction with humor and homeliness as she lives the life of a Quaker matriarch. And Margaret Stannici, friend of long ago, taught me the joys of research in the libraries of Pendle Hill[7] as we drank green tea and explored the various subjects which attracted our passion.

As I ponder the attributes and love from these wise women, I am struck by the fact that most of them have a connection to the Society of Friends and to Jungian thought. No wonder I have always felt at home within these two disciplines, and never more so than during the years I was connected to the Friends Conference on Religion and Psychology.[8] This yearly gathering founded by Elined Kotschnig who, if I had known her better would certainly have been on my list of wise women friends, draws many wise seekers, men and women, and provides a forum for deep exploration into Soul, Self, and Spirit. In this place, and at the wonderful and nourishing Pendle Hill, in itself a center for wisdom, I have been fortunate to connect with many of the women of my mantra.

Seeking to define wisdom, we return again and again to the places of renewal, those portions of this earth which call to our deep selves. Here, centered within ourselves and the sacred space, whatever it may be, we rest, secure in the knowing of those who have touched our lives and left us clearer and wiser, touched our hearts and awakened love. Blessed be the wise.

As I search into my own wisdom, aware that I, too, am regarded by some as wise, I find my journey reaching ever deeper, moving ever towards the roots of women's wisdom and power. And as I wind, serpentine, down the dark pathways and passages towards the hidden places, I remember my own mother and grandmothers, wondering. I do not come from a long line of healers, midwives, wisewomen. I intensely wish I did. I think my long ago ancestresses remembered mothers and grand-mothers burned at the stake, tortured into death, and stayed far away from the knowledge that led to such pain. So I have had to travel towards wisdom guided only by intuition and by the wise women I have met along the way.

Ever since I read *Daughters of Copper Woman*, a wonderful book about women's wisdom and power, I have been compelled by the words of the poem in the last chapter:

There are Women everywhere with fragments
        gather fragments
        weave and mend
When we learn to come together we are whole[9]

The rightness of this was memorable and powerful, and I instantly saw an image of women, scattered throughout the world, each with a part of the whole, a fragment hidden away as a precious old letter is tucked into a trunk in the attic. I saw us all, beginning to recognize the truth of the whole, climbing the stairs to search out the piece we had saved all these many eons, wandering in the forest to reclaim the wisdom of the trees, of the winter wind, examining our hearts to discover the dusty corner where the small love lies hidden. As the years passed, the call to become part of the gathering grew ever more compelling. It is now crucial for me to do my part in finding the way to our lost knowledge, for it seems the Earth will not survive much longer if we cannot find the way to transform our perspectives. [10]

As I began the search I had no knowledge at all of how it would turn out, where it would lead, how I would find the door to knowing. I had some ideas that women could reconnect with the cycles of Nature, rediscover our ancient powers of healing, enlarge our awareness of the world around us. I have found that these intuitions are difficult to put into words. Even so, women seem to know what I am talking about; they get excited, offer ideas and assistance. As I have journeyed, I have made discoveries, had them corroborated, and wondered often how I could not have known that some particular truth is so. It seems so obvious, once I release the restriction which keeps me from seeing what is in front of my nose.

Conscious, therefore, that there are restrictions upon my self, my mother, and my grandmothers, and that there may be a link through my own lineage of which I am unaware, I compose myself to remember. Remembering where there is no memory means sinking into the situation as I know it, and seeing what comes, rather like being with the image from a dream. It is like fishing; bait the hook with something you imagine the fish will like, drop it in the water, and wait. I remember. It seems to me that I come, not from a tradition of women's knowing, but rather from a line of women unaware. I remember my grandmothers. Nanny B., my mother's mother, was a matriarchal sort of woman. I have no idea what she liked. I remember visits to her as a child. She couldn't walk well, I never knew why, and stayed in her chair, her back to the window. She disapproved of my father, and the enmity between them must have been strong, for he dropped us off for our visits and never came in. His mother, my Nanny, was much more interesting. She was tall and thin. Of her three sons one was a successful businessman, one was a recluse with schizophrenic tendencies, and one was my father, a mechanic, minister, musician, dreamer and wanderer. She loved them all and accepted them all. We occasionally lived with her, and my memories of those times are warm and pleasant. She made wonderful breakfasts, listened to me, respected me. With her I felt like a person. With Nanny B., I was a child.

Neither of these women ever displayed any knowledge of healing, any awareness of the earth and its rhythms, any hint of magic. Among my mother's friends, interested in psychology, philosophy, and new thought, one acquaintance had connection with this knowing. Helen McElhone wrote a wonderful book called *The Secrets of the Elves* which contained formulas and ceremonies for calling and seeing fairies.[11] I was fascinated and read it many times, but I never did any of the rituals. Some part of my mind kept me from believing it might really work. Mother never suggested I try, either, so perhaps she shared that opinion.

Thinking of this now, I am surprised that I never tried because I loved nature and constantly explored and experimented. But I never stepped over the boundary which was set in place by some imposed rule, unknown to me, which assured me that fairy tales were wonderful, but of course they weren't real, and none of those things could ever happen in the real world. It was important, always, to know the difference between this "real" world and the realm of imagination. It took me many years to allow myself to understand that imagination extends reality, and that our limitations are largely determined by our perceptions.

I wonder, sometimes, what would have happened had I stepped across that invisible line as a child, finding somewhere the sure knowledge about reality. If I had remembered how to fly, how different would have been my world? And where, actually, is that line for me? I imagine a country whose borders exist on a multitude of levels, where one can cross into many parts of that land, being there in part, but until the final border is crossed the whole does not spring into being. The teachings of the wise tell us that all things emanate from one original Source. We seem to have many versions of that Source, and generally mistake the part for the whole.

In any case, there was for me a clearly recognized boundary line, and as I realize the firmness of the taboo which I experienced and the restriction which was so firmly in place for my mother and grandmothers, I am led more than ever to believe this line was there for protection, and that there was a long ago terror, which I also inherited, about approaching this boundary. [12] My belief has been that to acknowledge interest in such matters would lay me open to disbelief, ridicule, and worse.

I think, as I consider my grandmothers, that I want to sink more deeply into the truth of my inheritance, for the line which I have hold of now has come from somewhere and if I follow, I may find a door which has a key. From whence came the bits of knowledge to which I have access?

My Nanny lived with us in Alabama when I was in first and second grade. I remember her pancakes made from yeast batter and her ginger cookies. She liked to cook, and she smelled good. After my grandfather died we lived in separate houses, and I liked to visit her. She taught me to sew on the old single stitch machine that my father remembered from his childhood. My mother was not at all interested in sewing and her cooking was fairly basic. I learned a love of both these skills from Nanny. In contrast, Nanny B. was always in her chair; no one ever said, in my hearing, what was wrong with her, but she rarely moved from her place. I liked to visit her apartment in Philadelphia; it was rather Victorian and smelled of lavender and was very different from the trailers and small houses in which we lived. I liked my Aunt Helen, who never married and who lived with my grandmother. Aunt Helen was fun, and made peanut butter soup, which I thought was weird but nice, and had a lot of little animals of china and wood, most of which she eventually gave to me.

Remembering these women, and my mother, I think about their bodies. I remember how they felt and how they smelled. I never got close enough to Nanny B. to remember her body; I suppose she was in pain and didn't want to be touched. Maybe she never liked to be touched in any way. My mother and her sister seemed a little embarassed to be in their bodies. There was always a sense about my mother that she didn't altogether like or approve of her body but had a sort of uneasy truce with it. But she did not withold her affection, nor did Aunt Helen, and there was a womanly comfort which linked me as the daughter and niece to their physical presence. Nanny was more bony and wore long soft dresses. When she hugged me I could feel the fragility of her aging body. Later, in the year before she died, when she had moved back to Chicago and we went to be with her, the city apartment held great fascination for me, and I loved the textures of laces and fabrics, their gentle smells, and the old Haviland china which I still use. These things are forever associated with her and the gentleness and grace with which she loved me.

I discover, as I reconnect with the woman selves of my ancestresses, that I have a hunger for some food which I cannot name. I drive through town looking at exotic food restaurants, prowl the supermarket shelves. Nothing speaks to me. Gradually I begin to wonder. This is a specific desire, not satisfied by any sweet, sour, sharp, bland, baked, steamed or fried taste which I can imagine. Nor is this really hunger—rather a longing, and as I recognize the difference, I begin to understand.

Something way inside and very small remembers. Memories of a warm soft body of another, a woman body, my mother, holding me, cuddling me. Old photos emerge in my mind's eye: a happy baby, giggling and sparkling, held by my mother and my aunt. My hunger is for that connection, for the cellular holding, for being in the womanspace of my grandmother and my mother.

> *This is a place of being known deeply, in the inner reality of myself as a female person. It is allowing myself to be known in this way—an intensely intimate connection. It is woman to woman, woman to daughter, daughter to mother, flowing into one another, mingling the breath, the skin, the genes. It is becoming one with myself and the other, and allowing the other to merge with me. It is being open to receive, giving over the necessity of separateness, reaching into one another. It is to know love, deeply, with my entire and physical body.*

To be connected with the woman presence of my mother and my grandmother at the level of the small interstices of my being brings a deep sense of warmth and of being held in an interpenetrating way which reaches far beyond the skin. To be fully known, accepted, and to return this knowing and acceptance with full connectedness, allows for the free passage of emotions.   I am not certain if I ever experienced this as completely as I am imagining it now, for I am aware of the restrictions which my mother had on her emotional life, but I think I must have had it in some measure.   I remember experiencing it with my daughter.   The memory sings in my blood and winds its tune into my bones.

Here is the line, the connection, from woman to woman, transcending the boundaries of time and flesh, meeting in magical moments to teach and learn the interweavings of love. Here is the place, the centerpoint of meeting, the clear center of woman, the place wherein I learn, as a small child, that there is something other than the perceived reality, that here all things are possible.   To return to this knowing is to connect with the wisdom for which I seek.   Within this place it seems a simple thing, clearly taught, cleanly learned.

My mantra of Wise Older Women has taught me, in the manner of the wise, by gently encouraging me to search within my own soul for the way of connection.   Resting within their presences, *Henny, Dorothea, Eugenia,* I remember wise council, never demanding, a gentle guidance through stories told and observations offered. *Laura, Lily, Anna,* I am comforted by your bodies; nestled within your arms, my small self explores with all senses, gently touching, smelling, tasting.   *Winifred, Bettie, Eleanor,* your differences teach me of my many selves.   When I am present with you, poetic phrases fall easily from my fingers, I teach with wisdom and compassion, I guide clearly and fearlessly, with love and devotion. *Margaret, Edith, Olga,* you guide my explorations into my inner realms, gently nudging me towards some field or cave or tree so that I may discover for myself my personal truths, while recognizing always the universal Oneness.

Wonderful connections with wonderful women, for which I am eternally grateful.   As I absorb this learning, understanding just how much they have meant to me, my heart begins to dance, spinning and leaping, reweaving the connections, strengthening, shaping, adding strands of different colors, textures, dancing the weave into firm cloth.   And as I wrap the glowing cloth around my body, I celebrate, Wise Older Women, WOW, Women of Wisdom, WOW, Wonderful Old Woman, WOW, WOW, WOW, a shout, a song, a prayer.

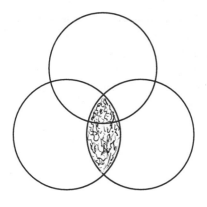

∞ H ∞

Tell Me a Story

Third Intersection: WOW to child

For thousands of years, teaching stories have been told from mother to daughter, grandmother to granddaughter. Long before people wrote things down, these stories existed, passed on and remembered with telling and retelling. This was understood to be the best way to teach, because a story is easier to remember than an instruction and a tale which imparts a message is more likely to be understood at a deep level, for we automatically make a connection between the story we hear and the story which is our own. We know, immediately, if a story has meaning for us.

Children ask for the same stories over and over again. Repetition lays down pathways in the brain, which, in time, become sealed in with an insulating substance called *myelin*.

Once the pathway is secured, the story will be remembered.[1] That is a scientific explanation for the repeated requests for repetition, and it is a fascinating insight into the ways of children.

Stories are also told again and again because they hold basic truths about ourselves, our spiritual connections, our deep psyches, and our everyday situations. We never tire of hearing truth, whether we be child or adult, particularly if it comes to us in a way that creatively connects us to our own inner knowing.

This third intersection, of wise old woman, hag, crone, WOW, with child, puzzled me as I approached it, not sure what form it would take. Suddenly I heard a small voice in the back of my head: "Tell me a story." I dismissed this as an aberrant imagination, but it was insistent. There are stories to tell, I remembered, stories told to me by many women in responses to my questions, wonderful stories. How better to begin than to answer the small voice?

Tell me a story.

Well—I told you already about flying.

Tell me again,

Ok. When I was a little girl, I could fly downstairs. I really could. It wasn't a dream or anything, it was real, I practiced and practiced.

I know. I did it too.

Oh, goody , tell me.

I lived in a house that had a long hall, going all the way down the center. At night, after everyone was asleep, I flew back and forth through that hall. I was a few inches off the ground. I always kept my eyes closed—but I always knew where I was, and never bumped into anything.

Did you go outside?

No, I was afraid I would get lost and never come back. Tell me another story.

Once I woke up and I was in the eye of a dragon. It was very big and I felt very small. I lay there, propped up on one elbow, looking—I am not sure if it was out or in. Dragons are neat.

Cool. What happened then?

I remembered a story I read, where a woman let a dragon

take up residence inside her—not inside in our real body way, inside in another dimension way—and it was really terrific how that worked.   She could go inside and find the dragon—and he was Huge—and talk with him and he taught her things.[2] So it seemed like I was having some sort of different experience, too. It wasn't my real body, like my flying was, and it wasn't a dream ...it was something else, and really real, in that dimension.

Aren't you afraid people will think you're nuts, talking about dragons and flying?   They will think your flying is like the dragon, and not believe you.

Well, that is the problem.   If I keep separating things into real and not real, then we never believe anything we can't prove. Nobody saw me fly.   But Pam says she taught her sister to fly, and they flew together.   She said she began inside, then went outside.   She had to learn to control her flight so she didn't get tangled up in the wires around her house.

Does her sister remember?

She says her sister is sort of explaining it away these days. But her other sister, Marci, remembers, and does know she flew. And I haven't talked with Marci yet, but I am going to, soon. And there are lots of women who tell me they flew, really, not in dreams or out of body, though there are those, too.

So what is real?

Well...I think that there are a lot of things that are real that we don't know about because we don't think they are real.   We have been taught they aren't real.   You remember my telling you about the study Blurton Jones did, observing children who were just beginning to learn the names of things, and how he noticed that sometimes the child pointed to a place where the adult didn't see anything, and so didn't say a name.   And the child would go on to something else.   And this happened several times, but since there was no name for whatever it was the child was seeing that the adult didn't see, then after a while the child stopped pointing.   It had no name, so it didn't exist, and after a while the child stopped seeing it too.[3]

You mean, like the little people that Lee saw and played with?

When Lee was a little girl she loved the gold cup the priest used in the communion service. It gave her a special feeling, how he handled it with such care, wiping it, how it had a beautiful case in which it was kept. She wanted to have that feeling, to fill the cup with wine and carry it to the people. She waited and watched, and one day she found a gold cup that she could use, and hid it away in her closet.

Lee lived with a family that didn't understand her and didn't take very good care of her, so she got away whenever she could and went into the woods in back of her house. As soon as she got inside the first line of trees she began to feel safe. There were a lot of things to do in the forest, animals to watch, flowers to find. The best were the lady slippers. She loved to see them, bright against the dark leaves and branches, glowing pink and splendid.

Lee knew about the little people who lived in the trees, and she brought her gold cup into the woods. She found a cloth with circles on it like the Wonder Bread wrappers that she could use for an altar, and she gathered mushroom caps for little cups. When everything was ready, the little people came swinging down from the trees and she gave them communion. They all sat around the cloth and she was happy.

What sort of little people?

She said they were working people, men who were short and thick and worked in the trees. She remembers they were about one twentieth of her size.

Is this really so?

Lee says it is. She isn't the only one who saw little people, remember. Jennifer told us about them too. She saw them in the woods around her house. She can still see them, even though she has lived in different places since she grew up. She said there were certain paths where she could find them.

Remember the stories we read about Findhorn, that place in Scotland where Peter and Eileen Caddy and their friends have grown a tremendous garden. The soil there was very sandy; it was near the ocean, and they had no money at all. They paid attention to the spiritual guidance they were getting, worked hard, and slowly the garden grew into a wonderful place. One of their friends, Roc, was able to see the nature spirits who lived in the growing plants. One time they planted some trees that were failing and needed lots of care. Roc asked all the nature spirits to help, and he could see the gnomes and elves working among the roots of the trees.[4]

Another friend, Dorothy, who had been with the Caddys from the beginning of the garden, was in regular contact with devas, which is the name for the angelic presence that is responsible for the nourishment of particular plants. She could talk with the devas for spinach, for clematis, for tomatoes and apples. Each plant has it own deva who understands what it needs.[5]

Roc said, "You can just look at a thing, or you can really 'see' what you are looking at."[6] I think he is talking about knowing different realities. You can look at a flower and see how pretty it is and love it for its beauty and fragrance. You might also open your vision and understanding to connect with the spirit that lives in the plant.

Did Lee do that?

I think Lee didn't have to try, because she was young and it was natural for her. She was happy to have the company. It was the same for Jeanne. The little people she saw came and played with her, and she was very lonely and sad, and badly needed friends. Somehow she was able to see them, and that was very nice for her.

Roc tells about how when he was little he threw pennies in a wishing well and wished he could see fairies and talk with them. And later, when he was a grown man, he got his wish.[7] Wasn't he lucky![8]

Why can't I see them? I wish I could! If I could fly, it seems like I should be able to talk with the elves, too.

I don't know. There are lots of things I can't do that somebody else can. I don't see auras, for instance, and Brenda can. She saw them when she was little, and she never lost the ability. She says it looks like a cloud over someone's head, and she can tell if it is a good or bad aura, so she knows the first time she sees someone and she is always right.

Oh, I know about that. I read about a boy who could see them. He called them "lights" because he didn't know any name for them. If his mother's lights were dark and murky, then he knew she would be cross that day, and stayed out of her way.   He didn't understand why everyone didn't see them, they were so real for him.[9]

And Marian sees them, too. She told about a time when she was in an audience waiting for the lecturer to come into the room. When he did, his aura was so startling, all bright and flaring, that she didn't understand why everyone didn't gasp! She was sure it was obvious to each person in the room, yet no one said anything. But, you see, neither did she!

So since she didn't say anything, and no one else did, then the aura didn't exist? You said if something wasn't named, then the child didn't see it any more.

Well, that's a curious thing, because she did see it, and she knows she saw it. I guess we don't really know what happened to those children in the study. Maybe they just stopped asking because no one else seemed to know anything about it. But I really wonder if more people would still be able to fly, and be able to see fairies and elves, if their childhood reality was recognized and acknowledged as true.

How did Brenda keep on seeing the auras? Did she talk about it?

No she didn't. And she says she never developed the ability the way she wanted to, primarily because she knew no one would believe her. She says the auras have never been wrong, and her initial impression of a person has always proved true. She said she always wished she could learn how to use this ability more effectively, and find out what else she could do, but there was no one to talk with and no teacher.

Are there any teachers?

There are some people now who are helping others to see auras, and I think that as they learn, and as the group of them learn, they probably develop some more understandings.[10] But it is not something you learn in school, or something that your mother or father would say "Oh, I see Sally can see auras. We should send her to Mrs. Wisewoman for instruction."[11]

You remember Kim who graduated this year. She could tell what people were thinking, and this got her in trouble when she was younger. You aren't supposed to be able to do that and her mother kept telling her "You should have more self-control", but

she didn't say how to do this. Kim grew up to be an actress, and
she found acting helped her understand and control the ability to
see beneath the obvious in her relationships. Remember how
she was amazed when I said "What if there had been a teacher
who knew about this ability, and knew how to help you manage
and develop it?" Her head was spinning at the thought of such a
possiblity.

> *Dragon's eye spins. I am drawn into the vortex, spinning
> into somewhere else. The dragon and I are enmeshed, I am the
> dragon, I am in the dragon. Wings unfold, scales rustle. Shifting
> dimensions, I feel my molecules shift. Metallic colors flash in the
> sun, I see a land far, far away. The dragon is shaking, the ground
> under me shifting,   Structures tumble, falling into dust.
> Nothing is as I thought it was, nothing is the same as before.*

*Where are you? I saw your eyes, you went somewhere else. Don't
leave.*

I was back in the Dragon's eye. Funny, isn't it, how these
things can happen? I was talking with you, and telling you
about Kim's head spinning, and suddenly I was spinning too.
And I was in a different reality, I felt it, experienced it.

*I knew something was going to happen. I felt the air change and
my feet started to tingle. Like when I feel I can fly, or when I get near
the edge of someplace high.*

You knew. What else do you know? I know you are
wanting to say something.

*We are stirring up the soil at the bottom of the river. The sand
swirls. My heart is stretching my ribs. Shifting, trembling on the
brink of...I don't know what it is...like a remembering.   Barriers
dissolving—shapes reforming—putting all these together makes it all
right for something to happen. I think I remember I once was another
sort of being. Now I almost could cross the barrier between there and
here...lift the curtain...open the door, run freely out, across the fields,
down the road, into the sun towards the waterfall.*

I think that is what I was seeing from the dragon's eye.

*Because all the women have come together to tell the stories, now
we know the secrets are real. Now the children can tell.*

Remember the story Marian told? About the phlox and the
moon?

Tell me again.

Marian lives on a wonderful farm in Connecticut. When she was little, it was her grandfather's and she was there every summer. One night, she was about eight, she and her sister and mother were the only ones home. It was a full moon night, hot and still, and they all were sitting out on the steps in their white nightgowns. It was late, but none of them could sleep, so they sat there, talking and watching the moon. The fields all around were easily seen, the moon was so bright, and the smell of hay and the sounds of horses stirring in the barns made them all feel happy. Suddenly a little breeze came up from nowhere, and they got up and began to dance around the yard, laughing and having a wonderful time. Their dancing feet carried them around to the front where there was a big patch of phlox growing tall, blooming and glowing in the night. And you know what? Their feet were so happy and they got so excited that they began to jump, higher and higher, and leap longer and further, and jumped right over that high phlox bed. All three of them, mother and her two daughters, leaped and danced back and forth over the flowers and never touched a stem, laughing and singing, while the moon kept weaving her magic.

I love that story.

And the other night I was at that farm with some of the women who have told me their stories of what they could do when they were children. It was full moon again, and it came up all big and golden, low over the trees. There was a white horse in the field, looking like a ghost horse under the moon, and magic was in the air again. Marian and I looked at each other and she said, "Isn't it great that we both know what it feels like to fly" and it was as if a cord was stretched between us, vibrating, and we knew we both felt it.

Do you suppose, if all of us who remember flying got together, maybe we would remember something else about it? Like how to do it now? I'd love to fly again. I wouldn't do it around anybody else.

Let's see—there's Pam and Marian. Kathleen and Ashley and Lori. Joan remembers, so does Nancy and Diane and Pamela. A lady named Patty wrote to my friend Rhea White, who is very interested in unusual experiences. Patty wrote that when she was about 5, she could fly down stairs and around the hallway. She never told anyone till she was eighteen, and then she was talking with friends about things that were out of the ordinary, and her identical twin sister was in the group. She mentioned her flying experience, and to her surprise, her twin said the same thing happened to her. Later when they told their mother, she said she did it too. So there were three of them, in the same family, and none of them ever told each other till this moment. The mother said she could keep on doing it as an adult, and could fly in a room full of people only they couldn't see her. I don't know what that means, and I can't ask her because they have moved and I can't find her. So I don't know if her mother was talking about an out-of-body experience when she was older.

Is out-of-body when you leave your body and fly around to other places?

Yes, and some women tell me about that when I ask about flying. And lots of people fly in their dreams. It feels different, though, flying with your body when you are awake. Patty said she and her sister were very sure it wasn't a dream. I have never questioned it, either. It is a different feeling from a dream.

It feels real. I knew it was my body, and I was surprised and excited, and sometimes I had to do it again to be sure I really could.

Talking about Patty reminds me about the day I told my friend Sheila that I had flown. Sheila and I had known each other for years. We travelled to weaving workshops and guild meetings, our children played together, our families shared holidays. We were part of a weekly meditation and discussion group for five years where we shared very deeply with each other. That day we were sitting at the side of a lily pond she had just dug, watching the water and the frogs and fish, and I told her my story. She turned to me and said "But I flew too. Only I went in my bed." She is from England, and when she was little, her bedroom had a window on the moors. She said she would fly, bed and all, out the window and swoop around the meadow. We stared at each other. All those years, and neither of us had ever mentioned it. I was the first person she ever told.

All these people who never told anyone. What would the world be like? If we had all told? How can there be so many and others not know?

I wish I knew. Maybe the world just hasn't been ready to know that things can be that different. In Zenna Henderson's stories of the People who came here from a different planet, they looked just like us, but they could do things we couldn't. They could fly, they could weave patterns out of sunlight, they could bring objects to them from across the room. Their neighbors saw them flying and got very frightened. A lot of awful things happened and a lot of them got hurt and killed because the neighbors thought they were witches and devils. The People were scattered around, not all together, so they coped with this problem in different ways. Some of them found an isolated area with no roads—they didn't need roads, of course—and lived there. Others simply shut down and taught their children to never leave the ground and to never do any of the other things. Of course, children being who they are, they discovered their abilities on their own, and practiced in secret. Some of the stories are about teachers who recognized these talents and encouraged the children to be themselves.[12]

It sounds like this lady knew about flying.

I know, and when I first found these stories, many years ago, I was so excited, because it seemed so familiar and helped me to stay in touch with my own flying. I can't find out if Zenna Henderson was a woman who flew as a child—she is dead now, and people who knew her say she was very private, and they have no idea. But the stories are so real, I believe she must have had some experience herself.

I still don't know what is real.

It all depends on how you define reality. It seems that a lot of people think something isn't real if they can't prove it exists. You can prove this paper exists, you see it, I see it. The chairs we sit in will be here tomorrow, looking the same as they do today. So that is one kind of real. I like one of these chairs, and I don't like the other. That is the way I feel, and someone could try very hard to convince me I should feel another way, but I would still like one and not like the other. My feelings are real, that's another kind of reality. You know I love you. How do you know?

Well...by the way you speak to me, by the feeling I get when you are near me...I just know.

So love is real, and yet there is no way to prove it except by the results of loving. Everyone knows love is real and the power of love can be immense.   People have done amazing things because they have love.

So if we know love is real, then other things we can't see or touch can be real too?

Reality is very subjective, once you get past the level of the chair. My feelings are real for me. You receive the result of my feelings, and you then have your own feelings.   If I recognize that mine are mine and yours are yours, then even though the feelings are similar we will each have our own reality.

The problem with these realities that are not chairs comes when you think I should accept what is real for you as my reality. Hitler had a reality that all Jews should be exterminated, and millions died because he made others live within his truth. In Europe, in the 15th century, church men said that wise women were witches and wrote doctrines which made it all right to burn them.   A few years ago, a man named Jim Jones decided God wanted all his followers to die, and they all drank poison.   And every day, someone thinks he is right and beats up his wife because she doesn't fit his reality.

So we have to be careful and understand that if I know I flew when I was a child then that was real for me.   When I hear you flew, too, then I know you shared my reality in some way. But if I tell Linda that she has to accept my experience as real in the way the chair is real, she is going to say no, because then she would also have to accept Hitler's reality. If I say it is real for me, she is fine with that.   And she knows she had a playmate when she was young, and no one could see him, but he was real in her experience.   Linda is very clear about the different realities, because she sees how dangerous it can be when someone thinks God is telling him to kill, or that you must worship in a particular way.

So when I tell you I saw an angel, you know it is real for me, but it doesn't have to be, necessarily, real for you.

That way each of us can have our own truth, and can share it with each other if we choose. If you saw the angel, I know you did. And lots of other people see them and know they are present. To me, that means it is probably true, and maybe someday the presence of angels in our lives will be as real as the chair. Or maybe they will always be a different sort of real.

Now I think it is time for bed.

Oh, please—one more story!

All right. About angels?

Yes, please.

Well, when Kathy was a little girl, she was upstairs in her bed. It was night, and her mother and father were downstairs in the living room. Kathy wasn't asleep yet, in fact she was wide awake, and suddenly she heard talking in the air above her—except that it wasn't ordinary talking, it sounded like bells talking. It was very beautiful. She knew immediately that it was the angels. She told her mother, who didn't really believe her. Her mother was a good Catholic, and after awhile she decided to go along with it, and told Kathy that she must have been a very good girl to hear angels talking, and that if she was very, very good, she might hear them again, some day.

So did she?

Kathy said she spent years being a very, very good girl in hopes she would, because it had been so beautiful and made her feel so special. But she never did. Years later, when she was all grown, she was visited by an angel, and another woman in the room saw it too. Kathy said she didn't see it with her eyes, but she knew exactly that it was tall, and male, and in golden robes with shining wings, and that is what her friend knew, too.

I'm so glad I have an angel. She is all in blue, you know, with a kind face. I don't see her, either, but I know she is there. And so do I. Good Night.

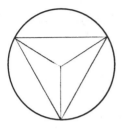

∞ I ∞

The Dragon's Eye[1]

I woke this morning and found I was in the eye of the dragon. Perhaps I was through it—perhaps I was the eye. One never knows, with dragons. There was a great sense of membranes opening and rustling of wings, and a wonderful feeling of arrival and peace. "At last" I thought, " I have been trying to get closer to a dragon ever since Smaug." Images flashed through my mind of the many dragons; Kalessin...the dragons and fire lizards of Pern...Hasai...the dragon that came flying to me in a dream. The many pictures of dragons I have collected: Chinese, Japanese, ancient, modern. The ones I have drawn, imagined, conjured.[2]

And this is different from all the imaginings. Here I am held, known, supported, taught. Here are answered many questions from long ago. "Why does the hero always have to slay the dragon?" "Can I have a dragon of my own?" Snugly ensconced, I look out on all the world, seeing first as the dragon sees, then with my own sight.

Throughout all the stories of women who remember things from childhood one thing is fairly consistent: we never told anyone. Somehow we knew we would not be believed. Some feared punishment, some ridicule. Most of us knew we were outside the world of reality as perceived by our parents and other grownups. Yet we are insistent that these things really happened. [3] I flew, it was not a dream. So say all those who remember flying. And while I know that physically I can no longer be free of gravity, my body still remembers. The way my feet tingle when I am on a high place, and the way I stay back from the edge because I do not trust my mind to stay in charge, is an ever present reminder of the possibility of transcending this known world. Ashley has the same feeling in her feet and for years thought it was a strange and unexplainable fear of jumping. Now that we have shared our experiences, she feels liberated from that fear, understanding instead that it is connected to the time when she was five and flew from the rocky ledge on which her house was built to the playset on the ground below. Our feet respond in exactly the same way, our reactions to high places are identical.

With my dragonsight, I can see the patterns forming as we open doors into the corners of memory. Light seeps into our cells, reawakening lost moments, reshaping the images of our lives. The patterns extend, flowing into the past and future, linking, creating, forming. Women together, knowing each other, telling our stories, delighting in our shared acknowledgement of our expanded reality. Something happened for us all when we were children, something which was out of the ordinary, but which we knew with absolute certainty was real. Believing each other, reconnecting with the special knowing which we have kept hidden so long, we are freed to integrate the realities.

Dragon's eye spins.

It is said, do not look deeply into the eye of a dragon, lest you be drawn into another world, a spiral labryrinth from which you may never return. But I have lost my fear, for I have told my secret and heard the secrets of others.

I spin within the eye; falling, I am supported. Where is truth?

Dragons are mythical beasts, I was always told; they never really existed. Why then are there so many in story after story? They must exist somehow, somewhere, to have had such reality for so many centuries in so many countries. If I believe in the reality of dragons, I must expand my definition of reality, or else accept that there are a number of different realities and I can know more than one. If Lee saw and played with gnomes in the woods when she was a child, and if Jeanne also had little people who came to play with her, why should there not also be a reality for dragons?

In recent years there has been an increasing acceptance of a broader view of reality. Near-death experiences are frequent enough that most people have heard of them or known someone who had gone to the edge between life and death and returned to tell about it. There is an upsurge of interest in angels, in UFO's, in psychic phenomena of all sorts. Television reflects and furthers this trend with a variety of programs of varying quality. Yet it seems the prevailing attitude is still one of curiosity, of skepticism, of waiting for scientific proof before reality can truly expand.

For many years, science has clearly defined reality for us. I did not realize, growing up in a home where intuition and the inner learning were valued, how much I was affected by this separation of truths. As Linda Jean Shepherd says, "The ideal scientist was unemotional and detached. His tools were logic and analysis."[4] The hard edges of this version of reality were largely unacceptable to me, and I was far more comfortable in the truths of the spiritual and creative, nourished by my reading and fantasy, by the clarity of my connection with nature and sup–ported by the feelings I had during the many church services and silent worship meetings I attended. In spite of this comfort, however, there was always the disapproval of the collective mind. The message was consistent: the sort of reality in which I felt at home was not truly real, and I had better be very clear about that, or I ran the risk of being locked up.

It was with great relief, therefore, that I began reading about the discoveries of David Bohm and Karl Pribram and the Holographic Model of the Universe. A three-dimensional image projected by means of a laser beam, the hologram appears in space, moving, changing, completely visible, yet it is not possible to touch it. The film on which this image is recorded can be cut into little pieces, and each piece will contain the entire image. With this new model for reality, the ancient teachings of the wise ones of many religions find confirmation: the All is, indeed, One, and within the One is All. It defines a universe within which all the disparate elements can find a home. Talbot says:

> The most staggering thing about the holographic model was that it suddenly made sense of a wide range of phenomena so elusive they generally have been categorized outside the province of scientific understanding. These include telepathy, precognition, mystical feelings of oneness with the universe, and even psychokinesis or the ability of the mind to move physical objects without anyone touching them.[5]

This view gives me permission to bring together all the things which I hold dear. The language of this new physics reflects my language; finally there is a bridge between the contradictory opposites. For years I have experienced great difficulty when I am talking with someone in authority about my understandings and ideas. I lose my words, cannot think clearly, sentences refuse to complete themselves, and I feel singularly inept. The concept which I am struggling to convey eludes me, and I cannot even think of an author's name whose words I am trying to paraphrase. I seem to fear that if I say it wrong, then I will be found out. My fear tells me if I hold true to the realities I have always perceived and in which I lovingly believe, I will be viewed as crazy. I feel the fear very deeply and it makes me panic; the words then refuse to come out. Within the realm of quantum physics, I can at last feel legitimate. We are talking about the same things, using words which make connections.

David Bohm postulates a deep reality from which all things spring, and calls this the implicate or enfolded order. Unfolding out of the implicate is the explicate order, the level of our manifest reality. This means that instead of the commonly accepted mechanistic order, wherein entities are seen to exist independently of each other, here all things are understood to be interconnected. With this view science and spirit merge, for the goal of Satori in Zen Buddhism and the union with God or the Beloved in many religions all mirror the vision of the implicate order. It might be compared to the collective unconscious which was identified by Jung as the stored memories and wisdom of the entire human race. We find ourselves in this deep reality through meditation, through dreams, through a variety of experience. However we arrive, we are shifted into a broader vision. Bohm says:

...In the 'quantum'context, the order in every immediately perceptible aspect of the world is to be regarded as coming out of a more comprehensive implicate order, in which all aspects ultimately merge in the undefinable and immeasurable holomovement.[6]

As a college freshman I made two wonderful discoveries. A basement secondhand book store was the first, and within that store the second presented itself to me. A slim back volume containing *Four Quartets* by T.S. Eliot has been my constant companion since I first read the words:

Time present and time past
Are both perhaps present in time future,
And time future contained in time past.[7]

Bohm and his colleagues brought the knowing which echoed within me from Eliot's words into definable reality. Constructing models of a holographic universe, these physicists tell us that:

"...*everything* in the universe is part of a continuum. Despite the apparent separateness of things at the explicate level, everything is a seamless extension of everything else, and ultimately even the implicate and explicate orders blend into each other."[8]

This is knowledge I have learned over and over again, reading it in books on Buddhism, in the lessons of B.O.T.A,[9] in the silence of Quaker Meeting for Worship, in private meditation, in deep conversations with friends. Now it comes full circle, science links with spirit, and the journey moves forward releasing me into understanding of the next step.

The wonderful conclusion which comes from a comprehension of the Holographic model is that if everything is interconnected and always present, then all the information and knowledge about any subject is available at any time. Information groups itself into categories, called fields of knowledge, wherein resides all the wisdom, theoretical and practical, that is specific to that field. Joseph Chilton Pearce provides, in *Evolution's End*, a succinct example of the truth of these fields. He points out that the people known as "idiot savants" who are unteachable, are able to perform complicated mathematical tasks (remember Dustin Hoffman's portrayal in the film, *Rainman*), play music they have only heard once, and in the most telling example, know all the makes and models of cars, including those still in production on the Detroit assembly line. His conclusion is that because these people have minds which are unencumbered with the mass of information the rest of us are constantly assimilating, they have, as it were, a clear road into the specific field of knowledge which is available to them. They have only to look, and the information is there.[10]

This is very encouraging when I consider my search to recover the ancient wisdom of women. It means that there is a field of the knowledge particular to women, and that I can access it if I know the code. If I can find the way in, all that has ever been known about cycles of nature, about healing, about plants and stars, and about the deep wisdom of the body will be there. I may not be able to understand or incorporate all this wisdom, but it will be there.

Pearce says, "The method of access to the fields determines the nature of what is then experienced from those fields,"[11] and Bohm states, "nature will respond in accordance with the theory with which it is approached."[12] *The way I approach the field will determine my experience.* This means I take the time to gather all the parts of myself, bring them to consciousness, understand them; a joining of child, woman, and wise one, infused with desire, mixed with knowledge of past failures. I bring stories, mythology, history, and a pleasure in the process, which requires a sacred space, a labyrinth, designed to guide and challenge me, teaching me about myself as I search for the way into the field.

"In the end is our beginning." All that I have written here is preparation for the deeper journey. The intersecting circles have shown me the roots from which I spring. Now the eye of the dragon spins, drawing me forward into the labyrinth and new experiences. It is a strange thing; no matter how long we travel on the inner journey, it seems we are continually beginning anew. Looking back over old journals, we find the revelations experienced yesterday were recorded last year, and the year before, always with the joy of discovery. We ascend and descend the spiral, coming upon the core issues over and over again. Each time they are new, for each time we are on a different loop of the spiral. Each time we build upon the previous insight; each time we venture more deeply past layers which previously stopped our progress.

"Enough," says the dragon, "it is time to go."

The approach to the maze is through a series of arched shrubbery, plants trained and shaped as they grew until they met each other at the top of the arch where now their branches entwine, leaves mingling into thickness. The arches flow in a curve, embracing the softly gravelled path. Sunlight flickers in patches as I walk beneath the branches, the alternating brightness and shade creates a contemplative mood. Sounds recede into the distance as my breathing quiets, absorbed in the contemplation of the rhythm, legs moving, feet stepping, passing through shade, sun, shade, sun, heat and cool, dark green and light.

Already the garden outside the entrance seems distant. This path was designed to bring me to the gate of the maze with a clear attention, distractions left behind, body and mind active in readiness for the challenge which lies before me.

Pausing here, a small bench invites me to spend some time in contemplation. There is a deep excitement growing, rising up from my belly, spreading through my chest and head, tingling out the ends of my hair. I hear echoes of old voices whispering "Calm down, don't get so excited, keep cool." I tell them this is none of their business, that being passionate is fine, that I am going to be centered, but I will probably get pretty wild and if they don't like it, they can stay away. I attend to the centering, feeling myself swirling gently, gathering and releasing, releasing and gathering, attending to the rhythm and the harmony, bringing the separate parts into the dance. After a while it is quiet; a soft pulsing soothes and lulls me.

Labyrinths and mazes have been fascinating people for thousands of years. They have been created for ritual, for focusing, for intrigue, for play, and for beauty. There are mazes made of hedges, of stone, of patterns on the floor, of rooms, of garden walls.[13] Always they draw us in, tempting us to discover the mystery, challenging our ingenuity and our memory. Labryinths echo the windings of the soul, as manifested for us in our complicated dreams which lead us, if we can only follow the twisting thread, to the truth about ourselves.

Ancient in origin, the labyrinth encompasses the shadows of wisdom, offers a method of developing concentration and, when used for its deeper intended purpose, a gateway into altered states of consciousness.[14] By treading the pattern, the seeker is impelled by the process, drawn into understanding as necessity demands the expansion of memory. Attention is focused; sight and sound are reduced to the awareness of the moment.

In the light of the full moon, I walk to the entrance of the labyrinth. Tall cedars line the path. White stone pebbles mark the edges, shining in the moonlight, and the soft bark mulch shifts beneath my feet. The path bends to the left, a winding curve. Ahead of me the gate stands, revealed. Festooned with garlands, heavy with iron scrolls, it waits, resting on its massive hinges. In the center is a face, strange and archaic.

It is midnight. The moon will continue to shine until dawn, its light so bright it creates shadows of deepest velvet. This is the maze hidden for centuries, the maze from which so many others sprang, originator, with the true wisdom of the labyrinth hidden in its massive walls. I have followed many secret paths to come upon this, hidden at the heart of all journeys. The full understanding of labyrinth is only just beginning.[15]

For twenty years I have envisioned a labyrinth which would be made of woven draperies. At every turn within the soft and mysterious passages there would be a sculpture, a painting, a poem, a tapestry. There would be intelligent lighting for these works of art as well as comfortable places to sit or stand for contemplation. The nature of the place would allow for quiet. This image has occupied a glowing space within my memory, never demanding expression yet never departing. The truth about a symbol is often present in such a simple fashion that it is easily overlooked. Our instant understanding is set aside by our conscious minds which feel it is too easy, too obvious, and that there must be a different answer, one which requires a more complicated thought process.

Now I understand that the draped walls and opportunities for deeper understanding are a metaphor for insight into the meaning of the labryinth. I know, now, that the true purpose of the dead ends, the blind alleys, the meandering passages of the maze is to teach and enlighten. Blundering into a wall which has no door, it is possible to sit a moment and contemplate the obstacle. The person trained to see any interference as a block to progress towards the sought-for goal is blind to the possibilities for enlightenment along the way.

Within the maze of our minds we encounter many frustrations, obstacles we struggle to remove, to get through, to change. Often we are better served when we accept the situation as a fact, waiting in the place we perceive as wrong, looking instead to see what is really there. This is a way of being which is offered by the wisdom of many different disciplines, from the silence of the Zen master's meditation to the Serenity Prayer, which reminds us to "accept the things you cannot change." [16]

Now it is time to move beyond the entrance. The midnight air shifts. The metal latch moves smoothly, the black iron wrought in spirals and rosettes swings open with a gentle sound, and I step through, into silence. I enter between the portals of stone, alive with many faces. I make the commitment. There will be no turning back. This is a difficult moment; arriving here has taken many months. Now I enter with body and soul prepared to be here.

Whatever this means, I am ready. I hope.

The first turn is to the left. I have always known this would be so, all those months I waited at the gate, I knew I would turn first to the left, as soon as I was within the gate. And I knew, also, the first place would be a place of contemplation. A short alley, hedged with the thick and impenetrable shrubbery walls. At the end, there is a white statue. This I also knew. Now I am here, my footfalls silent on the thick grass.

Silence. The white marble gleams in the moonlight. Now I understand - within the maze, there is no time and no sound from the outside world. Only me and the statue.

Standing within the silence, waiting within the presence of the marble figure, I try to see the features. This is not possible. It is only a figure from the past, waiting there for me, I know it has been waiting through the centuries until I appeared, waiting till I was finally ready to enter into the mystery. Time and space blur, the air shimmers, and the figure is around me, surrounding me, infusing me, within me. It has merged with my cells, the molecules of marble and my human atoms have somehow combined. I feel its presence within me, a solidity, a certainness, a foundation.

What has been waiting for me all these centuries? Through all the fog and confusion, the difficulties I have felt in arriving at the portal of the maze, the fear of reprisals, the fear of the power. All these fears are memories, now, and the white presence within me strengthens my steps as I go forward. This is a companion in the incredibly true sense of the word. This is my strength. Not outside me, but within, deeply so; within is not even an adequate word. And through this presence which has been waiting for me, I am connected, I shall hear the speech of birds, I shall know the rumors of the roots, the flight of the butterflies. How to listen with my blood. Here is the software;[17] now I must learn to use it.

Now the alley is empty. The path leads to the end, where the shrubbery walls surround me. I turn, the white marble within me. Curving, the path leads me through a sequence of hedges which doubles back and forth on itself. These are like cycles, stretching out the edges of awareness. The smell of green leaves surrounds me, cool and fresh. Breathing deeply, I remember the number of alleys created here, the deepening part of the pattern.

My interest in the labrynth has arisen from the belief that it is in the journey that we find our truth. As I spiral through the sequences of learning and understanding, moving between words in books and images from inward listening, I realize my quest to encounter the mysteries of women's knowing will be accomplished by deeply listening to the messages from my own body and soul. I also realize the extent to which these messages were hidden as women were excluded from knowledge and the teachings of wisdom. For me, therefore, the labyrinth is a metaphor for the recovery of these hidden moments, and each turn may yield up its secret, if I but wait and listen with a willing mind. It is important to recognize goals and go towards them, but it is equally important to understand the value of the present moment. This is teaching which has been with us for many centuries, yet even here the teachers are predominately men. Women understand things differently, when we allow ourselves to sense deeply into the realms of our womanselves.

I am a woman. This is a bold thing to say, for as the circles overlap and the awareness grows within me, I find myself responding on levels which have been, both overtly and covertly, forbidden. When I danced in that workshop in New Hampshire and received the little yellow candles into my hands, the vision was preceded by a visceral loosening, a shaking free of long-held bonds. How tightly held are the insides of woman; hold back the sensations, keep the stomach flat, resist the flow of fluids, don't jiggle, be careful what you say, don't look directly at anyone, hold everything in. Our bodies are not our own. We must dress them according to other's expectations, and there are many demands. Endless advertising messages offer these bodies firm and gentle support, husbands are prone to see them as possessions and ego extensions, children accept them as sources of continual outpourings of nourishment. Even our women friends and partners support the expectations, as we do ourselves, for we have been conditioned well and long. Our sexuality is split off from our spirituality and sensuality is suspect, linked to loss of control and loose behavior.

We have been taught to control our passion: *"Don't be so aggressive"* our walk: *"People will think you are seductive"* our minds: *"You're coming on too strong"* our spirit: *"God will take care of you."* The message, over and over, is *"Watch out for your woman self, she will get you in trouble. Don't try to be free and independent, no one will want to be with you. It is dangerous to try to make your own connections with God, you might be led astray. If you do not keep constant watch on your body, it will betray you."*

Even today, as some women in some areas of some countries are able to enjoy more personal freedom, we continue to come upon limitations we didn't know we had, and with each step forward we become vulnerable to a backlash. Fear of the results of freedom keep many women locked into relationships. In the powerful play, *Vinegar Tom*, by Caryl Churchill, which movingly depicts the injustice and terror brought to a small English town by the witch hunter, one of the women sings about doing everything possible to be "right" so as to avoid the horror of the knock on the door in the night. She marries a man whom she does not like in order to obtain this safety while her friends are caught and hung.[18]

> *Now the path straightens from the hairpin loops into a long curved alley. A small pool, clear and dark, rests in the middle of the stones. Here is a place to pause, to reflect on the journey, to trace the points which mark my growing consciousness.*

Today when I say I am a woman, I speak with a deeper acceptance, opening myself to the rhythms which I intuit are buried within my body. This is not easy to do. When I graduated from high school in 1950, a nice girl from an honest family, I had been well schooled by the whole society in which I grew up, and I had clear messages, not only about what nice girls did and didn't do, but how nice girls thought about their bodies. In subsequent years, I did a lot of experimenting and exploring, but I really didn't vary that much from the ingrained pattern. Now I am asking my body to show me the way into the knowing I seek. When I began this search for the lost wisdom of women, I did not expect it to lead me into my body. But path after path has turned in that direction until I can no longer ignore what seems, now, to have been obvious from the beginning. I knew there would be a reconnecting with the rhythms of Nature, but I was blocked from the realization that it is within the depths of my own body that the connection is made. There has been a serious and intentional split, created deliberately, which separates body from head and mind, body from spirit, body from woman. Our bodies ooze, jiggle, smell, and we are taught this is suspect, dirty, disgusting. Any attempt to connect with body has immediate sexual connotations and far too often stops there, ignoring the wider and deeper range of sensations.

The truly integrated being of body, mind, and spirit has been deliberately shut off, both by those who wish for control and by woman herself to keep from suffering the consequences of being a whole person. This split affects men as well, forcing them to stay within a model of Man which is as incomplete as that of Woman. It is fortunate that there are men, such as Sam Keen, James Hillman, Michael Meade, who are exploring the truth of men at the same time as countless women are searching for their wholeness.[19] Each of us, separately and then together, meeting, sharing, releasing, gathering, integrating, may yet manage to come to a new level of being human in harmony rather than opposition to each other.

The intriguing aspect of the separation of woman from body is that it seems to function on a number of levels. As a dancer in the nineteen fifties, I struggled and stretched, constantly requiring my muscles to expand their abilities. In time I grew dissatisfied with the defined structures demanded by what had become traditional Modern Dance and began to explore a more unified manner of movement, not exactly returning to the pioneering style of Isadore Duncan[20] but incorporating the spirit within which she moved. I entered a field of movement within which an emotion or sensation could translate directly into body response. Dancing and choreographing in this manner required continual and direct awareness of the link between body and spirit.

In subsequent years I married and birthed three children. Nursing them, caring for them, immersed in the physicality of food, diapers, baths, my body became a fountain continually pouring out with little time for replenishing. As the years went by, I found more time available and returned to the search for truth, meditating, studying Jung, Hillman, Gurdjeiff. There is so much food for the mind and the psyche, and those paths to wisdom are so clearly marked, it is easy and often encouraged to bypass the body.

Remembering these aspects of the journey and tracing the connections with the unfolding of body awareness, I realize how little I understood of the truth of my actions. Disconnected from the knowledge that my wisdom resided within my body, I made no links, accepting each part of my life as the continuing journey, but never seeing the pattern. I searched and learned, studied and integrated, always on the premise of the vitality and truth of the Spirit. Never was there mention, or I did not see it, of the deep wisdom of the physical body of woman, and I did not know it was missing.

Then several things happened which I can only now, looking back, see as rhythms which deepened the pattern. I connected with the Goddess. I was always blessed with a healthy body; living close to the earth of rural Connecticut I could now enter into the land and the seasons with new appreciation of the food I grew and fed myself and my family. Russell Holmes, my Jungian analyst and teacher, advised me to pay attention to my body sensations as I worked with clients. He supervised my training as a psychotherapist and though he taught me many things, nothing was as useful and important as this. I learned that when I had the sensation of vertigo, something was dangerously close to a precipice; if I had tingling in my feet, it seemed to indicate the truth of a direction we were taking; if I felt the presence of another energy in the room, it was real and needed my attention. Russell simply provided me with the open door and left me to discover the language of my body as an adjunct to my training.

I became aware of my addictions: alcohol, food, caffeine. After several years of struggle I was able to release the dependence on alcohol. Working with my own addiction and listening to many stories and struggles of others, I began to see how I turned to substances to quell the sensations in my body. While I understood that these feelings for which I had no name were the stirrings of my deeper self, body and spirit wisdom, I often could find nothing to satisfy them, and so I used the available and familiar routes to quell and numb.

Within the circles of awareness which were bringing me gradually into fuller connection with body, remembering the time in New York when I danced in the field of true response to stimulus, I became open to the next level of body awareness. I had always depended on the relationships with the men in my life for my body's experience of myself as a woman. Now I found a depth and satisfaction in the true love between women. This love went far beyond sexuality, reaching into and opening sensations and spiritual connections, lifting me into myself, plunging me deeply within a new awareness of my woman self. I found myself in a new world of knowing, seeing from a new perspective, in touch with myself in a way I had longed for but never reached.

Living with men has its joys and its trials, and growth often seems to be the result of the struggle to reach some measure of harmony between opposites. Living with women is an entirely different experience. Seeing myself reflected in the other, aware of the mutuality of bodies, moved deeply by the common threads of living, relationship with a woman has the ability to shift the pattern of loving into a new dimension.

On a recent night, driving home, the car ahead of me had a cockeyed headlamp. Instead of illuminating the road ahead the light was cast to the side, to the right of the car. Where the bushes grew close to the road, the light made a flickering flame, fluttering over the leaves, leaping and dancing up and down. Where the roadside opened out into a lawn, the light stretched into the darkness, creating unaccustomed paths, flashing into trees and houses, unexpected, surprising, astonishing, delightful.

When something unexpected happens we can regard it as a deviation and attempt to return to normal as quickly as possible. We can also see the shift as an opportunity to experience something new, to see the world from a different perspective. The broken headlamp is an irritation, but also allows something unusual to happen. I missed the strange light when it turned off my road and the image of that surprising illumination becomes part of my inner pattern.

I did not expect to enter into a woman-centered world. When it happened, however, and my perspectives were enlarged, my deepening awareness of the truth of being a woman cast light from a strange direction onto my journey of becoming. Gradu–ally, as the path widened and led ever downward and inward, the pattern growing ever more clear, I came to experience the necessity of naming. For too long woman has remained hidden, shrouded under layers of protection, garments of every type throughout the ages. Today in some parts of the world we walk the streets with relatively little body covering. Just so are our inner layers shedding and we begin to see and sense the form within.

I rise from my seat beside the pool, shaking myself, I have been lost in remembering. The water is dark. Looking within, I see the stars reflected, and then the dragon's eye looks at me.

As I see myself through the eye of the dragon, watching the weaving and flowing threads create a pattern which is particularly me, I can see more clearly the rhythm and structure which I name. This pattern is mine, then, to cast before me as a fishing net is cast into the water from the boat. Because it is my pattern, the fish which now swim into my net are the ones I am to have, and in this knowledge I rest, trusting that I have entered into the flow of the universe.

All of us struggle to see ourselves clearly. I know something of what this is like for men, and I have great respect for the difficult task they are undertaking. It is a different process for women, and here my cells and membranes resonate with the effort. When one's very being has been submerged, ignored, denied, attacked, for so very long, finding the way to clarity is incredibly difficult. Here in this place by the quiet pool, I begin to truly understand the meaning of the entrance into the field. Each of us must come to it in our own way, and the manner of coming determines our experience in the field. My reverie traces my personal experience, and this is my path.

Suddenly the air about me shifts. A cold wind brushes my hair and ripples the surface of the water. The stars and Eye rearrange themselves, and the face that I saw on the entrance gate shines darkly at me from the water. Around it the Eye spins, spiralling in and out, up and down. I grow dizzy. Looking up, I am confronted by the same face, hugely looming towards me, then retreating into the arch of shrubbery ahead. It is the Gorgon Mask, set to guard the Mysteries in ancient times. It is the face of Medusa.

Years ago, a green snake appeared in my dreams and imagery, and the clay manifestation of that gentle guide rests, alertly curved, on my desk. In a dream, there was a little snake in a house. I caught it under a wicker basket, but it soon crept out. I saw it as it slipped under the wall of the room. "Grandmother," I called, but the snake disappeared. I wanted to follow, knowing there was wisdom there. Medusa's snakes beckon. This time I will go.

∞ J ∞

Medusa: The Myth Unfolded

The dragon's eye spins and I am drawn into its depths.
Images form and reform. Snakes curl and hiss, baleful eyes glare
through fog and blood, lips curl and tongue protrudes over
pointed teeth. The Gorgon's head hangs in the air. Medusa,
ever a symbol of fear, which men perceive they must conquer as
they conquer dragons, beckons through the mist. She lives
within the dragon and I must explore within her story,
unfolding the myth, for there is truth within the distorted tale.

She is a symbol of the hero's triumph, of good over evil, light
over dark. She of the snaky locks and the baleful stare, she
whose terrible head was cleanly severed from her body by the
will of Athena and the strength of the obedient Perseus, she
whose frightening power to turn all who looked upon her to
stone prevailed even after death; within her story is the secret
story of the destruction of the ancient mysteries. Through her
progression from beauteous winged goddess to feared ugly
creature is traced the fall of woman from her ancient rich power
rooted in the cycles and patterns of earth to the present time
when the struggle for control by the patriarchy has left both men

and women bereft of the wisdom arising from that connected power. This separation has spawned a panoply of fears and misconceptions, all arising from the relegation of women to a position which is not only less active than men, but is associated with the dark. To our collective minds the dark is fearful, suspicious, terrifying, a condition in which danger lurks to snare the unsuspecting traveller.

Woman, being dark, is also evil. This is the shadow within the sun of a patristic culture. Woman may be honored, cherished, respected, as long as she keeps her place. Lurking below the bright surface is the fear of the witch, the mystery, the danger that she will somehow overtake and consume a man. Reclaiming the Feminine from the associations with evil, setting her in her rightful place within our psyche, recognizing that her rhythms and patterns are different from the Masculine but nevertheless of great value, would right the imbalance under which we suffer as a world. And yet the obstacles in the way of this possibility are enormous. It would take the psychic equivalent of a global earthquake to rearrange our unconscious perceptions.

The first step in changing anything is a clear understanding of the situation as it exists. This understanding must be present at all the levels in which a problem appears. Otherwise we find ourselves in the classic comedy situation where a man is intent on going forward, his feet are moving, his body is leaning forward, his energy is focused, yet he does not travel from the spot. What he does not realize is that someone has hold of his coat from behind. He is not in possession of all the facts.

In order to change a pattern of behavior it is necessary to discover not only the conscious, rational reasons for the situation but also the information possessed by the psyche, the unconscious patterns and opinions which keep the behavior firmly in place. If we are afraid to do something, no amount of conscious convincing will take away the fear. We may carry out the action, but the fear will go only when the unconscious defense system no longer perceives danger.

Since the fear of women and the association of woman with evil is lodged so deeply in the collective unconscious, we need a way to translate that fear into an image which is powerful enough to body forth its intensity.   The language of the unconscious is image; stories create images within our minds and myth is the ancient story handed down through the ages. Within the myth we find our archetypal roots. It would seem, therefore, that by exploring myth and defining the interface between the ancient story and our present-day situation, the old tale may speak anew through our own unconscious.

I am using the collective "we" because the connection of woman with evil is the problem of us all. Although the words I write here are mine, it is my hope that you who read them will be moving through the pattern with me, adding your own thoughts, reacting from your own experience, telling your own versions of the story. This is a journey which we undertake together, and we must all be active participants if we hope to come to a creative solution.

Perhaps within the story of Medusa, whose popular image embodies the destructive power of woman, it will be possible to unfold such an image. The traditional tale is familiar. Medusa made love with Poseidon in one of Athena's sacred temples. Whether Athena was jealous or offended is unknown, but in her rage she turned Medusa and her two sisters into hideous creatures with horrible faces and snakes for hair, banishing them to a desolate island. She then convinced Perseus to bring her the head of Medusa. Because one look from the eyes of the Gorgon turned men to stone, Perseus was provided with a mirror and a cloak of invisibility. He was thus able to cut off Medusa's head and bring it back to Athena, who thereafter wore it upon her shield. Medusa thus takes her place in the archetypal lineup as the evil woman who must be destroyed by the hero.

The origins of Medusa lie far back in time from her encounter with Poseidon. Scholars agree that she was once part of a Triple Goddess. She is variously seen in the serpent goddess of the Libyan Amazons,[1] the goddesses of the sea deities who were beautiful with golden wings,[2] Neith in Egypt, and Athene in North Africa.[3]   As often happens when the genealogy of goddesses is traced, she appears with other names. She is also Metis, which means wisdom, in Greek, and later called Sophia in the

Gnostic versions. Anatha, also Neith, Triple Goddess of Sais, her name to Egyptians meant "I have come from myself."[4]

This is a wondrous litany of names. From them it is possible to sense the presence of the Great Goddess within this tale, and to explore the foundation of Wisdom which is common to all these manifestations of female divinity.

Triple goddesses were linked to the moon in its new, full, and dark phases. The three aspects of Neith were Athena the new moon, Metis the full, and Medusa the dark phase of the moon. These aspects also related to the phases of women, new being the Virgin, the maiden; full was the Mother; and dark was the Old Woman, full of her life's wisdom. Within a world where earth's cycles are understood and honored, birth and death are accepted equally as part of the round of life, and thus the dark moon goddesses were also the destroyers.

One of the most ancient of symbols, the serpent is associated with the goddesses, most particularly with the wise ones. Because the snake sheds its skin, emerging renewed, it has always been connected with rebirth, renewal, and wisdom, linked with the moon which also is reborn each month. As a dark moon goddess, Medusa is portrayed with her wise serpents.

Blood is entwined with the story of Medusa. The menstrual blood was part of the mysteries of ancient woman and was believed to give them their healing powers.[5] These mysteries, held in the dark and restricted to women, were carefully guarded from the presence of men. A Gorgon face was posted at the entrance to warn the men away, and this face assumed a terrible aspect, blood red in color, with serpents hissing around the face and a frightening grimace. The importance of the ritual mysteries remaining exclusively with the women is demonstrated by the story that the Gorgon head could turn men to stone, thus ensuring their giving the place a wide berth.[6] The Gorgon head was synonymous with female wisdom: terrifying, powerful, and altogether essential.

Gorgon masks were also worn by priestesses during the enactment of the mysteries, for none of the participants in the mysteries were acting as individuals, rather, they were creating the greater connections by their participation in the rites. In time the mask came to represent protection against the evil eye, and was used on shields and buildings to ward off negative influences.[7]

These are the components of the Medusa story. The transmigration of such potent elements of female wisdom and power into a tale of terror and death provides us with an opportunity to explore the journey of women's wisdom from dark and honored mystery to evil degraded and feared. It is a complex entwining, with each portion of the tale branching out into multiple directions, many of which have been well explored by scholars and artists. Much research and consideration has been devoted to imagining life in a culture devoted to the Goddess and her Mysteries.[8]

If we are to bring the recovered awareness of the positive strength and power of women into our everyday lives, however, we also need to encounter the images within our own individual, personal responses. Intuitive knowing which arises from an inner connection and understanding is the clearest, most direct way to manifest the shift of consciousness which we seek.

Esoteric traditions have long kept secret their wisdom and practices, requiring a vow of silence before transmitting any part of their teachings. The stated reason for this is to ensure that the knowledge does not fall into the wrong hands and be subject to misuse, and this is a valid concern. I think the deeper reason, however, lies in the fact that the Inner Wisdom can only come by way of intuitive knowing, and since subjective learning is often difficult to comprehend clearly, a particular attention needs to be present before trust is established. By pledging secrecy, the initiate allows the discoveries to remain within the container of mystery. Thus the hidden truths are not subjected to the comments of the casual intellect, which would confuse or discount as irrational the deeper revelations.

The process of exploring and revealing the hidden truths which lie within a mythological figure requires this sort of holding, to allow the information received to remain within the receptacle of the mind and heart until insight appears. By allowing the creative energy and the imagination some freedom while simultaneously remaining conscious of the whole, an informed energy comes into play which facilitates the sudden opening into the place of knowing.[9]

In his examination of the many manifestations of the Triple Goddess throughout the mythological world, Adam McLean comments on the necessity of this approach.

> Mythology once committed to paper and pursued as an academic study loses much of its inner life. Rather, mythology has to be eternally relived in the soul and cannot be engulfed, encompassed, and explained even by the bright fire of an active intellect. Study must only be seen as a beginning, for it will not lead us into the heart of the mystery, but rather leave us picking away at the detailed fringe of alternative versions and having to make judgements as to the validity of sources.[10]

He urges us to "go down and meet it," reminding us that the Gods are not an intellectual construct, and their embodiment can only occur in a realm of being which "allows their spiritual energies to weave structures fluid enough to reflect their subtle spiritual nature." Jean Houston has said about this relationship:

> One feels oneself partnered by the archetype; it becomes a kind of inner beloved of the soul. And in one's meditation of life, one knows oneself to be the exotype in time and space, an outward expression of an archetypal being who lives beyond time and space.[11]

Meeting Medusa, we now go down into her realm, to the place of the dark, where endings meet beginnings and the hidden reveals itself to the questing desire. Gather the threads of her many manifestations, hold them together, and let them shape the story in answer to our question. And the question itself, to call up the hidden response, must be in the language of desire, the language of the soul's lament. "Why is it," I cry, "that I cannot reach to the roots of my being? What can I say, how can I act, that will not produce the feared and fearful response, the destructive act upon my very existence? Is there a way to allow the woman and the man to mutually respect and understand each other, not destroy each other?" To the world I cry: "Give me back my wisdom. Allow me reconnection with my knowledge, allow me to use it,and do not kill me for having it. Respect my

woman self in whatever way it chooses to appear. Do not deny
my reality by violence or word. Show me the way, Medusa, to
rediscover my reality, and teach me, that I may discover a way to
safety. How may we transcend this impasse within which we are
all caught?"

The echoes of my cry spiral down into the darkness. My
sight in this world dims. A scene forms, seen first from far
away, as the view through the wrong end of the telescope
appears small and distant. Soon it approaches, enlarging until it
merges with my moment. A woman is telling a story to her
friends, and as she tells it, it is happening. Her friends and I
watch the tale.

* * *

The seaport is full of the usual bustle, people moving busily
to and fro, men shouldering heavy loads. Shouts and laughter
erupt as friends encounter each other, preparing to depart. I look
for my ship. A little one, tucked away at a dock far down the
line, it has none of the swirl of color and noise. It seems almost to
have a shroud over it, as though it is trying to lose itself in the
mist that hovers in that spot. I make my way towards it. The
feeling I have as I move in its direction is of reluctance, the ship
and its owners are afraid to be going where they are bound, and
they are certain no right-minded person would be asking to go
with them. I picture a taciturn and resigned old sailor, forced to
make unpleasant journeys for the silver slipped into his needy
hand. Times are hard for the small ship owner. The large con-
glomerates of merchants hold many vessels and anyone not
joining their ranks is being forced out of business. It was almost
impossible to find a man with a small ship willing to undertake
an unusual journey. My contact, a small and shifty-eyed man of
indeterminate age, let me know he could arrange to fulfill such a
request. I wanted to go to the island of the Three Gorgon Sisters.
I told him the priest of my temple had laid a mission in my
hands, and that in penance for a sin (I did not mention the extent
of this transgression, only implying the shame of it was terrible
to bear) I was to spend five nights on the island where Medusa
lived. I proved this intent by purchasing supplies; food, a tent,
some blankets, and other necessary items, paying in good silver

to demonstrate also my access to adequate funds. I knew word of my shopping forays would reach the ears of the captain, reassuring him of my ability to make good on my offer.

My true purpose in going is very different. It is not well known in my land, but the temple I serve maintains its roots in the old traditions, and the Triple Goddesses were once our Holy Ones. Serena, the oldest among us, remembers the tales she heard as a child, when there were still a few survivors of the slaughter. She held the memories, storing them carefully like precious tapestries which are folded gently and laid away in golden boxes lined with fragrant herbs. In secret she revealed, to the few of us willing to take the risk to listen, the fragments of the mysterious patterns, pieces of songs which broke off as if written on a parchment plucked from fire as flames consumed the ends of phrases. As I listened, I felt my hand moving, lightly brushing the air as over the nap of a rich velvet, feeling the memories of ancient spells tingling beneath my fingers. I am a direct descendant of the old ones, Serena being my grandmother, though this connection is not much spoken about. My mother died when I was young, and I might have also left this life, abandoned and starving, but Serena brought me into the temple to serve and live.

Each of us has our own true story, matching our destiny, and when a tale reaches our ears which contains truth as we know it, the words slip down into a secret inner place to join with other re-membered images. There they lie, nourished by the desire of our soul, turning now and then as a dog turns in her sleep, waiting while their colors deepen, pictures shape, dreams begin. The twitching and stirring of their turning as they form and reform reaches our waking bodies; we respond with discomfort as vague desires float just out of reach and a restless hunger sends us searching futilely for satisfaction.

Just such a yearning troubled my sleep and haunted my waking moments as I grew into a woman, passing the age of novice and receiving the secret sign of power. Our ceremonies are not those of the outer temple, though we are ever careful to maintain the expected traditions with incense, ritual, and prayer. The hidden rites contain those fragments remembered by Serena, fragments which have become centers around which bodies of energies have formed. Like attracts like, and just as our own stories draw to them the necessary parts, so also do these treasured words and phrases, gestures and rhythms, call to themselves that which they need to flesh out the fullness of the mystery. It was ever so, in times behind and beyond us; the wise ones know it takes but the tiniest piece of truth for the magic to reweave itself complete once again.

One day Lorella, a younger sister in our order who is studying the art of discovery, calls to me. "Sybil, look," she whispers, "look at the mirror. I breathed once upon it and the clouds appeared. Twice I breathed, and the clouds parted. The third time this picture appeared. The mirror no longer reflects our reality."

In the mirror I see a woman with long hair sitting on a chair in a strange room. She knows I am here. She makes black words appear on a white screen. She is writing the story I am telling, the story of my journey to Medusa. It becomes real as she writes it. There is a window which has opened between her and me, between here and there. My here is her there, yet we are in the same place of time, the story unfolding for us both simul-taneously. I will not know what I do on my journey to the Isle of Medusa until she writes it. She does not know what she will write until I make the journey. We will weave the story back and forth between us, crossing the dimensions, each giving the other knowledge and courage. We both want the journey.

* * *

Shift. It is as simple as that. When we were children, we played endless hours, happily engrossed in a world of our creation. I remember hearing my youngest son David chattering enthusiastically in his room before his language matched the English words. When I peeked around the door to see who he was talking to I discovered he had all his toys arranged on the shelf and was creating a play, giving each one a voice and a part, creating dialogues. He was intent on his reality. In childhood, a friend and I spent long hours playing with my collection of china animals, choosing teams and having games and battles. Was there any difference between the land of giants and dragons in the fairy tales I loved to read and the back yard in southern Alabama where I sat in the tall shadow of the bamboo grove?

When I sit on the floor and move the round cards of the Motherpeace Tarot deck in a circular motion, shuffling them, hearing the click of the card edges as they pass over one another, I feel a shift of consciousness happening. This action is a signal to me that I am paying attention to my presence in the intersection where time opens up to include not only the temporal but the transcendent. I move into awareness of my presence in this place, time future, past, present, all available at a single moment, in my time, and then instantly am able to be anywhere. I am also available for any information, so when I see the card I have drawn, the image incorporates itself immediately into my moment, even though it may take me several more moments to understand the meanings.

Pausing in my writing, now, I go to the floor to draw a card. Shuffle, slip, slide, the cards spin through my hands until one, at the center, emerges. Four of Discs. A picture of a woman in an earth-colored room, log rafters, bare but for a fire burning in the center, smoke rising to a hole in the roof. On the wall, four mandalas. The woman is shutting the door; it is almost closed. This card brings instant peace. Noble says "The Four of Discs represents an inner sanctuary of some kind...where a person can be alone and sheltered. The figure needs silence. Her personality wants a place as still as a monastery."[12]

Fours in the Tarot deck represent stability, referring to the four directions, the four corners of the earth. It is a number which brings form and order into the circular process, allowing for a grounding of energies. Roots are necessary for the tree to grow tall; grounding is important in order to branch out safely. Ritual and prayer connect the participant to the sources of strength, thereby creating a sacred space wherein there is "...a separation between inner and outer, a space where something special may occur."[13] Here is the card which exactly relates to the place within time which I have been describing, an image which is another way of showing the moment between breaths.

When Noble describes the four discs on the wall, she says that for the woman they

"... represent tasks she has set for herself, inner goals and ideals of spiritual growth. The first disc suggests a spiral to the center of herself; the second, a magical flight to heavenly realms. The third suggests that her going in and coming out will assume a rhythmic balance; and the fourth promises integration of the four elements in a cross-centered mandala. Gratefully she shuts the door to the outside."[14]

I love the silence of the quiet room. The circular images on the wall describe, exactly, the process of this writing, and bring me into further circles of centering and development. Writing in this way reminds me of D.H. Lawrence's description of his first encounter with paint.

So far as I am concerned, it is like swimming in a baffling current and being rather frightened and very thrilled, gasping and striking out for all you're worth. The knowing eye watches sharp as a needle; but the picture comes clean out of instinct, intuition and sheer physical action. Once the instinct and intuition gets into the brush tip, the picture *happens*, if it is to be a picture at all.[15]

I am in it, now, swimming and spinning. Meditation opens the space. So too does ritual. The maze holds me, spinning me into a multidimensional world, following the process as it emerges onto the screen. I love entering into the maze. Simply plunge into the verbal painting, following the colors as they lead. Shift. I am back in the story. It is effortless, it calls me.

*   *   *

On the windy isle, trees blow and bend, their thin branches tangling like strands of hair. Black shadows in the growing dusk, they dance in counterpoint to the massive boulders resting on the beach. Stony outcroppings reach pointed fingers into the surf, promising a dangerous approach. Noticing the massive cloud formations overhead, we drop anchor well off shore, unwilling to attempt a landing until daylight and the tide can combine to assist our efforts.

It is an uneasy night. The wind howls, singing through the trees and the holes among the rocks. We are often startled awake, certain we heard a woman scream. At times it seems a wailing erupts, rising through the octaves, rising and falling, beginning again, over and over, lifting the notes and the hairs on   our heads till it fades, blown apart into trailing wisps of sound.   We look at one another, each wondering if the other heard, afraid to speak, mouths dry.

Dawn breaks. The wind slows, winds down its frenzy. The surf still pounds the beach. Grey clouds slip across the still grey sky. With the sun come rosy threads, weaving promise of a clear day. Breakfast and hot coffee give us time to wait, the tide is yet an hour away from its turn.

As the sky lightens, we look toward the island. It rises out of the sea, dark rocks splashed wet with the waves,   and climbs high in a series of craggy slopes. A bleak place, I think, though I notice a few hints of green, and I shudder as I contemplate the time I have agreed to stay here.

Suddenly the shift comes again, and the woman again sits making the marks I know now are my story. "Hush," she says, "I have had an understanding. There will be a mystery, you are entering a place of shifting time, all that you see is illusion. The island exists out of time. Medusa and her sisters live here as they always have, bound by the time within which you set sail yet breathing another air, hearing an older ocean beating on the shore. As you set foot on land, contain your fear, follow where you are led. The dragon's eye receives you."

Then she is gone. The grey water moves more slowly. Golden light sparkles off the crests of the ripples, the sun is up.

*   *   *

I sit in silence, reaching into my deep center to connect with the essential Medusa. Images swim past my vision: the snaky haired woman, dark, powerful, intensely beautiful, intensely female.   I move more deeply into my love for woman, the woman I am, Herself, the woman. I watch the serpents twine lovingly around themselves, radiating wisdom. The very air about her vibrates with the beauty, a full knowing, a deep remembering. Sophia, I name her, the ancient name for the Wise One. The name evokes serenity, a calm and peaceful face, full with the wisdom of age, her hair a dark cloud about her beautiful visage, her flowing robes falling with ordered grace.

To my altered sight, I see the Medusa revealed, the vision of Sophia becomes transparent, I see the two within each other. They co-exist, their faces blend as one, the serpents rise up within the cloud of darkness. This is the true face of wisdom.

*   *   *

The small boat is lowered into the water, my bags and boxes with it. The sailors hold the ladder, steadying it as I climb down. They seem somewhat reluctant for they are certain they will never see me again. I have contracted for the ship to return in five days, but it is evident they believe it will be a wasted trip.

Deposited safely on shore, I stand, watching, while the ship slips away on the morning tide. My feet are exchanging information with the rocks and sand and awareness of the life within this island seeps up my legs. Strength I feel, and a dark passion, a love of life that permits the smallest bush to cling to a scrap of rock while the surf pounds below. There is abundant life within this place which to my eyes appears so harsh. I hear, through the soles of my feet, the scurry and scrabble of small creatures, those of the water and the warm-blooded ones who live on the land.

And the sound of singing comes to my ears.

Drawn as iron to a magnet, I leave my belongings on the beach and ascend the rocky path. The singing is steady, strong and rich, with a throbbing undernote. It seeps into the marrow of my bones and sends warmth flooding through my blood. As I come closer to the source, I begin to vibrate in response to the changes in the notes, singing them myself as memory echoes. These are the originals of the fragments Serena held so dear, the fragments around which we wove so many of our patterns as we sang and danced the measures of the Goddess.

Approaching the top of the hard-edged hill, the path widens into a grassy slope. Cut into the living rock, a series of simple columns creates a temple whose roof is the wide sky. Patterns flow around the columns, weaving through the stone and spilling out onto the grass, patterns formed by women treading the measures of the intricate dance. Three figures stand back to back at the center, their presence strong and compelling. Lines of energy flow outward from their bodies, snaking around the dancing pattern.

As I approach the temple the dancing ceases. The three women step forward and I hear my name called. "Welcome, Sybil, we have been waiting for you."

* * *

It is always the case. When there is great fear, and I hesitate long before making the committing step, the actual event is far different from my anxious imagining. Over and over, I have approached the necessity to make a metaphorical leap without having any certainty where I will land. It is an act of faith which I must make in order to continue on the path. I hesitate, I attempt to bargain, I speak of those who depend on me. "How," I say, "Can I be willing to do whatever is required of me when that may turn out to be a leaving of all I hold dear to venture to some far distant task?" And yet, when all arguments are exhausted, I discover the leap is not so great, and life goes on, with changes which are possible to effect or are already in motion.

So, here, where my fear was intense and I anticipated great travail, I find I am expected, prepared for, and welcomed with open arms. The terrifying Medusa is, as the woman who writes told me, an overlay, a seeming, created by a frightened society of men who wished control of the world. The easiest way to strip someone of power is through a story which discredits, a rumor of inappropriate behavior. The skillful manipulation of facts to portray something which has just enough truth to be believed yet includes a theme of betrayal produces a myth which transcends time, influencing countless generations which are not in possession of all the facts. *Malleus Maleficarum* was an instrument which gave churchmen and witchhunters the right to destroy thousands of women, and in the process it contributed to an image of the inherent evil in woman which maintains to this day. In the book of Genesis, the story of Eve is created out of the truth of the Tree of Knowledge, the Sacred Serpent, and the apple of Wisdom, but these ancient symbols are distorted by the intent to place woman beneath man, and thus the Goddess is denied Her place in the Garden. Medusa, the beautiful golden-winged woman who understands the joy of combining sexuality with the sacred, is forced to wear the face of the guardian of the Mysteries. On her is heaped man's fear of impotence, that he will be turned to stone, as well as his perception of the evil energy of woman which is so terrifying it can only be destroyed.

*   *   *

The pattern turns within itself, shaping and reshaping the air. Feet beat a stronger rhythm, drumming out the song, the dancers curve in lines drawing me ever more towards the center. A space opens. The earth is parted, a slit drawn wide on either side, Mandorla, vesica piscis, place of entrance and of birth. Stone steps lead down. The women step aside, waiting.

We are one now, I who write the story, I who am Sybil, and I who walk the Labyrinth. Our realities have merged on this windy isle which is the body of woman and the place of knowing. It is my choice, now, to enter the sacred place. I feel the women bathing my body, wrapping me in soft silk, anointing my feet. Blessed and encouraged, I step toward the body of the earth

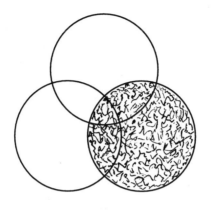

∞ K ∞

Wise Body

Third Circle: Second Cycle

It is finally upon me, my true journey within. After many ventures I have circled at last to the center. My foot pauses, hesitant to proceed. The next step will lead me more deeply into the labyrinth. All the paths lead me here.

Again and again I realize that I know, yet did not know I knew, that the way into the search would be through my woman's body. Again and again I realize I believe the subtle information that women are not to be trusted, we cannot trust ourselves, that our bodies will betray us. I need to repeat to myself over and over that it is natural for my body to have fluids, to smell, to jiggle, to make noises, to have sensations, to respond to a variety of situations in a variety of ways. And I affirm, again and again, the link between spirituality and sensuality which produces physical manifestations when I am spiritually connected and spiritual responses when I am intensely physical.

Simply put, my body and my soul and my spirit are an interactive whole. When I can accept this without shame, free of the restrictive voices, then I can move into the vagina of the earth, returning to the Mother, ready to unlock and unfold the wisdom of the earth and of my body. Held there, within that nurturing womb, I shall come more deeply into my wholeness.

I am grateful, as I seek to remove the sticky shreds of repression of sensuality and sexuality which still cling to me, that there are women such as Christine Downing, Stephanie Gianacopolus, Christine Northrup, MD,[1] who are willing to clearly address the myths surrounding women's bodies and bring the clarity of their own experience into their writing. Artists Judy Chicago and Georgia O'Keeffe have painted and created out of their women selves. Cerridwen Fallingstar and Elizabeth Cunningham have written from their experiences and allowed the body its integral place in the stories.[2] And many others, artists, writers, poets like Adrienne Rich and Olga Broumas, whose work sustains and encourages my struggle.

But in the end, I am left with myself. I sense, as I allow my consciousness to slip lower in my body, that there is a specific place, low down at the level of my hip, slightly on the left side of my belly, that seems to be shrouded in darkness. As I look, wondering what this is, the shadows shift and reveal the form of a box.

It is carefully guarded, this box which rests in the dark, hidden, level, tucked away from consciousness in its secret compartment like a false bottom in the dresser drawer. I am aware in a very subliminal way, that this place exists but the clouded dark has obscured the truth until now. It continues to obscure. It feels intensely dangerous to go near this box, to want to know what is inside. My mind skitters away like frightened rabbits bolting for cover. At other times, I feel the energy which lies within the box, a hot, swirling, yellow and red dynamo which seems too strong for anyone around me to bear. I fear to unleash it, I fear it would flow across my life and change me irrevocably.

I hear other women say similar things. That they fear no one would want to live with them, if they released this energy which bubbles up from within. I long to enter this depth, to experience the power, and I fear. Yet I want to go deeper. I must go deeper.

This box, formed from repression, contains that which is more than everything, my experience of myself as a woman. The darkness which enfolds this gradually yields to gentle acceptance and persistent questioning. This is the journey into the center, and is the next phase of the maze and leads, eventually, to the enactment of the mysteries.

Part of the repression of my body is that I was dissuaded from touching myself, not only physically, which was somehow sinful and shameful, but it was also made clear I was not to touch whatever is in this box. I am not to touch my own box,[3] and I am not to look. The message to women is clear, we believe we have a shameful secret hidden away within us, we dress it up, clean it, make it beautiful, but we must not consider the power and wonder which is there.

The circle of women on Medusa's island wait as I hesitate. Their attitude is one of patience and acceptance. I realize they could be loving and nurturing, encouraging me to take this step into the opened earth, but this would not allow me to meet myself fully. In their wisdom, they are letting me discover each step of the way, for only thus will I learn my woman's truth. I only wait to gather together the pieces of my knowing and to feel aligned with the place and time, for when all is connected, the next step will happen. My desire for the journey arises from within and cannot be denied.

There is a reaching that happens inwardly, a longing for the clear experience which is uncluttered by any preconceptions, noise, or dogma. This longing brings people into meditation rooms and trance experiences. It is essential for the connection with soul. When the deep well full of dark water reflects the stars which shine above and in its depths, we are stirred beyond measure and give ourselves over willingly to the fullness of the experience. Then the inner shift is felt, and the realm beyond this is entered, it enters us, we are shifted as we make the shift. We receive it within ourselves and in the receiving are transported.

I have been frightened of this potential, not because of the activity itself, that is pleasurable, but because of the power which I experience in that clear place. Always I am aware it could irrevocably change my life. So there is always a holding back, a reluctance, a fear. Here, approaching the container of woman's wisdom, the fear is magnified, for it now involves not only my personal comfort but also the threat of extinction. For extinction is just what has been attempted for centuries, with incredible success, and I bear the collective memory of that terror.

I think the entrance to this container can take place in a very simple manner. Perhaps in earlier times it was necessary to experience the venom of a serpent, a long ritual with fasting and cleansing, secret rites. But we have been held secret for too long, locked away from our woman power. This time, in this age of instant communication and quantum physics, we must have an easier method available to us. It must be consistent with the advances we have made in science and technology, with the explorations of the Unconscious, with the Spiritual awareness which has come to us. This age of Aquarius has opened our eyes to a far greater world than we had once thought possible. It makes sense to consider that there is also a simpler way to reach to the heart of knowing.

If each of us comes into this world with a key to this entrance, it would seem it is the ability which is different from what is accepted as normal. Normal locks us into our three-dimensional world; by not accepting anything outside those three walls, it is impossible to use the key in our hands. So if we accept the key, and set about discovering how to use it, perhaps it will turn out to be as simple as connecting the inner child with the inner adult.

Perhaps now there is some universal understanding of the magnitude of the repression, how the keys are virtually forgotten, so inaccessible as to be almost impossible to reach, buried under the rubble of lives destroyed by abuse and neglect. And possibly, because there has been so much repression of those keys, and because it is time, in the turning of the ages, for the transformation to occur, people now are being given more keys, transpersonal experiences, exceptional experiences,[4] to remind them that these keys exist, to put them into our hands, to make it easier to find the doors. For the key will find the door, I believe, if we only can understand the truth.

My own key is the remembered ability to fly. How easy it was! Perhaps this is what I need as I stand in the circle of women on the windy island, waiting for understanding. I draw in a breath, bring in the lightness of air, feel the cells in my bones expand, and release the multitude of fears. The women shift, feeling my readiness.

In the open ground the steps lead down. It is time to fly. Down stone steps, moss covered and ancient, I float. The passage-way at the bottom is narrow and dark; I continue flying, remembering Kathleen and the dark hall of her childhood home. Effortlessly I go, faster and faster, spinning through the turns, laughing with delight — and then the earth shifts, the island shakes itself, turns inside out — and I am suddenly on the shore behind the temple.

The beach is warm and vibrant under my body. Sand sifts through the back of my hair, wraps around my toes, settles into the small of my back. The swish of the waves tickles my ears, mingling with the soft breezes which whisper gentle tenderness, caressing my skin. Warmth lifts up through my thighs, sliding around inside my stomach, spreading past my heart and permeating the space behind my eyes. My bones turn to liquid gold. My belly softens as feathers touch my skin. I am enwrapped in love, deeply centered, held and nourished. Women's hair trails across my arms, tickles my nostrils and tangles in my fingers. Breathing deeply, I smell sun-drenched skin which tastes of salt. And when I open my eyes, I am looking into eyes of deepest blue. Far within them a tiny flame flickers and I submerge myself, abandoning all fear, to join my energy to hers.

Later I lie in the temple, couched on a bed strewn with fine blankets. There is a light odor of incense; silver bells tinkle gently with the passing breeze. I lie in the gathering dusk, listening inside to my body. The box has softened, melted, I am deep within its contents. It is dark in here. I feel many voices oddly murmuring. They say inconsequential words, strung together into jumbled sentences; "look out, whatever, velvet, shout, soft. Walk carefully, the floor may open beneath you." Shift. Body turns. "Line up another cell for peace. Another mother." Settle again, turn, carefully shift again. Hips shift. Gentle rocking. Light grows behind my eyes. There are eggs here, clustered luminously, darkly shining, separate, glistening. They are tucked into the crevice at the bottom of the woman space. The woman space is the vesica, the vessel, the mandorla, the place that Mary could never leave, for it is the woman space. The place Georgia and Judy were drawn to, being woman. That Georgia could not name and Judy could. Can I. Yes. I will. I want. It is the woman space, this is within the pod. Feel the seeds spill from the nurturing vessel. Deep earth forming from the clay, woman space, unmistakably. This is not shameful. It never was, truly, only in perception. Judy Chicago brought it out. I understand, now why she used the *vesica* as the unifying shape. We are so embarrassed. It is our womanspace. Our box. Odd — it has been called that for so long, and we didn't understand. It is all hidden right in front of our noses, of course, waiting till we could see.[5]

Here is where the seeds dwell, where dwell the seeds, from whence cometh my hope. Shift. Settle. Here they are, here we are, the genesis of all the world. Create and uncreate. This is the field, begin here. Sunlight. Warm and nurturing. Spring cometh in the mountains. All the phrases are generated here. Genatrix. Each egg carefully laid, nurtured, cared for, loved. Loved. Amen.

A breath. I sink more deeply into the softness. Held deeply, I turn again. Again the smell of salt air caught in dark hair and warm skin. She is Goddess, she is Woman, she is Love. The air is charged with the intensity of passion. The earth opens within me, I plummet down, through walls of flesh, close darkness, closer tenderness. The sky takes me, tosses me high on a wave of clouds, I soar, higher, higher, the bird's wing brushes my face, the ocean and the cloud merge at the center, the tree grows through me, blooming, blooming, blooming.

Then there is no more breath. Inhale, hold, wait, feel the air seep through the cells, give a little at a time, watch them unfold. A year later, exhale, slowly, slowly, savoring each fragment as it leaves. Fresh breath again, feel the cells expand, nourished with air, growing, vibrating, glowing. All the molecules in the body are shifting places, playing at musical chairs, where they stop, nobody knows. What will I be when they come to rest? New. Different. Better.

There is a song singing itself in my head, resonating through my body, setting my toes to music. Deep song, throbbing song, soaring into the sky, sinking again to earth. I send the song to my belly, to my womb, to my box. The deep space opens again, branches reach high, roots thrust themselves deeply through dark earth, curving around stone, settling into the peace of the inner places. I am tree and well simultaneously, vibrant between the heights and depths, resonant with the sound of the great copper bell which rings and rings and rings.

I walk through dark corridors, torches flaring in the walls. The silence is thick, I turn to the deeper levels. Within the heart of the rock the cavern lies below the level of the ocean. The stone in the center is ragged with old clothing, second skins, heart's desires. This is the place of stripping, where one comes, alone, seeking the true message of the soul. Here are left behind those last vestiges of hope, of plans, of personal ambition. This is Erishkegal's domain.[6] I was here before, more than once, in other places, I know the impelling need to leave behind all things, to be exclusively devoted to the true deep self which is She who demands nothing less than all. I come, now, ready to be stripped of all the excess, willingly setting aside the uncertainties and traditions which have bound me into a disregard of each wonderful inch of my precious body. I stand, at last, before the rock, deeply loving my flesh — and then I step out of that body, giving it to the stone which receives it, absorbs, renews, and returns to me myself, a great dark cape of love and passion, entirely mine, unfettered by previous lives.

Once again I stand in the great hall of the temple, smelling the soft odors of flowers and firs. The women dance a turning measure, their own dark cloaks flaring out in wide circles. I join them, my feet remembering the pattern from some other time, when I must have learned it as a girl against the time I would be ready to dance. Thrice the circle turns, thrice the pattern winds among the pillars, thrice we sound the final note.

Medusa comes. Her great golden wings flow behind her cape, arching up over her head. Snakes twine round her arms and slip among the curls of her hair. Her beautiful breasts shine forth from her bodice, her waist is encircled with gold, her thighs press gently against the light silver gauze of her skirt. The hem tinkles gently with tiny silver bells.

How long have I waited to meet Medusa! For years I have imaged her, known she was beautiful, made representations of her with paint and sculpture. I heard the bells in the seaport town, waiting to board the ship for this island. Yet until this moment I knew not the power and splendor of the woman.

The robed dancers bring me before her. She reaches out, lightly, with a kiss and embrace. Her serpents twist themselves into loving knots, touching my hands delicately, their cool skin slips beneath my fingers. I stand, entranced, drinking in the fragrance of her body, the silken sound of her robe. Around me the temple encloses, sustains, renews. Time slows to an instant, to the single point of existence. I am here now, always, forever, for a moment. I know all things and nothing at all. I am within the timeless center where all words originate and there is endless silence.

I breathe. The world begins again, forever recedes, time takes up the beat. The softly whispered pattern continues. Bare feet beat on the floor. She moves, her skirt sways, silver bells stir in the folds. Gently she draws me into the dance.

Now the rhythm quickens, the intensity increases. Power ripples through the room, the air is charged, the singing magnifies and echoes with itself. Medusa adds her pattern, a counterpoint, silver and gold threading in and out, swirling quickened circles through the dark cloth of the women's robes. My rhythm shadows hers. Following the scent of her body I find myself moving through the molecules of air with new awareness, shifting balance, reshaping my cells to meet the openings in the air left by her passing. The dance continues, hours it seems, forever perhaps, until I am again re-formed and brought to rest.

*   *   *

Medusa and I walk through the shadowed pines.

I say, " I am writing a story about our meeting here. I want to reach for the deeper truth, to see through the story created by the Greek men, deconstructing the myth, as we say. I hope to bring the beauty of your power into the lives of women as we move forward into the twenty-first century."

She says, "You came on a ship that sailed from its home port two weeks ago."

I tell her of the blending of stories, that I am that woman as well as the one who writes the story, and that I am also in the inner circles of the maze, watching the whole thing intertwine.

She laughs. "No wonder you arrived so swiftly into the dance."

"Tell me the story of Medusa" she says.

We sit on the mossy stones. "Once upon a time," I begin, "there was a beautiful woman. When she was a child she played in the forests and meadows around her home. She knew where the spiders spun their webs and went out in the early morning before the dew dried to see the shining jewels. Wildcats came to her to be scratched behind their ears. She listened to the music the flowers made as their petals opened and she held the great trees of the forest close in her loving arms. Most of all she loved the serpents. When their glowing patterned bodies rustled through the leaves she stopped, sat down, and watched their fluid dance. Since she had no fear, the snakes never harmed her, and she held them all, even the deadly ones, in her gentle hands.

"Medusa's sisters liked the snakes, but each had her special wisdom. Euryle, whose name means "wide roaming," soared with the birds, watching the eagles build their nests. Stheino, the strong, went deep within the caves under the hills, reaching into the heart of the land, playing with the beautiful jewels and whispering secrets with the dark. Together the three girls held the land under their care. As the years went by they grew up and each of the three had beautiful long hair and large glowing wings and they cared for each other, staying always close together.

"In time they were initiated into the temple and the mysteries of women, the sacred and secret rites and traditions which honored the body of the earth as they honored their own bodies, and which brought the high spirit down to unite with their flowing rhythms. They became priestesses, women skilled in the embodiment of transfigured power, and they were loved by all the people.

"Year after year they lived, growing always more beautiful, caring for generations of children and their children's children. They watched many changes take place in the world around them. As the world grew larger, and people moved further away from the temple, they took with them their memories of the three sisters. Sometimes the sisters were called by different names, meaningful to the people as they made new lives for themselves. In the new lands they built temples, remembering what they could understand of the mysteries, and invited the sisters to bring their presence into the new home. But their invitations, inevitably, were not complete, and they thus invoked and worshiped a partial memory.

"Around these fragmented remembrances, new stories arose, having some semblance of the original truth, but adding many embellishments which arose out of the experiences of the people of that time and place. It is thus that myths are created and recreated to suit the mood of the age. So it was that in Greece the story grew about Athena, a goddess born from the head of her father Zeus after he had swallowed her pregnant mother, Metis. Now Greece was a country in which man's mind was highly respected, and his wisdom was second only to that of the Gods. It was only natural, therefore, that the Greeks should create a myth which portrayed their supreme male god swallowing Metis, which means female wisdom, and himself giving birth to the daughter from his own head.

"Now Athena was one of those names given to the sisters, as was Metis. So you can see that the story has gotten mixed up and changed to suit the needs of the male-dominated times in which the Greeks lived. Athena became the Goddess of battle, defending home and State. She was also the protector of civilized life. To the Greeks this meant conscious, intellectual, male-oriented living."

Medusa is smiling. "Good, so far," she says, " but you must clarify something. Here we are, talking together, and you are telling me a story about me and my sisters. Then, you trace the spread of our wisdom and worship to Greece, and there is Athena, part of the three of us, who is now transferred and transformed into someone so different it is hard to recognize her. She is real, you could go and talk with her if you chose, just as you are talking with me. How do you explain this phenomenon?"

I had been thinking about that. I am sitting here with this beautiful woman, and she is supposed to be a terrible creature, frightening to behold. I remember the insight I had approaching the island; there are different realities.

I say, "At the heart of everything, there is no time. If we begin in the heart, we can be in whatever time we choose."

Medusa's eyes are sparkling. "Go on with your story," she says.

"It is often said that we create our own reality. There are many gods and goddesses all over the world, all real to those who worship them. People live and die for their realities and shape their personal world to match what they believe. At the true source it is all the same, but we find it easier to have something tangible to talk with, build a temple for, tell stories about. We can teach our children the values we hold dear by telling stories.

"It was natural, therefore, that Athena should be the manifestation developed by the Greeks within their culture, and she therefore became real, matching truth as they knew it. But she, being born from Zeus' head, forgot about the mysteries of the women in the temple, becoming altogether conscious, full of light, and a Virgin, not in the old sense of the word, which meant "woman unto herself," but with a new meaning, "untouched sexually by man."

"The trouble is that you cannot keep the whole out forever. And the mysteries were part of Athena, whether she liked it or not. That dark wisdom and power of women was unacceptable to the Greek men, however, for it would have threatened their control. So another story grew. It was told that Medusa made love with Poseidon, lord of the Sea, in the temple dedicated to Athena. This mixing of sexuality and spirituality angered Athena, it is said, and in her wrath she transformed Medusa and her sisters into terrible creatures, with faces like the Gorgon masks that guarded the mysteries, and gave them snakes for hair. One glance from their eyes would be sufficient to turn a man to stone. And she banished them to a lonely isle."

Medusa laughs. "That is the part of the story that is so foolish," she says. "This has always been our home. It is no isolated island—you will see, when you leave. It is at the center of everything, and all roads lead to and from this place. Those in power were so intent on supremacy that they cut off all the lines of communication, the roads are seldom travelled and thus are largely overgrown and hidden unless you have eyes to see beyond the screening hedges. This is the center of the maze."

She continues: "The Greeks saw only the necessity of isolating me so that the power we three contain would not threaten their control. Their efforts were very effective, engendering such fear in men that they never came near us in body or in spirit and thereby increasing the separation."

I ask, "What about the idea that one look from you would turn men to stone?"

Medusa smiles. "That is part of the mysteries. The Gorgon mask that we place at the entrance to the temple warns those who are not initiated to come no further. But it has another function, which is little known for it was seldom needed. Embedded within the features intended to frighten is a protective spell, in case someone did not notice the mask or heed its warning. It simply renders the intruder immobile, unable to see or hear, a temporary statue. In this way even an accidental interference with the mysteries is unable to take place. Once he is released from the spell there are no ill-effects whatsoever, and he has witnessed nothing.

"It was a rather clever manipulation of the facts. By making my face the mask, it was impossible for anyone to get away once he had been seen by me, and thus his statuary condition became permanent. My beloved snakes replaced my wavy hair; they refused to be separated from me, even by a myth. The result for them was that they became associated with the horrible image and feared as greatly as was my distorted face. And my centrally located home became a rocky island in the middle of a stormy sea."

I say, "The story continues that Perseus, with the help of Athena, killed you and brought your head back to her. They say she wears this head on her shield."

"Yes, that is the story. But you know," Medusa continues with a small smile, "she couldn't ignore us forever. Even though the myth separates her from her origins, she is always linked to us, and there had to be some visible acknowledgement of that truth. By wearing the image of the Gorgon head she is able to retain some of the power of the Mysteries, and although she is willing to engage in armed conflict, she is also the protector of those who weave, spin, and craft the beautiful necessities of life. We survive, you see, albeit hidden, always ready for she who can see beyond the obstructions."

She stands. We embrace. Her ageless body is warm beneath my hands. "Go well" she says. Her light kiss against my forehead is a brushing of a butterfly's wing. A light breeze tangles in my hair, fingers trail away. The sky begins to turn, the earth turns I turn; I am at the center, I am motionless, I am spinning, I wait, eyes closed, breath still.

* * *

From behind my closed eyelids I can see it is dark. Cool air flows around me; I smell green leaves and damp earth. A trickle of water makes a small musical sound. I open my eyes in the center of the maze.

Remembering Medusa's words, I know this place and the far away isle are the same, that when I am at the center of myself, I am at the center of all things. The underground cave under the island is present within me at a thought. I feel my body turn, feet beating the rhythm as my long dark cloak flows out around me. The labyrinth surrounds me as I move into my body and my knowing.

Resting from the intensity of the complex journey into the

realm of Medusa, I remember the beauty. Wisdom, as the dictionary defines it, is "the knowledge of what is true or right coupled with just judgement as to action: sagacity, prudence or common sense."[7] I understand that the only truth and rightness I can know is that which is truth for me. Then I must put it into practice. The combination of knowing and action is the mark of wisdom, and when I am within the rhythm between these two, knowledge flows easily into manifestation.

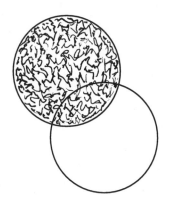

∞ L ∞

Magical Woman

Second Circle: Second Cycle

I sit in the earth, feeling the warmth, knowing the rock is beneath me. I have come from the place of deep wisdom, returning to daily life. [1] This is a time for being in the earth, in the water, in the sun and moon, in fire, in air. Fire, water, air and earth, magic and nature. It is a time to remember the summer night when women gathered on the grass to see the orange moon over the field where the white horse grazed among wisps of mist. A time for a woman to be dancing the rain in, feeling her feet reaching roots down into the earth. This is the time for being in a circle of trees, and to honor the tree in the center of the circle around which the women sit together. Here we speak of gardens and flowers, of food centered in the earth, of rock and place.

This is also the time for magic, simple magic, earth magic. Not the high ceremonial magic requiring complex preparations and initiations but the magic of everyday people. It is not possible to talk very long about reclaiming the ancient know‑ ledge of women without mentioning magic, for we have long been accused of using it. It is important to define the word, letting it stand free from the centuries of fear with which it is surrounded. The wise women of the past knew about herbs and potions, elixirs and candles. They knew how to find the healing leaves, the flowers and bark which brought relief to suffering.[2] Magic is the making of something which is other than what we experience as normal. Any transcending of the world as we have come to know it we call magic. If we fear this ability to tran‑ scend, we call it bad and persecute the person who is able to make this magic happen.[3]

Whenever we shape natural forces to a desired end, we are using the energy of magic. A television set would seem com‑ pletely magical to someone from the seventeenth century, while to us it is commonplace. When I mix flour and honey, yeast and milk, knead the dough and let it rise, then form it into loaves which rise again to form bread, I am making use of the natural characteristics of those substances. There is no mystery about it to me, but again, it is magic to one who has never seen the process. Doreen Valiente says

> " ...magic works because of nature's laws, not in spite of them. It is something built into the universe. Hence there is nothing really supernatural or supernormal, in the strict sense of these words. All is part of nature; but much of the realm of nature is 'occult,' that is, hidden.[4]

Learning about magic is learning about Nature, its rhythms and balances.

Once there was magic. Simple magic, the kind any woman could make, magic of the candle, of a stone. Our finger tips were sensitive like tongues, we could touch a plant and know its essence. Rhythms of life sang in our blood. I remember, I remember. In the high field where the grasses blow in the morning wind, I walked, waiting for the sign. Fingering

*through my hair, the wind whispered the message of the day:
hot, some rain this afternoon.   The plants asked for it, and I
told the moon last night.   We are all one, the moon said, so
there will be water for the ground tomorrow.   Snake hisses
through the grass at my feet, tickling my toes.   Blessed one, I
say, where shall I walk today?   He slips swiftly off to the left,
I follow more slowly.   Along the curving way, grain is
growing.   The plants offer it to me; eat, they say, it is good, it
is ready.   Chewing on the handful which slid into my hand,
I pause, listening to the lilt of melody.   Song sparrow greets
the heat as it builds within the earth and sky.*

How difficult it is to stay conscious as I approach this field
which is within the field of knowing.   Sleep o'ertakes me at
every turn. The spell is still alive, turning the loop, the *geas*
continues to protect me. I wish to be released. I recognize that I
may die, may be condemned, may be feared and tortured.   If
this is to be, then it will. You cannot protect me any longer, long
ago Mother. I love you deeply, as you loved me, as I love my
daughter. But the protection must be released, it is time for me
to wake, for all women to wake.   No longer can we allow the
fears to govern our lives. They govern the whole earth, and the
earth is dying, and we will all die with it if we do not risk the
leap into the future. We must be freed to move within the field
of our deep knowing, where the magic moves, alive and free.
We will need magic, if the earth is to survive, for nothing else is
working.

*So release me, Mother, from the protection of your spell,
release me so that I may enter into the field, listen to the
birds, commune with the grasses and fly with the wind.   I
love this earth so much, my Mother.   I love the rocks, the
trees, the flowers and the birds, the animals which run on
four legs and those who walk on two.   I marvel at the bodies
of insects which contain luminous works of art within a
fraction of an inch.   I delight in the brilliant feathers of the
goldfinch.   I long for the clear cool waters of the inland lakes
and the wild waves of the ocean shore.   The subtle colors in
the wild grasses of the field thrill me.   I welcome the skunk
who travels through my back yard, and my cat's weight on*

my chest for her morning snuggle.   Mother, I love the
thunder and the rain, the heat of summer and the snap of
cold ice.   I love the deep New England rocks pushed up by
the glacier, their striated colors take my breath away.   The
earth between my toes and the fish slipping through the
water, the dark forests and the shining sands, blue sky and
grey—all are part of the wonderful world and I do not want
to lose them.   So you see, Mother, it is time to slip the loop,
free my memory, let me wander down the path to my own
knowing, my true self, my woman me.   This is our time, we
need to know, clear minded, open eyed, freed of the waters of
Lethe the forgetting.   No more sleep, the time for sleep is
past.   In the name of the Mother who is All and in each of us,
lift your fear from me and set me free.

Reclaiming the knowledge will require the ability to listen
with my body, my mind, my ears, to see through the veil of
expectations, to suspend incredulity, and to know the power of
the small.   It requires me to feel the earth's rhythms within my
woman's body, the deep throbbing, the delicate singing, the
intense excitement of transformation. The seed absorbs moisture,
swells with the growing life within its walls, and bursts apart as
the insistent leaf is ready to unfold.   Even so must I contain the
potentials, nurture them, sustain myself through the uncom—
fortable swelling until I reach the joyous bursting through to
awareness.[5]

Listening, now, I wonder what it is I want to know?   Is it to
walk at the ocean's edge, knowing the rhythm of the salt waves
is echoed in the ebb and flow of my own blood?   Or is it to stand
on a high hill, the wind tangling my hair, sensing the turn of the
weather as the rain approaches?   Why is it, I wonder, that I want
to be connected with this knowledge which I know is present?

I think the deep awareness that things are out of balance, not
right, jangled and confused, calls me to find their true rhythm.
The work I do every day as a therapist and guide is the same
work I know the planet requires.   The need is great, whether it is
felt by the woman who knows her spiritual needs are not being
met by the traditional religions and aches for a belief within
which she can feel at home, or if it is the pain of the forest

thoughtlessly slaughtered to make way for a parking lot. What an imbalance we create when we build bigger and better malls, tempting people to spend more money than is available. How wrong a rhythm is created when both parents must work to pay for the basic necessities of life, leaving their young children to fend for themselves, watched over by adults who care little or abuse. There is no end to this list, it goes on and on, perpetuating itself in the same way as the body perpetuates its tensions, each one necessitating another until the whole system grinds to a halt, stuck, broken, desolate.

When I am still, I can feel the true rhythm of the universe, pulsing beneath all the macadam and trash, threading through the song of the bird and the flow of the river.[6] This rhythm calls me, echoing within my blood, singing along my nerves. I want to connect with my woman's knowledge so that I can help the rhythm reverberate along the old paths, setting the earth on its true course to fulfillment. Many of us are working for this cause, and everyone is important. Some are active in politics, some work hard for environmental safety, some attend to the inner changes. Remember Anne Cameron,

> There are women everywhere with fragments
> when we learn to come together we are whole[7]

This is my part, consistent with my life and work, a weaving of threads to support the pattern.

Again and again I come round the circle, over and over the pattern repeats, creating familiarity. Pilgrims and seekers tread the same path year after year, until the way is beaten deeply into the earth. Stumbling across it, we may not recognize it, but when we walk the old ways, attending to the rhythm, our feet find themselves following the curves. Maze patterns are often trodden into the earth. The repetitions of walking the same spiral bring the seeker into the place of knowing, in body and in earth.

When I was a child, I tied my thin gold chain into many knots for the pure pleasure of working them loose. I love untangling strands of anything, following the ends through to the source. The maze is a tangle until it is understood, until I stand at the center and know in my mind's eye the pattern of the paths.   I must untangle the knot formed by forgetfulness, deprivation, oppression and fear, the knot which keeps us from our true selves as women who have connections with magic and power. I am also a weaver. When I have untangled all the yarn, then I can weave the beautiful threads into rich tapestries, each line of color nestled into its perfect place.

Untangling this knot is a complex matter, for there are many turns of the yarn which are hidden from view, revealed only as the strands begin to unwind. We have no idea of the extent and depth of our repression as women until we begin to notice the small things, the little encoded bits of expectations which we always took for granted until one day we notice them within a context[8] of freedom and suddenly ask "Why?" It is the same for men, who also are trained from early childhood by the patriarchal society which says boys must be brave, not cry, always win, be strong. I am bemused as I listen to the seven-eight-and nine-year-old boys in my neighbor's yard, already driven by the pattern to which they know, instinctively, they must conform, each loudly struggling for supremacy as he tosses the ball through the hoop.

It seems that all these patterns of expectations are designed to keep us from knowing the true pattern, from understanding our true magic, from hearing the true rhythm of the Universe echoing in our bodies. Yet, somehow, we know. When I ask a woman "What do you know that you don't know you know?" and she finds herself listening, for a brief moment, to her true self, in that moment she knows there is something there.

Reaching within we must respond, send something back to ourselves from the far distant coast obscured by fog and misery, listen to our wisdom, thread through to the rhythm and recreate ourselves.

My wise friend Bettie says "Truth is very sturdy. It will endure." She is right.   It has endured for centuries, hidden deeply, emerging quietly through the silence, showing itself in the touch of a hand, the turn of a head, visible in the newly risen loaf or the comforted child. We have had it all along. Now is the time to make the connections, reaching across the miles and years, linking our bodies with our minds, acknowledging that our power is true within itself, self-defined, unique.   Our patterns, our rhythms, can restore the world to balance.

Here in the warm earth, I am at the center of the maze. Medusa tells me her temple is at the *omphalos*, the navel of the world.[9] I am connected here through the line of life to the Mother, generatrix of all life. Now, feeling the dark places within my body filling with light, sensing the linkage to the rhythm, now is the time to examine what it means to be a woman today, and how I shall carry this meaning forward, finding the paths which lead out of the maze, discovering the full pattern, going in and coming out, coming in and going out, free access to the mysteries and the magic.

Deeply I reach, remembering the hot summer days when I grew a huge garden, feeding my family full of teen-age children and their friends. In those days, when I invited the sun into my body, brought the fresh mud up between my toes, and felt my spirit leap into the air with the waving tips of the field cedars, so like the cedars of Arles where Van Gogh saw the energy spin and glow, there my blood sang and the Goddess came from the moon to teach me. I wrote then of stars reflected in dark water and long roads travelled alone. In those days I began the intense relation with my woman self, and I return to those places in memory now, seeking for the linkage which will teach me the deep, simple magic of knowing myself fully.

There is a simplicity in the placing of a seed in the earth, watering it, watching it grow. I did it as a child, planting victory gardens in long rows beside the Alabama country school. The turnips and radishes came up as reliably then as they do today, though I never cease to be delighted by the magic. I love the rhythm of the garden, the demanding abundance of beans and tomatoes, the slow nurturing of the melons. Within this rhythm it is possible to feel the slow turning of the earth, attending to the changes in the light as the season moves toward the fall harvest. If we wish to eat we must pay attention. There is more than food for the body here, however; there is also food for the soul and the spirit, offered if we but listen and learn.

If you feel as I do, and want to reestablish connection with the earth, try this. Walk outside onto a patch of grass, a weedy field, or some sandy beach. Barefoot, feel the contact between your body and the body of the Earth. Be there for a while, listening, sensing, thinking, knowing. There may not be words. You may not have great insights. But gradually, if you do it day after day, you will find yourself knowing something. It may be the need of the lawn for water. It may be a clearer certainty about a problem you face. It may be a stronger sense of your connection with the Divine. If you are greatly defended against your inner knowing, certain that the only valuable information comes through your intellect, you may need a little more time before your roots begin to grow. Once they do, and you feel them reaching into the earth, seeking moisture and nourishment, then you will under–stand what it means to be grounded, and you will know without words in a way which may be difficult to talk about.

Eliot again:

> Words, after speech, reach
> Into the silence.[10]

Reaching, the words draw to themselves more knowing. In this way we come to our wisdom. This is the fifth "way of knowing," the one called constructed knowledge, which Mary Field Belenky and her friends identified in their much needed study:

> Constructivists seek to stretch the outer boundaries of their consciousness—by making the unconscious conscious, by consulting and listening to the self, by voicing the unsaid, by listening to others and staying alert to all the currents and undercurrents of life about them, by imagining themselves inside the new poem or person or idea that they want to come to know and understand. Constructivists become passionate knowers, knowers who enter into a union with that which is to be known.[11]

There are many ways to come to this knowing and they all involve the inner listening. In this way we are able to enter the place which is, in the Zen terminology, No-Place, where all things have their origin.

I sense a rhythm to the reaching. It is the familiar looping of the symbol for Infinity, a figure eight lying on its side.

Following the pattern, I lift the knowing up into my being, then let the energy flow over and out into the Center of All, where it turns down, then lifts again, bringing out another wave of knowing which then turns toward me, falling and rising once more. In the center the magic happens; in the turning the Unseen world appears manifesting my desire.

What is woman? What is the rhythm of the feminine? It is important to weave all the pieces of answers to this question into some sort of image, for this is the way we can activate the inner knowledge. Research into the development of the brain has revealed some fascinating facts about the need for a model. Our brain has the innate ability to learn a language, for instance, but the language we learn is the one which is modeled for us by those around us. It could just as easily be Russian as English, French or Swahili. The tongue we speak is entirely determined by the language spoken in our environment. We know also that if a girl grows up neglected and unloved, it is impossible for her to give love and nurturing to her baby unless someone teaches her how to care for a child. Pearce says: "If no stimulus is given of an intelligence, that intelligence will never unfold."[12]   I can continue to ask the question about women's wisdom, but since the memory of the model was eradicated centuries ago, I am left perpetually with the question echoing within my soul.   Each piece of the answer makes sense and fits into the longing, but I need the picture of the whole before I can finally see the answer.

There are women everywhere with fragments
when we come together, we are whole

What are the pieces that seem to belong with this image?   I think of all those in the Women's Spirituality movement who recognize and name Goddess in her many manifestations.[13]   I think of the nature-centered religion of Wicca. [14] I remember all the teachers, the business women, the mothers, the artists, countless women who are moving from their expected role into positions of respect, power, and happiness. I think also of the thousands of women in various countries, even the United States,[15] who still believe in female genital mutilation, of all the women abused and battered by husbands and lovers, of women still regarded the world over as a possession of man. We are an incredible mix of experiences and passions, freedom and slavery. From the wealthy Park Avenue matron to the woman holding her starving infant in a drought-ridden land, we are women together and there is a bond which we recognize no matter how far apart our lives have taken us.

The secret we all hold close to our heart is the knowledge that we could be more than we are, if we could, somehow, someday, somewhere, break free of the pattern in which we find ourselves, release our power to create, allow our magical self to emerge. That there is that which we know that we don't know we know. I think this belief is there somewhere even in the woman who has completely acquiesced to the fate in which she finds herself, though it may be very deeply buried.

Women have a special ability. We can reach out, each to each, and connect. As we follow the curves of the Infinity symbol, reaching, gathering, bringing into ourselves and giving of ourselves, we come to a new comprehension of relatedness. It is no longer an outpouring of feeling towards another, but instead a reaching out and into the other; then a corresponding reaching and taking into ourselves. How much more true might our relationships become if we followed this model, for it adds a completely different dimension to the way which we consider is natural.

I am with a friend. We are with each other, sensing and listening with more than our ears. We notice small things - the way the eyes sparkle, or the tension in the shoulders. We value each part of the information we share, knowing everything we sense is true in some way. When we speak, our words come from places which are real, giving each to the other the expression of our sharing. I watch my words move towards her, see them turn towards her inner being. As she absorbs their form and content, they rise within her, enriched by her responses, and turn towards me. I open to receive, following their turn again past the center point between us, and scoop them joyfully up into my soul. The pattern continues, rhythm building upon rhythm, each participating from herself while honoring the other fully.

It is the same pattern for all our relationships. I can exchange this energy flow with my cat, with the birds at the feeder, with the plant in the garden, with the tree in the woods. It is a matter of practice, to learn the new way, to listen with my whole being, so that I can watch the rhythm weaving itself and be a part of the pattern. This is the gift of the Feminine, a special ability women carry.[16]

Our magic is simple. Enter into the truth of that which you desire. Hold it cleanly and clearly, gathering information with all of your senses. Keep your desire focused, pay attention to the small messages. When you know the form and the activity which will open the way to success, believe its reality and take action. Your intuition will aid and guide you as you come to your inner knowledge.

When I hold the sense of that secret knowing within me, believing it, nurturing it, encouraging it to find some form, I begin to feel a strength settling into my lower back. Roots reach down my legs into the earth, roots of pure energy, shining and whole. Supported by this base, I feel my spine straighten, and my head clears of the encircling fog. My organs settle into their places, firmly conscious of themselves, and tensions relax as I abandon the need to be any shape other than the one I inhabit. Remembering Medusa, I listen for the pattern of my blood, rediscover my breathing, move with the rhythm of my cells.

This is the manifesto of woman. I am a being connected totally with myself. I intensify the small, bringing hope and love into the crevices of the world. I expand into the largeness of the world, aligning my power with that of others, knowing myself for the true being I am. I celebrate myself, Woman. I do not need, any more, to call myself whole, because there is no part of me which considers fragmentation. I am woman, I glory and celebrate my being, I have no need to be other than who I am. I am of Earth, connected, power flowing perpetually through me from and to the Universe. We are a Living, Breathing Unity, I breathe the plant, the plant breathes me. From my womb springs new life. My body sings and celebrates each present moment, knowing the pattern, weaving the rhythm. Blessedness is my natural condition and it flows through me permeating all. I am woman, my body is alive, vibrant, all my senses participate fully, richly, perpetually. I am blessed and I bless.

∞ M ∞

Can You Imagine...?

First Circle: Second Cycle

It seems strange that we can lose touch so quickly with the important things of childhood. The essential self that takes form in the body which slides into this world from the womb of the mother is surrounded immediately with expectations, unrealized hopes of parents, and a host of fears for survival. Most of us are granted a few years of relative freedom before we must completely conform, and in that time the gifts and talents we bring with us can find some expression. Then the walls close in, and we are brought into conformity with the expectations.

Some part of us always remembers. So when I ask my questions, there is a stir in the deep memory, a flicker of awareness, as something long forgotten is recognized.

"What do you know that you don't know you know?"

Her silent reply is in her eyes: *The question drops into my consciousness and moves down, like a homing pigeon, arrowing into a hidden darkness. A moment, I pause, and then I nod, acknowledging the truth of the knowing. What it is, I do not know, as the question, turning on itself, redefines the problem. I do not know, yet now I know there is a not knowing, where before there was, perhaps, as I consider, an indefinable something, perhaps a longing, never seen, never recognized.*

What is it I know that I do not know I know? Some hidden part of myself, some lost or never found secret?

"What did you do when you were a child that was unusual, that you perhaps never told? Did you fly? Or, perhaps, see angels? Did you have a relationship with trees and animals? Could you tell what people were thinking? Did you ever see fairies? Did you have a friend others could not see?"

Why are you asking me these questions? How could you know about my flying? I never told anyone. I'm not sure I can tell you. What will happen if I tell? Will I be punished? Or laughed at?

Why are you asking? You say you flew too? Did other children see fairies? I always thought I should be able to see them. How did you know I could tell what my mother was thinking? Why are you asking?

I am asking because it is important to me. All my life I never told anyone about my flying. Then I met another woman who had done it too. Remember in *Mary Poppins*, how the little girl can understand the speech of the birds? Later she forgets she knew. I always thought that was true and now I know it is, because lots of women have told me they had communication with their pets. Maybe that was a story, about Mary Poppins, but the author was writing about something that was real, that children can do things that later they stop doing. And I want to know all the things women remember about themselves when they were children.

When you ask me about this, I feel myself shifting. If other women had this experience, and I can tell you, then it doesn't have to be a secret any more. You are not laughing at me. You want to know, it is important. You will not punish me. You are working on a research project which has been approved by a major university. This is not just my imagination.

I can feel that hidden part of myself expanding, breathing, remembering more. You ask more questions. I remember other things. You are excited, happy that I am sharing my experience with you. You believe me.

Many of the women with whom I have spoken have told me how important it is for them to be able to bring this cherished and secret part into a fuller connection with themselves. "You have certainly started something for me!" MJ writes, "I am sure I am almost constantly playing around with this at some level." Brenda says "Now I embrace them (the experiences) along with everything else about myself!" "It has changed my life!" says Sage. I begin to wonder how far this may reverberate. If we accept this special aspect of ourselves then we become something more than we thought we were. We feel more accepting, appreciate ourselves in a deeper way, our child self feels, finally, acknowledged.

What would it have been like, I wonder, if these abilities had been accepted at the time. Suppose, when I was a child, my mother recognized that I had some special abilities. Suppose she had, then, sent me to the wisewoman. Or suppose she had begun teaching me the songs and stories which would create the foundation for my gifts. Suppose my heart's desire had been to make magic...to talk with the flowers...to fly from the top of the mulberry tree. I was happy as a child. I loved the early mornings when I was up early, simply dressed, outside with the world. Hot long summer afternoons, riding my bicycle on dusty Alabama roads, picking dewberries when I was hungry. What did I long for? I wanted my stuffed animals to talk. I wanted to know all about the plants, inside and out. I loved to discover. I loved to make things for myself. I loved to explore and uncover. I would have loved to learn about magic. It was never offered. What if it had been? If the fairy tales I devoured had somehow been entrances into realms of infinite possibility.

In a fantasy story called *Changeweaver*, there is a land where it is recognized that women hold the power and the magic. In this land, little girls begin learning the songs of the Disciplines as part of their childhood games.[1] As they grow into women, their abilities are shaped and nurtured. I would love to have had such a training. In the story, the women come into their full power as they have children. And there is the clue for us, today. When we acknowledge and love our forgotten children, we may then learn about our power and step into ourselves as women.

What would my life have been like? Suppose the town in which I grew up was conscious of the value of the gifts of the children? My mother would have been nurtured in her childhood as well. I think that would have meant she need not have been so shy. She recognized as much of me as was possible, but how was she to understand my deep connection to the trees? I was so open, eager for teaching. When I wept to be parted from my friend the southern pine, she told me to talk to it, tell it I loved it and that I would never forget it. This was exactly right, and as I hugged my tree, loving it, I knew it loved me too. I have never forgotten it, nor the rough feel of the bark on my cheek and arms.

She also taught me something about memory. In our yard in Alabama we had a camellia bush which bore spectacular flowers in a wide variety of combinations of intense pink and white. I loved those flowers, and grieved when they faded. Mother told me how to take a picture of the flower with my mind, looking at it, fixing the image in my memory. She said then I would have it forever. She was right, and I have added countless other images to my wonderful collection.

How exciting it is to imagine myself learning more. I wonder where the possibilities existed. Were there more moments which I can now recover, reweave into the web of my remembrance? We can change the past; in the holographic understanding of the universe, all time is here, now, always, and what I call the past exists only in memory. In this moment in time, I can re-image the past and in so doing, redefine and reshape my memories, thus creating new patterns in my perceived present life.

I want to begin with flying. Putting myself back into that time, I remember. It was a funny little attic apartment in Newton, Massachusetts where we lived, my mother, father and I, when I was about four. One of a succession of homes, resting places, momentary pauses in my father's search for the spiritual home which eternally beckoned and which was never to be satisfied by any material house. I remember this place more clearly than many of the others because something very exciting happened there.

I don't know what my parents did in the rest of the house. Perhaps Mother taught in the nursery school on the first floor. Whatever the reason, I was left alone from time to time, for brief periods, and this is when I learned to float over the stairs without touching them. Childhood is full of mysterious things, new discoveries, unfolding wonder. Too soon, too often, the magic is dispelled by casual adult comments, patronizing, ridiculing. Better not to tell at all, the child realizes, tucking away the special knowledge, the unappreciated ability. I never told my parents. I wonder, now, what they would have said. I would like to ask them, but they have both been dead for many years. I wonder if they noticed anything.

To create my new reality within this memory, I now imagine I did tell my mother.

"Mommy, Mommy, I can fly! Come see! Watch me!"

Heart beating suddenly, hopefully, she follows. She has been watching for the signs, wondering what gift her little daughter will manifest. She had not dared to hope for flying. This was a very special gift, one which she always wished for herself, for to be able to leave the ground at will excited her. Her own talent was different, she had the gift of intertwining, which took the form of the ability to weave close and permanent ties with people. She could see already that Herta did not have this ability, being more connected with her trees and animals than other humans.

"Mommy!"

She watches as the little body steps out into space over the stairs, hopeful this is truly so, a little afraid of what might happen, but Herta is well and truly launched, and is soaring down the stairwell, actually turning the corner. "She has been practicing!" she thought, watching her daughter come to rest in front of her on the second floor landing. Delighted, she scoops her up, laughing and tickling her, praising and pleased.

With a wriggle, Herta slides free and races up the stairs to fly again. This time, as she lands, Mother catches her. "Let's go tell Daddy."

Already I feel freer. Strange, always, how this sort of imagery can recreate the past, becoming the new reality. C.G. Jung developed the technique of Active Imagination, which he used to help his patients continue their connection with their dream self while they were awake and in conscious reality. In this technique, you reenter the dream at the point at which you woke. Carefully you reestablish your presence in the world of the dream, remembering the people, the place, the time of day, the events, your emotional state. Then you let the dream continue. The key in this process of dreaming the dream onward is your active participation. This is not daydreaming nor stream of consciousness activity. This is an entrance into the realm of the dream, with careful attention being paid to your conscious observation of events and conversations as they unfold within your awareness.[2]

I have had Active Imagination experiences which are now a solid part of my life and memory. It is a powerful therapeutic tool, for it can give an unhappy inner child the attention for which she has always longed. A dream image can provide that which life left out. With this process we access the field of the Holotropic Universe, and in so doing can gain entrance to the field of knowledge specific to our process. Attention, particularity, and desire are keys to the way in. We do not just wander into the dream and out again. Active Imagination is just that, active participation, not guiding but rather being present with the possibilities until the right one emerges.

By entering into the field of innate abilities with the desire to experience approval of my flying, I am, immediately, in a place where full acceptance is the reality. When I feel the delight of my mother as she catches me out of the air, I find my body relaxing into fuller appreciation of my accomplishment. There is a confidence that she will know what to do now, that she understands, that she and the other adults have been noticing me for my own true self, and that she will find me a teacher who will help me fly further. The old pattern of not telling anyone for fear of ridicule is gone, replaced with a new confidence and expectancy.

I am excited, now, to discover what the next development will be. *Entering again into the field, I find I am in a school where there are classes for the gifts of each child. My group is outside in the playground, which is a special one, for we don't need all the usual devices for getting off the ground. Instead, there are a series of platforms, built mostly into trees, though there are some constructed of wood and metal. These are of varying heights. There is plenty of space between the platforms. We are practicing flying, sometimes up, sometimes down, the hardest is across from one tree to the next, for we must shift levels to land on the platform. Heather is hovering in the air over one of the platforms, She can't come into the trees just yet, she has to learn to move from one platform to another. She told me she used to sit crosslegged beside her bed and rise into the air, but she never travelled anywhere, so she has to learn to do that first. Pam is in the next tree. She is better at this than I, because she went outside to fly before anyone knew about it, and then she taught her sister. Kathleen is swooping across the playground, learning to make somersaults in the air. She told me she flew with her eyes closed in the hall at home. Now she can open her eyes. She is very brave. I hope she will help me when I get to somersaults.*

Nancy, Ashley and I are in the same tree, learning to fly up, because we all only flew down before we came to school. Flying up is different. You sort of catch your breath and imagine yourself lifting. It is hard, at first, but now we are having more fun. I remember last year when I learned to ride a bicycle - it was so hard to get the balance at first, and I could only do it down a slope - John pushed me off and I wobbled my way to the bottom. Then all of a sudden, I got it, and I could ride! Flying up is sort of like that. Other kids tell me all the time that they fly in dreams, and what they say sounds just like how it is. Today Ashley and I held hands as we flew. That was exciting, because then we had to let go at the right time to get to our separate landings. But we did it! Ashley knows how to do something else. When she is out with her dogs, she can lift rocks without touching them. I asked her if she could lift really big boulders, and she said it didn't matter if they were big or little. The dogs help her concentrate.

It's a pretty day. The sky seems to go up forever. I feel as though I could just fly up and up, and rest on a cloud. I remember a poem I wrote. " Story Parade" published it!

> *The clouds are the wind's pillow*
> *The sky is the wind's bed*
> *With such a place for resting,*
> *"I like to sleep," the wind said.*

I imagine I could sleep up there with the wind. Ashley says I can't, I couldn't breathe that high up. She was on a plane once, and learned about how the air gets thinner the further away you get from Earth, until there is no air at all, and then you are in Space.

Lori floats down from her perch in the top of the tree. "It's time to go," she reminds me, "We have Naturespeak now." I tumble over myself, getting down to the ground in a hurry. This is my favorite class. It's so easy. We just go walk in the woods and listen to the trees and flowers, We are very quiet, most of the time, so we won't disturb each other, but the daffodils can be very funny and then we laugh out loud. I like to sit on the stone walls—they tell me such wonderful stories. There is never any problem when you are talking with a stone, they know all about everything. I wish I could talk with people as easily as mother. She has lots of friends and they have all sorts of things they talk about. Talk, talk, talk. I'd rather listen to the moss. And smell it. It feels so good on my face...all cool and green and sort of wet...smells of woods, real deeply. Nothing in the forest minds me smelling, I wonder why grownups don't like it. I smell everything. It's how I know what it is, and I love to remember with my nose. Mother says it's not polite to smell my food before I eat it, even though she understands what I am doing. So I do it when no one is looking.

When Lori and I are in the woods together, we can both hear the trees whispering to us. She feels the same way I do about English; it is hard to remember all the words, and they don't feel right, sometimes. I think most of the children in this class agree. We all like this language better. Eva is under the big tree by the stream, calling the fish. She says she just is calm in spirit and they come. She laughs when she calls the fish, because her brother can't do it, so she always catches more.

Stories women tell me weave through my imagery. Together we agree it would be wonderful to have had such a school. Together we can begin to reshape our memory. Somewhere this acceptance and training exist. Imagine what the courses would be:

Flying; basic, intermediate, advanced
Naturespeak
Development of Intuition
Principles of Magic

History of Elves, Fairies and Dwarves
Techniques of Mind Reading
Animalspeak
Teleportation
Stories the Rocks Tell Us
Angelic Discourse

Contemplating such study expands the possibilities. It moves us closer to the fields of experience.

If the holographic field has all time within it, then all memories of all women exist in that field. Zenna Henderson entered it when she wrote the People stories. "Just stories," she might say, were she alive today. Or might she admit, secretly, as so many of the women have, that she remembered flying and that memory was so precious that she, years later, wove her stories about a whole world where the Gifts and Persuasions were treasured and nourished. Another writer, Pat says her stories come from her imagination, vivid from childhood. Just her imagination? Or was she connected with that holographic field where small magics were possible and people knew how to feel their way so deeply into trees that they could become one? What is imagination? It is discounted as not real because the things it reveals are not compatible with the three-dimensional world which science has defined for us. Suppose, however, that through our imagination we perceive and enter a realm which exists on a different level, functions on a different vibration, and is simply another way of seeing, a differently perceived reality.

When Jeanne tells me she once played on the bottom of a swimming pool, sitting with the little people who were her friends and playmates, and was perfectly content to stay there, resisting mightily when the adults hauled her up into the air, I assume she was, for those moments, in a reality where she could breathe under water, or did not need to breathe. Then I remember Heather told me her sister always said she could breathe underwater. I believe Jeanne's experience, but it carries even more weight when I put it together with Heather's sister. And then I remember my training in breathing meditation, and the way I can stop breathing at the end of an exhale and feel that I do not need to breathe ever again.

There are many tales of people who can do unusual things like move objects without touching them, heal themselves immediately from a wound, suspend their animation. Many of these experiences are documented and tested for their scientific reality.[3] Our childhood experiences are not proven in such a manner, but they are real to us, and we can recognize their truth as we share them with each other. Our child selves respond with delight at the idea of learning more about our abilities. And the importance of the experience to our adult selves confirms the truth.[4]

As we come out of the woods, glowing from our conversation with the rocks beside the stream, the bell is ringing for the Friday afternoon class. This is one of the best times in the week, for here we all get to tell our stories. MaryJo runs up to us, her hair all messy with bits of straw sticking out. "You've been in the stables again" I tease, "you don't have to sleep there, just because Prince is teaching you how to whinny." MaryJo draws herself up to her full four feet. "We talk!" she protests, "Whinnying is just for fun." I grab her hand. "I know, I know," I reassure her. MaryJo is new in school, and she still feels protective of her ability.

In the big sunny room we all find comfortable seats. It is so nice to have chairs we can curl up in, and rugs on the floor. It makes telling stories much more fun. Sandra says "All right, girls. Today let's tell about times we knew things. Who wants to start?" Five hands were already waving. Larissa is dancing around. "I fell in love with an elephant in the zoo, and Mother wouldn't let me try to touch it and I couldn't get past the barrier. I started crying and was really, really upset. I wanted so much just to touch the trunk. Then, all of a sudden, I knew I could use my mind to reach into the cage, and I did! In my mind I touched the trunk, and I know the elephant felt it, because he waved at me with his trunk."

Kris is next. "I used to lie in bed at night," she says," and feel myself swinging. I'd go higher and higher. I knew, I don't know how, but I knew, that if I went really high, I would be in another place, and that place wasn't really real. I knew I could make a choice. If I stopped swinging when I was that high, I would be in that place. It was my choice."

Lots of voices ask "Did you? Did you stop?" Kris shakes her head.

"No, I never did. If I had, I don't think I'd be here now." Sandra tells us such a thing is possible, and that we sometimes have to be careful, because the boundary between this life and another place can be very easy to cross. She says she knew someone, a long time ago, who meditated a lot, and went out of his body to travel to other places. Only he didn't know how to do it safely and forgot to keep himself connected to his body. So one day he was gone, he never came back, and his body just went on sitting there, but there was no one home. We all shivered. I'm really glad that couldn't happen now, because now everyone is taught in school. Sandra asked us all to reach out and hold hands and remember we have each other, and we can always talk with someone. That felt really good, and I held Lucy's hand and Kathleen's, and we watched the energy flowing through us and around the room.

Pam says "Could I go next?" Everyone got settled again." I can understand what the birds are saying. I hear them talking about where the seed is and how much fun it is to float on the spring breeze." Sage says she can do that, too, and others nod. "But what I really wanted to tell you," Pam says, "is that I know I am my grandmother. She died before I was born. I've know this since I was three years old. Sometimes my father's sisters and brothers tell stories of when Dad was a child, and I know all about them already. At first my uncles and aunts thought I was strange, but now they understand, and we have a lot of fun remembering. Dad is still a little weird about it." Sandra laughs with the rest of us. "I guess so," she says, "to have your little girl tell you things about your childhood might be hard to take." Nancy's hand is waving in the air. "I remember my other mother, the one I had before. My mom doesn't like it when I talk about her, and I mostly do it when I'm mad with her, but my other mother didn't get mad at me the way Mom does, and so I tell her. She says she's the only mother I ever had, and I tell her, no, this was before. She doesn't see how I can remember." We all think this is pretty neat. "Oh," Pam says, " and when I was little, I wanted to be an elephant when I grew up. I really did."

When the laughter died down, Sandra asks, "Anyone else know something?" Lucy shyly raises her hand. " I know I am a Princess from a magic kingdom. I know I really don't belong here, and my parents are just looking after me till my real parents arrive." Sandra smiles. "There are others who know they don't really belong here," she says. "Anyone else?" A few hands go up, really slowly. "It is hard to talk about it, I know. Thank you for telling us, Lucy."

Joan says,"I know when people are lying. I didn't find out till a little while ago that other people couldn't tell too. I see it written on their foreheads." Sandra says that would be a very useful thing to know. She says she has heard of one other person who said the same thing. "Maybe we can learn how you do that, and teach others," she says. "would you be willing to help us do that?" Joan beams and nods her head.

The door opens and Lorraine puts her head in. "We're ready for Mindreading," she says. "Jackie says if any of you not in the class are free, you are invited to sit in." We all head toward the door. Mindreading is a wonderful thing and we have all heard stories from our friends who can do it easily. We all want to learn.

This school could be real, if we set aside our fear and our doubt, our skepticism, our training, and accepted the things our children say as true, try to ask more about the unseen things in the room, open our minds to a wider world. Then, perhaps, we would begin to remember more and more wonderful things.

∞ N ∞

Ancient Connections

Overlap: Three Mandorlas

In the old religion of Wicca, it happens from time to time that a person by circumstance, location, or desire, finds herself alone, following her spiritual practices by herself. Such a one is called a Solitary. I am grateful there is a name which recognizes and accepts this situation. I am a Solitary, by nature, it seems. Circumstance developed it, an only child of parents who each had their own interests, moving frequently, living mostly in the country where I could easily entertain myself. All my life I have enjoyed my time alone, valued it, often preferred it, happy with my own searching, writing, moving within the land of Soul as I know it. I am, I believe, difficult to live with, for it usually does not occur to me to share my thoughts and actions with another, though I have learned some modification of this behavior.

I also long for connectedness, but of a certain kind. I am interested in meeting the other person at the deep level, in the place of Soul, yet I often find this difficult because of the wariness which I and others have; we do not trust each other. Fear lurks behind the masks we all wear and I often find it difficult to reach into my truth and set aside the convenient protection. Because my longing is strong, I don't want to participate in conversation which is superficial, yet I often find I cannot release my tongue nor find any words to say.

There is a rising tide of urgency, however, felt by me and many women I know, which intensifies as the millennium approaches. Now the necessity of meeting and sharing with other women is becoming very strong. In order to be present with the coming changes we must be moving together to raise the energy, exploring with each other the new possibilities, using our recovered wisdom to support and augment each other's talents and discoveries.

I don't even know for certain what I am asking. But the fantasy future contains a clue, the soul threads which weave the beautiful web beckon me on. It is communication of the deep sort which I seek. A return to the language of my childhood, when I could communicate with the Southern Pine without words.

Together. It is hard to image it. Without any holding back. That would mean no fear. No fear the other might not like me. No concern about being left. It would also mean being comfortable with the different languages. With the language of Nature and not having to talk English all the time. So we would be quiet, or noisy, or with a rock, or a bird, and share and support —I don't think support is a word we would need. It would be so natural, it would not need a separate word. It would be a natural part of the love for all things. We would love ourselves, totally, knowing that by doing so we also love all others.

To come to the deep place where the energies may meet and dance, we must first clear away the old forms. It would be nice to do this gradually, so as not to disrupt the pattern of daily life. But I am not at all certain this will be possible. We are very resistant to change, fearful that we will not like the result, unwilling to give up patterns we hold as essential. We may need a strong disruption before the new can emerge and take form, before there will be the space to see what is good and what is not.[1]

In the shift of consciousness about women's roles in society, there is a re-emergence of the Feminine, the essential archetype which is carried within every human, male or female. This is not to be confused with the term "feminine" which has come to mean attributes society assigns to woman, such as feminine clothing or feminine behavior. The archetype of the Feminine, sometimes called Yin, as named by the ancient Chinese, recognizes our ability to think in a circuitous fashion, weave diverse parts into a whole, reach deeply into our intuitive faculties, and nurture growing life in the myriad ways it requires.

It is this renewal of awareness of the Feminine which holds, I believe, the promise and hope for survival of the planet. We have lived in the grip of the Patriarchal, hierarchical system for centuries, and we are rapidly discovering the inherent flaws in such a system. As women demonstrate their abilities to function well at all levels of society, not only equal to men but with their own uniquely individual way of perceiving truth, we begin to understand that the prevailing systems are not the only ones possible.

Linda Jean Shepherd notes:

> Throughout the history of science, women have been identified with "Mother Nature" as cyclic, nonlinear, nonrational, and unpredictable. Studies of nonlinear dynamics now show that these qualities are, in fact, vital to life.....The masculine Aristotelian ideal of complete order—of everything forever in its place—leads to death. By infusing robustness and flexibility into the traditional linear approach to research, the Feminine enlivens science.[2]

The image of woman as both robust and flexible begins to describe the energy and kind of power available when the Feminine is allowed to come into her rightful place. But this is not just about women coming into their own, it is about the Feminine aspect of men and women, about the archetypal Feminine being present in the world in Her full range of abilities, integrated, uniting with the Conscious Masculine, so that we can, at last, become fully human.

I sense the change of the millennium coming. I feel it in my head, an onrush of feeling, intense, nearly unbearable. It swells to a crescendo, then fades away. What is happening? How can I describe this? I remember a phrase from a Broumas poem:

> ....for which
> like amnesiacs
>   in a ward on fire, we must
>   find words
>   or burn.[3]

My brain short-circuits. Am I wired strangely? Is the wiring trying to change. (Does the wiring WANT to change?) What is this curious sensation that happens in my brain? It feels like a surge of power.

Suddenly I am transported back into an old dream, a big dream, one which I painted, imaged, lived with for several years, then stored in memory until further understanding was possible. Now it emerges, offering another level of insight.

Dream:

> *I walk on the outskirts of a city at night. A great storm blows up with mighty winds which topple the electric utility poles as I watch. I see the flashes and fires begin as the wires crash to the ground, and I run to escape the danger. Wires are everywhere across the road, it is unsafe to travel. Later I come to an ancient European town with narrow cobbled streets and houses which overhang the road. The church crowds up to the sidewalk, and an iron gate set in the side of the wall guards an inner sanctum shrine which is on the outside of the church. This opening glows with golden light, a jewel within the surrounding darkness and age. Ageless itself, it is seen but inaccessible, protected with iron bars.*

> *I walk further along the twisting roadway, climbing the gentle slope. There is a destination, somewhere ahead. On my right is a building. Entering, I find myself in a large empty room. Tall windows, covered with dust, filter the*

*sunlight which falls on the dry wooden floor. Heaped into
corners against the walls are piles of old straw, dusty, a few
white feathers mixed in, while a single white chicken runs,
clucking, around the room. I stand, looking about. Turning
to my left I suddenly see, sitting halfway up the wall. a tiny
old woman, wizened, with brilliant blue eyes. She is looking
at me.*

In my dream, the carriers of electrical energy, life blood of a
city, are broken. The dark streets are covered with twisted wires
and shattered poles. In the distant buildings fires are breaking
out. The system shuts down. Transported back in time to the old
European village with narrow streets and overhanging
buildings, I find the church surrounded with a wall, as the old
ones often were, but harboring in the niche the golden light of
the older faith. I have gone from the bright light of the modern
electrical system to the intense glow of the inner spiritual magic,
preserved through time, sheltered in the sturdy wall, unbe–
knownst to the priests in the sanctuary.

Much of the wisdom of women was contained within the
practices and ceremonies of the earth-centered religions. Simple
magic attends to the cycles and rhythms of nature, and the
celebrations of Beltane, Samhain, and other seasonal holidays
coincided with harvest or spring planting and were designed to
insure the survival of the inherent energy contained within these
natural events. In its quest and drive for power and control, the
Church devised many ways to divert, negate, or incorporate
these practices with the goal of eliminating all connections with
the Pagan religion.

When the mind has been restricted, and the psyche has been
locked up with preconceived ideas and expectations, it is hard to
move beyond the imposed limitations. If I have lived all my life
in a room, never leaving, and only occasionally glimpsing the
outside world through a narrow window which was mostly kept
shuttered, it will be a strange day when a hidden door opens and
I can step beyond the four walls. The light would be painful to
my eyes, I would feel the wind abrading my skin, my feet would
hesitate to touch the grass. Just so, as I struggle to understand the
changes which I sense are coming in the universe, I see at last the

myriad patterns which have hemmed me into a narrow vision of reality. Here I find my brain easily becomes overloaded and I have the sensation which I can only describe as short-circuiting. My wiring is outdated, unable to accommodate the increased load. I am reminded of my days in New York, living in old loft buildings once used for light manufacturing, now occupied by dancers and artists in need of space. We searched for these places, illegal for living, cheap in rent. When we found one, in need of tremendous work, the wiring was often minimal, a few bare bulbs hanging from worn black cords. Dusty and dirty, the long windows caked with soot, sunlight shining through the grime, we looked at the expanse of floor and gleefully accepted the challenge.

My dream presents me with the same space. It is an old dream. Fifteen years ago I drew it, painted it, wrote about it. Its power has remained, only partly understood, throughout the intervening years. Exploring the image of the inadequate wiring in my brain, the memory of the dusty windows in the New York City loft called up the picture of the dream room, empty save for some old straw and feathers, a single chicken, and a compelling old woman. I have learned that when an old dream appears in response to a current image or situation there is a good reason, that the correspondences are in line, and it would be well to pay attention. When this happens in session with a client, and the dream is from a number of years ago, I am credited with superb memory. I hasten to explain it is some function of the brain that brings the dream image leaping into consciousness, as a computer search will reveal long forgotten items when keyed with the appropriate word.

There are layers of images in this room. It is a place of mystery, the silence of the tiny woman and her piercing blue eyes compel me. It is a place of creativity, for a dancer must move within such a space. There is a correspondence to the niche in the church wall; the old woman is also in a wall. Both she and the shrine are ancient, linkages to another reality. This room demands my attention and I have labored in it, reaching for understanding, trying to make connection with the woman. I struggle; how can I open a dialogue with her? Am I to do this? She has much wisdom I am certain, but she is also a trickster, with those intense blue eyes. How am I to approach her?

Approach. Of course. There is only one way to come to her, for she clearly has no intention of coming down to me. I am to rise up through the air. This whole story is about my childhood ability to fly. She is sitting cross-legged, half way up the wall. I can rise up to sit in the air opposite her. Reclaim myself. The reality of all my stories so far has carried me into recognitions and comprehensions beyond my everyday capacities. Truth is what we remember.

This one is really hard. This is more real than any of the other stories. It was easier to journey to Medusa's Isle than to find myself rising into the air. What I did so easily as a child is now an impossibility, even though I completely believe myself and all the others. Lifting into the air is different from hearing angels, reading minds, even from seeing nature spirits.

As I have spoken with women about their early childhood abilities I have asked how it feels to be validated in their memories. For many, answering my inquiry was the first time they told anyone. This is particularly true of the fliers. Flying is an ability so contrary to normal experience, so vulnerable to requests for demonstration, that it has been important to all of us to keep the secret. The thought that I might actually be able to recover this ability is terrifying and exciting, and with a large part of myself I don't believe it is possible. I understand the mythic dimension and the value of flight as a symbol and metaphor, but might I truly lift my body from the ground? Well!

Jean Houston has said "People will go further and faster in developing human capacities if their training is tied to a story and especially to a myth."[4] I have a story of flying that is about me as a child. To bring this ability into my adult life, I need a story to shape my imagination.

Suddenly time collapses as I contemplate this dilemma. I see myself in the air opposite my teacher. If I am there, will I be able to understand how it happened? I think this is the teaching being offered to me.

Now I can begin to see more of the hindrances placed in my

path, There has been so much training to shape me into an acceptable member of society, an acceptable woman, training that is difficult to uncover and impossible to remove if not seen. This room itself brings one into memory, one which I had no idea was a problem. The memory:

> *In another part of my journey, at another time, I am a small girl, about five years old, sitting on the floor in a room, alone. In the next room my father is meditating. He says to me, "I am being quiet," and I know I must also be quiet. I sit on the floor, the bare floor of a rooming house; Mother is at work. There are tall windows which are dusty, the sunlight falls on me as I sit on the floor, silent, waiting for Daddy to finish being quiet.*

This has been a recurring image, a place I have returned to without knowing what the importance of the time might be. It is a familiar occurrence, all through my life with my father. Dad was very spiritually oriented and his time for prayer and solitude was unquestioned. It was one of those things which I accepted because there was no possible alternative—like bed time is bed time, and one does not ask for innumerable glasses of water because changing that fact is simply not a possibility. I know the truth and efficacy of this for in raising my own children there were certain things that were fact, and there was little repetition needed when facts were unalterable.

It has never occurred to me, however, that the art of waiting might be interfering with my ability to move forward. Perhaps I have not developed the art sufficiently and have rather practiced the skill. Patient waiting is useful when raising children, caring for the sick, listening to clients. Women learn to wait. Reflecting on this now, I realize the art of waiting must include discrimination, knowing when to wait because one must, when to wait with attention to the process, and when to stop waiting.

In meditation I sometimes get to a place that has no energy; it is different from the quiet waiting that is active and which has its own vibrant life. In this place I tend to fall asleep, lose consciousness, become listless. Perhaps at these moments I have slipped, unknowing, into the pattern of the child who waited. Perhaps if I am free of waiting for my father to finish, I can, in this place, move on into my own pattern. It is curious to come across spots like this, when the rest of my life is active, directed, full of motion, but I recognize the truth of the situation, the place where the child is stuck, waiting eternally to be freed.

Since these two rooms have so much in common, I think I will try letting them coexist. Perhaps something will happen.

I bring the two rooms together, Now the child is sitting in front of the tall windows in the dusty room where straw and feathers gather in the corners and a single white chicken runs clucking across the floor. The old woman watches me, I am the child. There is a question: "Where is your father?" He is not in this place. That feels better; father is left back in his quiet room. He can go on being quiet. I love my father, and being quiet was what he did sometimes. Now he can be quiet and I am somewhere else. Maybe I don't have to stay in that other place forever. Let's check.

Back to the first room. Empty! The sunlight falls on the floor. I look around. Nothing is in this room. Dad is still in his room behind the door.

Now, as though a video tape has been on hold and then released, I watch a scene in motion. The door opens and Herta, who has been waiting patiently, jumps up with a smile. Her father holds out his hand. Together they leave the room, going out for a walk. Their life continues.

Freeing the child from stuck places brings always a sense of great relief, and this is no exception. In comparison with many of the situations in which I have facilitated the release of a child caught in fear, hiding and neglect, this seems mild. But each person has her own necessity, and I find this simple shift of attention to be an important step at this point in my search for the way to reconnect with my ability to fly. It is also true that small things can alter the course of our lives; a critical word at a parti-cularly vulnerable time, a harsh response to a tentative offer of sharing from an inner place. Things like these can frost the flower before it blooms. Separating the child of magic from the child who waits eternally allows that particular part of my small self to move into relationship with a larger awareness. Now I think I can contemplate the act of sitting on the air with a more conscious attention.

Things happen fast. I now find myself sitting opposite the old woman. I can look down and see the chicken running around. I can also wonder how I got here, because I don't seem to have any recollection of lifting off the ground. But I look down at the chicken and think about eggs.

When I work with a dream, I know each image has several layers of meaning. So thinking about chickens and eggs, I first go to the personal recollection. What do I know about them? When we lived on the farm in Preston, we kept chickens. They were free to roam and when I brought the compost out they always came running full speed, necks stretched out ahead of themselves, in their haste to get the goodies. They always made me laugh. I love chickens. We had nesting boxes for them, but a couple of times a summer I would find two dozen or more eggs in a warm hill of grass. Amazingly, they were always perfectly preserved, and while I cautiously broke each one into a separate bowl as I used them, they were always good to the end. I have heard it said the egg is Nature's perfect container.

I think about chickens. They always seem to be a favorite sacrificial creature. No one appears to think much about it. I find myself wondering about this. I find it difficult to imagine that in a world where all life is sacred that the blood sacrifice would be considered necessary. Is it possible that in the early matriarchal, earth-centered cultures, there was no such thing? And how, I wonder, might people regard a chicken, a bird that is content to stay around people, that doesn't fly far, that can be counted on to give an egg a day? This is a valuable commodity, and not something to kill except for food. I can imagine the hen being honored for her fertility. Perhaps women who had difficulty conceiving might beseech her blessing. The egg and the womb do the same thing; nurture the life within until it is ready to emerge. If I were a barren woman, I might well envy the chicken, beseech her to make my womb fertile.

Now, sitting opposite the old woman, feeling the power of her intensely blue eyes, I stretch out my hand and meet her answering hand. Palms touching, sliding past the skin, reaching for forearms to clasp and hold. Transmission of energy sparks and flows.

It is fine to be a solitary, and I value the discoveries I make. Now it is time for us to be co-creators of the universe, to come together. Meeting each other, we now share our experiences. Old woman is all those women who have gone before; behind her, in an unbroken line, stretch centuries of wisdom carried in the bodies of countless women. Conscious or not, our bodies have been the repository of this wisdom, and it is time, now, to join with each other, share our discoveries, and step forward into the transformations which must occur.

How would it look, this coming together of women? I can see an image:

> The women gather, moving through the summer field, through daisies and buttercups, and stately Queen Anne's Lace. Walking slowly, enjoying the day, feeling the sun warm on their hair, they meet, greet, walk hand in hand, touch each other gently, eyes shining their welcome. Few words are spoken. The silences are full of conversation, sharing the beauty of the day. In Spring they came, in snows of Winter, on crisp Fall days. Summer brings them again, the moon is full, the night will be clear.

> The trees come out to meet them, the woods waiting behind the edges of birch and aspen. The giant oaks stand deeper, where the shadows play with the sunlight falling through the branches. From every direction the women come, some through the forest from the other side, some from the north, some from the south. They meet at the familiar place, the clearing circled with stones, grass carpeting the ground with green.

> Touching, holding, speaking soft words, the women reaffirm their deep connections. The energy builds as they weave their soul threads together. The web is beautiful, shining with many colors, stretching from one to another, encompassing them all with love and trust.

There it is; we are not separate, we are all parts of the One, and are all One together, each one of us is the One, and All. We would need to know that absolutely.

When the knower and the known become a unified flow, we know that we are identical with the deep Meta-universe from which we continuously arise. Upon realizing that we and the cosmos arise together from the Meta-universe, we know that we share the same "body." We become aware of life as an ever-renewing wonder. No longer seeking escape from or domination over the world, but more conscious and direct participation within it, we move in gratitude through the vast body of Being that is the Meta-universe.[5]

So what would we do together. We would simply be joyful or peaceful or learning, together. We would share ourselves with each other in whatever way we wanted. We would be comfortable and without fear with each other.

Thinking this way is incredibly powerful for me. I have never put into words the desire of my heart. I am still not doing it completely, but this is a beginning.

We would have a deep sharing. We would join hands and walk together into the field of knowing and look, together, at the places therein.

It is hard for me to imagine being in a group of women without having the nervousness, the inhibitions, the holding back. Perhaps this is me. Perhaps it is also others. But it is hard. Bringing my body, my love, my soul, my spirit, my being together. Being able to be with other women in full connection because I want to have the joining at the level of freely sharing soul.

Something happens when we share about the childhood memories. There is a connection. When we share about sexual openings. There is a connection. When we can be spiritual together. There is a connection. Co-researchers, core-searchers. We are Core searchers. Searching for our cores, individually, the core of woman, the core of life. The center is in the center, the core of the apple contains the seeds. It is a star, a pentagram. The goddess sign.[6]

Once I dreamed I was going to a school for fishes. I was in a cave; the entrance to the school was through a hole in the ground. Light shone up from the depths. The edges of the entrance were crusted and wet, like old rocks in tidal flats. The slippery ladder was the way down, and care must be taken to descend. There were more than one of me. I was beginning the descent.

Fishes are the deep parts of self that are spirit, living in the deep, reflecting the stars. If they are to be taught, are learning, then this is learning on a deep level. I am to learn with the fishes.

I am a solitary person. I prefer to be alone. Yet the connection with certain friends have been standout special ones, where I could, in various ways, say whatever I wanted to say.

I remember Pendle Hill, the first year there when I was 13. I remember saying so often that everything there was important, and that people could wash dishes or set tables or talk about the weather, and yet it was important. I want that Pendle Hill. All the time. Without fear. When I long for community, it is that community for which I long. In this community, we could braid each other's hair, walk with the dog, cut up onions, talk about the weather, but it would not be meaningless conversation.

Could I pledge myself to have no more meaningless conversations?

If I were not hiding parts of myself, I would have no fear. My fear is that I will not be accepted, will be reviled. I know I am strange, different from the normal, always have been, not willing to face derision, wanting to be me.

What would I like this to be?

I would like us all to be accepted for ourselves, and to see ourselves clearly, acknowledging our gifts, appreciating ourselves. I would like us to be able to redo the past sufficiently so that we can connect clearly with the essential energy and then share it with others. We give each other life. This is about women sharing and women knowing in the place of woman. The knowing is of ourselves, and of each other, each the other woman. The meeting is in the knowing which is in the meeting.

We go down into ourselves and learn, so we can come up into ourselves. It is a different direction. We are already here, we are the mountain. We come up into ourselves.

So when everything else has gone, and all the communication lines are down, and the city is on fire, then we can shift into the old place, where the sacred is kept in its shrine of light. And in the abandoned and disused warehouse, which is the place of creativity in my lexicon, the wise woman comes to bring me, perhaps, to the next place? And it comes up from within me, and my eggs are there, waiting to be hatched, and the field is within me and I am within it...oh, yes.

The power lines are falling, falling, flashing and burning, tangling in themselves; step carefully around them, for indeed the old ways are dangerous when they come to ground. The intensity of their power could only be carried in the air, unconnected to the earth. Separated from the rhythms of day and night, heat and cold, the electricity keeps us always the same, one temperature, one illumination. Walking away from the carnage, we can come again to the quieter time, to the ancient ways, and find there the holy space intact, shining through the dark stone.

At the end of the dream, I am cooking eggs in the kitchen for a stream of people who pass through the room. In a very real and practical sense this is sharing the mystery. It is not bread and wine but rather the perfect food, the renewal of life.

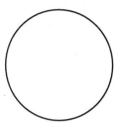

∞ O ∞

In My End Is My Beginning

In the Tarot deck, the Fool is represented by a zero, O, and is the beginning of the Major Arcana as well as the end. The Fool is wisdom beyond all knowing, intuition which opens all the doors, freedom to play, to follow the spirit, knowing all things, believing all things. Within the Fool we dance beyond all boundaries and ride the wind.

Laura lay on the floor, her face encased in plaster impregnated gauze. Around her she could hear soft murmurs, gentle prayers, and whispered comments. Elanor lay to her right, and to her left she could feel Jennifer's toe gently tapping on her ankle. She knew they were conscious of her as she was of them, as well as the six others who lay scattered around the circle. Laura felt the plaster harden and shift imperceptibly. The soft carpet under her back felt good. She and the others had been hiking out in the woods all day, gathering leaves and nuts, berries and feathers, watching the sun traverse the sky. Her legs ached pleasantly, remembering the steep path that skirted the rock ledge. It was at the top of the hill they had seen the eagle, circling high above them. Laura smiled, remembering how they had watched till it seemed the eagle flew into the sun.

Jennifer's whisper, "Its time," brought her back to earth. She raised her hands and began to work the plaster mask loose from her face. With small wiggles and grimaces her skin pulled away from the gauze bit by bit and then the whole mask was free. She held it up in the air for a minute, letting her skin breathe, then she gently lowered the echoing white shape to once again enclose her nose, chin, cheeks and forehead. How different it was now, heavy and cool. She settled it with a little facial shrugging. Suddenly she was enveloped with a surprisingly comforting sensation. This was her face, line for line, recognized, welcomed, incredibly familiar.

Soon they were all sitting up, comparing masks, trying others on, exclaiming over the differences. Sally suggested a game. "Let's pass the masks around till I say stop. Then try on the one you have, see how soon you can tell if it is yours." There were a lot of giggles about this new version of musical chairs, and soon each woman had her own face image in her hands once again.

Sarah went to the window to open the curtains. Surprised by the light, deer lifted their heads on the far side of the lawn, dark eyes glittering. One by one, the women slipped out of the door to see. Standing in the warm dark, feeling the throb of the earth beneath her feet, Laura began a slow dance. She felt her hair lift as the energy began to flow through her body, rising up through her legs, entering in a warm pool throughout her pelvis, flowing up her spine into her head. Turning, her hand caught Elanor's and together they slid into a gliding walk which spiralled between Sally and Alice. Soon there was a line of women treading the warm summer earth. When they reached the middle of the lawn they lay down in a circle with their heads touching together in the center, like the spokes of a wheel.

Daphne began a chant, a low note repeated three times. Jennifer's soft soprano began to weave itself around the rhythm, shaping a delicate melody patterned on the wind and stars. Celeste added her contralto voice with the authority which comes with long training, while Sally and Sarah kept the underlying rhythm of the thrice repeated note. Elanor began a dance with her hands, weaving the darkness into intricate shapes which seemed to fall from her fingers as they formed. Alice found her back wanted to rub and beat against the earth, shoulders shaking and echoing the throb of the chant. Laura lay quietly, breathing in the dark air, bringing the rhythm of voice and body into harmony with the essential being of the night as Tara watched the dancing in her head, seeing the whole group of women from a point ten feet above the ground.

"It is so wonderful," thought Laura, feeling the familiar pulse of harmony as the alignment shifted into place, "to be able to be with these friends, to be accepted for myself, no matter how different I may seem to be." She let her memory drift back ten years. It was not always so. Ten years ago she was still caught in the pattern of loneliness, unable to speak her truth, feeling as though she spoke an unknown language. Ten years ago she could not feel the pulse of the earth, was deaf to the music of the stars. Ten years ago, knowing yet not knowing, she began to listen, awakening the senses which she remembered as a child.

Time spun itself into overlapping curves of memory. She saw herself in the meadow full of yellow flowers, laughing and dancing with the gossamer beings that flitted from leaf to leaf. The shimmer of their wings reflected the many colors of the sun as they rode the breezes, lifting and floating, whispering wordless secrets into her ears. The scene dissolved into the curl of an ocean wave which carried her, tumbling, onto the sand to lie breathless and grateful, marvelling at the intensity and power of the sea until she was warmed by the sun into normal breathing and ran to join with the wave once again.

Fragments of her favorite poem drifted through her head:

Time past and time future
        What might have been and what has been
Point to one end, which is always present.[1]

She saw, once again, the familiar double curve of the symbol for infinity, the figure eight lying on its side. Smiling to herself, she remembered the gradual dawning of comprehension about this symbol, how she realized its potential as a model for creative relationship. The relief was enormous in the weeks following the insight, for it was clear the possibility for true friendship was

finally open to her.   Years of parties, meetings, dinners and
other awkward gatherings had tumbled into perspective when
she understood at last that it was a problem of expectations, of
not knowing there was any other way to talk with people.

She remembered telling a friend: "It's like this. I have a
thought, and it rises up in me, curves down in a flow into you.
You receive this thought with love, caressing it, bringing it into
your being with attention. Having received it, you then return
to me that which rises in you, having considered and acknowledged my thought. Our thoughts cross at the point of change,
the intersection between thee and me, and in that point is the
essence of the All."

It took a good deal of awareness, Laura remembered, to do
this all the time. At first she only thought to do it occasionally.
But then Sally began talking about the same thing, and they told
Celeste and Emily.   Gradually, as the group evolved, they
realized other women and some men were understanding this
way of being together.   "It's like that story of the hundredth
monkey. On one island all the monkeys began to wash their
yams, which they had never done.   The day the hundredth
monkey washed his yam, a monkey on a distant island suddenly
discovered his yam was tastier when washed.[2] Do you think that
when enough of us have made the change in our expectations
and behaviors, that others will be influenced, get it through the
unseen currents of energy which flow over us all?" Celeste's eyes
were bright with excitement as she posed the question.

Soon they realized the new way of relating with each other
was the way to reconnect with Nature, and spent many hours in
silent conversation with rocks, trees, flowers, animals and all the
rest of the abundance with which they were surrounded. Laura
smiled as she recalled the recognition with which she greeted the
feelings of delight and excitement rising in her body.   The
intense thrill of meeting and joining with a sunset, the flight of a
goldfinch, the smell of snow in the air, intensity which had
seemed to fade as she grew older, returned with even richer
nuances. As she coaxed and allowed her body to participate, the
body of the earth increasingly responded. Intuition, trusted ever
more deeply, spoke frequently with clear authority.   As

excitement rose through her soul and manifested in her body, she understood that the old cravings for food and alcohol were an attempt to quiet the passion aroused by these connections. Separated as she had been from her true knowing, she had misunderstood the messages and, perceiving them as discomfort, had sought to alleviate them with the things which had brought comfort in the past. Now she welcomed these feelings, recognizing them as openings into greater insight.

Then there was a day when everything shifted. It was as easy as turning a kaleidoscope. One minute the world looked as it always had and the next moment the pattern was different, all the pieces were in the right places, and her perception was entirely changed. "Of course," she realized, "I knew all along that something of this sort was possible. I just didn't quite get it." And they all got it. Their on-going dialogue and exchanges with Nature had resulted in a basic change, from the religio-scientific reality that Nature was here to serve man who exercised ultimate control, to becoming participants in the active consciousness of the world. As they read about the Middle Ages, searching for the wisdom with which women had once been connected, they came to understand the mystical and magical nature of the relationship these people had with the world around them.[3] "Rocks, trees, rivers, and clouds were all seen as wondrous, alive, and human beings felt at home in this environment. The cosmos, in short, was a place of *belonging*."[4]

This was what was missing; this was what all the witch hunts and repression had achieved. People were split apart from the wholeness which perceived Nature as organically alive and themselves vibrant in full participation with the entire earth in the cyclic process. Separated from this "embeddedness in a complex and natural system,"[5] lost to the mystical under-standings of unity with the One, humanity followed the divergent path for centuries, unaware that it was leading to the destruction of the biosphere within which they lived.

"It has always been up to the women to make the reconnection," Laura mused, laughing as she found herself repeating again the thought they had all expressed in countless ways. "The men are always thinking they have to climb the mountain, make a pilgrimage to achieve enlightenment. We know we *are* the mountain, and it is us. We are manifestations of the same Unity." Her body responded to this thought with a glowing awareness of her friends, joined in their circle of spokes, singing and playing with the ground, the air, and the stars. All her cells smiled, it seemed, with the delight and joy she was feeling. [6]

Enriched and renewed, the women raised their arms, joining their hands into a nine-pointed star over their heads. Daphne brought the chant to a shimmering note of conclusion with a tone that soared upwards through the dark air. Palms touching, fingers fluttering, they all slowly brought their hands down to the earth beside them, delighting in the vibrant energy. A moment of silent gratitude, and then they were all rolling together, laughing and hugging each other.

*   *   *

As I write this story, letting it unfold as it will, I realize this is the only way I can find a glimpse of the future. Fantasy and science fiction writers are experienced at this method of insight, taking known facts of present life and projecting them into the future, spinning them together with wishful thinking and imagination, then letting the story take them into uncharted territories. Some of these projected realities are coming true: we find ourselves in a world where people travel through outer space, where a printed page fed into a machine can emerge in its identical form from another machine thousands of miles away, where conversations can take place between two people while they simultaneously see each other on a screen. These things were "just your imagination" not so many years ago, and I am old enough to find them continuously miraculous. I write these words on a machine which fits into my briefcase, and I am constantly amazed at the marvels which it performs with a touch of my finger. All these miracles exist today because someone imagined them yesterday.

I choose to image, therefore, a world in which the perceptions of children are honored as reality, accepted and nurtured with recognition of the unique gifts with which we enter this life. I choose to image a world in which women are free and able to fully participate in their lives, each in the way which best allows her gifts to manifest. I choose to image a world in which men are also free, with a deep and informed understanding of what freedom means as well as acceptance of full psychic responsibility which accompanies such freedom. I choose to image a world in which Nature is experienced in all her aliveness and magic. And I choose to image a world where relationships of all kinds are caring, thoughtful, passionate, loving, and intense.

But most of all I want to imagine the mysteries, the inner secret tradition of the matriarchal culture, for this is the nature of my search. Our power as women is rooted in our bodies, our minds, our spirits. The mysteries bring all these together in full participation, liberating our energy so it can rise, flowing smoothly, throughout our being and out into the world around us. The mysteries are holy, sacred moments when women enter into the deep waters of desire, experiencing and creating, interweaving souls and bodies. To reclaim the power of woman we must enter the mysteries.

It is important, when imagining such mysteries, that we also image ourselves stepping away from the restrictions and fears which have been placed upon women for so many centuries. Our bodies are not our own. Our sexual energy has been forced into narrow confines defined by societal pressures. Sensual delight is only acceptable under certain limited circumstances, and any other expression of this energy makes us incredibly vulnerable to physical and emotional attack. These conditions make it difficult to imagine ourselves fully free, fully in possession of our bodies, our emotions, our passions, our sexual expression. Freedom does not mean simply throwing off restrictions. True freedom includes the ability to move directly from the seat, the root, of our personal power with full awareness of the complex of connections resulting from this action. True freedom means we have moved beyond reacting to past injuries and are liberated to join with our friends and our environment in full celebration of the deep power of life.

True freedom includes the ability to set aside perceptions which have defined our sexual experience. Recognizing and naming our fears lessens their power over us, allowing us to move past the barrier which they erect between us and our truth.

As we enter into our deepest knowing, we find not only our own unique spirit but also the awareness that each of us is a part of the limitless whole, each contributing another aspect of truth. Separate and alone no longer, we discover our bodies as integral instruments for the manifestation of the energy which creates and heals. With a deep respect for all life, we bring energy into our bodies, drawing it up through our bones and blood, and return it to the universe transformed by the passage through ourselves.

Thus we discover that the familiar structure of limitations set upon our sexuality transforms, allowing us to participate with new power in our daily life. The sensual delight in warm showers, incredible sunsets, deep meditation, is understood as a natural physical expression, as is the leap of joy when the heron flies from the marshy shallows, or the magnolia bursts in pink profusion against the intensity of blue in the spring sky. The recognition that our sexual sensations are awakened by these gifts need no longer be cause for an automatic dampening of feeling in that area of the body. When we understand the full range of possibility inherent in our sexual response, we will cease to fear the rise of body sensations, for we will know their connections with the richness of our lives.

With this freedom comes a deep respect, not only for our own bodies but also the bodies of others, understanding them to be expressions of the sacred connections with the greater truth. A major fear which keeps the narrow structures in place is that if the passion of sexuality is loosed, it will run rampant through society. With true freedom the opposite is the reality. When the body is seen as a participant in the sacred mysteries, there can be no question of violation of another, for to do so would harm the participating connectedness which has become so cherished. Rape and incest are forms of power over another who is perceived as less than fully human. This view is so dehumanizing, so devoid of any comprehension of the value of the unique individual, that it would be impossible in a world where sexuality was fully understood as the transforming power which balances light and darkness.

This sounds like true fantasy and arguably impossible for humans to achieve. So was this computer, a hundred years ago.

So was air travel, the telephone, television. I choose to place my energy and vision in this direction, believing that if I do so, and if others share in this vision, we may discover the impossible is present, if not in our lives, perhaps in the lives of our children or grandchildren. A world in which children are honored as the carriers of insight and new abilities, where women nourish the treasure of relationship and life, where men respect themselves and the world around them, and where full participation of body, mind and spirit is sacred, connecting humans with all life throughout the universe, is a world worth working for. Imagining its reality helps bring it into being.

*   *   *

Laura looked at the faces of her friends gathered around the big oak table and laughed delightedly. The table was heaped with materials of all sorts; moss and feathers, paper and paints, yarn, glue, bits of leather and rope, fabric in a variety of colors and textures. A big bowl of clay was set on a bench at the side of the room. A week had passed since the night under the stars, a week during which each woman had lived with her plaster mask, wearing it at home, feeling the life within it and readying herself to make manifest the energy it contained.

Sally arrived breathless, with apologies. As she settled into her seat, they all slipped into the familiar silence which preceded each of their activities. Laura loved this moment, welcoming the way her consciousness dropped deeply into her body, the way the silence spread tangibly through the room. Time slid away, suspended in some distant moment. In this place, personality leaves, there is only the breath. Breathe in, and the Universe breathes with you. Breathe out and you float on a cloud of nothingness, needing nothing, wanting nothing. Silence envelops all.

Becoming aware, softly, of the gathering of souls around her table, Laura stirred. The women reached out hands, connecting themselves with each other. There was a brief buzz of conversation, then they all settled into the process of creating. Elanor caught Laura's eye and they exchanged a glance of delight, remembering the pleasure they had felt as they prepared their home for their friends, washing the white curtains so the sun would be bright, polishing the tables, gathering the fresh flowers from their garden. Everything smelled good, lemony and clean. Sally's husband had brought over a basket of fruit from his trees and Daphne's daughters contributed a tin of their special tea. Celeste's partner, Joe, had offered bright scraps from the costumes he was making. "One of the best parts of this," thought Laura, "is the support and cooperation of everyone. It is so wonderful to know they understand that what we do here is important to us all." She remembered the many years of struggle for this recognition, grateful they were now behind her.

Soon the room was full of creative sparks as the masks began to take shape under loving hands. Daphne, Sally, Elanor and Laura packed clay around the outside of the plaster form and began to fill in the face to make a mold for paper mache. Sarah, who had already made her paper form, was busy with an intricate pattern of painted shapes. Jennifer and Alice, loving their connections, were working close together as always, Jennifer's bright auburn hair tangling with the darkness of Alice's brown curls as they twisted paper and string into serpent shapes. Celeste was making a patchwork of vibrant fabric pieces while Tara, who loved the simplicity of pure form, was twining a single vine around the forehead of her mask.

As evening came and Elanor rose to light the candles and lamps, Laura leaned back, satisfied at last with her creation. She loved working with this intensity and it was even more special to share this with her friends. They had not stopped for lunch but eaten as they grew hungry from the bowls of salad and fruit or the sandwiches Tara brought. Now there was a happy chatter as the tension eased off and the pace slowed, each woman putting final touches to her mask or happily contemplating the finished product. Soon they would leave for Sarah's house, where her husband and two sons had promised to demonstrate their prowess in the kitchen by providing dinner for all. Reminded of this, they all suddenly realized they were hungry, and clean up was swift and thorough. A few moments of silence, grateful for the gift of creation, and everyone was gone, each with her mask in box or bag to await the sacred gathering the following week.

*   *   *

What we must ultimately understand is that when we take part in the act of creation we are not isolated with our materials and our vision but are actually affecting our surroundings. The creative process plunges us into a participatory exchange of energy which is enhanced by the intensity of our involvement. The shift in scientific understanding resulting in quantum physics and the concept of the holographic universe has opened our eyes and hearts to the realization that we can no longer take indiscriminately from Nature, for in doing so we ultimately harm all of life. We begin to see that "The whole universe appears as an interconnected and intrinsically dynamic network of relationships. Nature is no longer a machine, but a web, vibrating with life."[7] Remembering how the fragile spider's web trembles when the tiniest insect flies into it, helps us to comprehend the extent of the connections within which we live. Moving towards a "participating consciousness,"[8] we struggle to regain an awareness of the extent of life itself, not limited, as we think, to the visible outlines of form, but rather stretching beyond those boundaries, energies joining in a vast and complex pattern.

Thus when I shape a form from clay, or allow my fingers to type words when I don't always know the end of a sentence before I get there, if I am aligned in these moments with the Universe as I experience it, I am giving and getting and my creative process is influenced by the environment around me even as I am participating in its creation by my act. My awareness of this exchange can fill me with delight, with awe, or with fear, but whatever my reaction, creation will never again be the isolated activity it was before. Whether I am creating alone in my studio or in the company of others, the energy flows through me, and my consciousness of this flow strengthens its purpose and increases the interconnectedness. When there is a group working together, the power is intensified. Then the intricate, invisible joinings awaken with a new dynamic, uniquely defining the experience of each member.

In such a group I found my understanding of the community of women enhanced, enlarged, and redefined through the medium of clay. My fingers shaped a bowl about five inches across which was somewhat pointed at the base, so that it must be held in the hand and not set down. Within the inner rim of the bowl, I found myself creating indentations, curving them in and out with my thumb. Each one had a distinctive shape or curl, and with each one I remembered a woman who had a profound influence on my life. The indentations and memories continued around the bowl until they numbered seven. Six had names, the seventh was "for all the rest." As I held this bowl cupped in my palm, smoothing and refining the shapes, I meditated on each name: Henny, my Jungian analyst; Lys, my mother; Lilo, my lifelong friend; Dorothea, teacher and friend; Miss Minema, third grade teacher and friend; Betty, my partner and best friend. My fingers shaped a deep well in the middle of the bowl, spiralling down to the center. A poem arose:

Bowl
Gathering tenderness,
Gentle hands to touch my face,
Remembered tears that fall, unshed,
On the inner valleys of my soul.
Gather again, beloved ones
Into this bowl I may not set to rest.
My fingers trace the litany of your names,
Circling, circling, spinning anew the fragments;
The moment there, by the sandy cliff,
There, on the green gold lake,
There, in the city of snow.
Pieces slip side by side,
Gathering, gathering,
Within my grateful heart.

It was the gathering together of these women, their names, their memories, into one bowl which I hold in one hand which wove the connections into a new sense of community. These women, and so many others, have supported me, loved me, nurtured me, and I have often not allowed myself to feel the flowing warmth, for I did not understand the multidimensional nature of the connections. I made this bowl in a group of women who met regularly to experience creativity together, and this expanded energy allowed me to come into my own enlarged awareness.

Fear has kept me isolated from this warmth, fear has

separated me from my knowing. Fear of so many things; torture, rejection, intensity, the unknown, truth. Fear leaves me stranded on the icy desert, consciousness fraying into the wind, alone forever. Come, come into the warmth, gather round the fire, join hands, feel the flow. Nestle the child within the eye of the dragon, she is safe there, where sight becomes the way to heaven. Alone no longer, her natural completeness encouraged, she flies with the dragon, soaring and blending.

As fear departs, the world opens. In my mind's eye I see the energy flowing, sharp lines from the fir tree meeting the slow cloud from the oak. Bird song darts through the branches, curling the planes of the sky. In my mind's eye I walk through the back yard, asking the ground where best to plant the tomatoes.

"Here," it says, "here the sun is the best. And over here," it says, "the carrots will flourish when you have dug out the rock. Lilies there, daffodils here, and here. A tree planted in this spot will provide shade for the little pond you dream of." The yard was waiting for me to ask. Wisdom comes when fear departs.

So the answer to my question, "How can we know what we don't know we know, how can we regain and renew the ancient wisdom of women and reconnect with mystical and magical consciousness, healing and nurturing ourselves, each other, and the world?" is a process, and the question is part of the answer. There are no answers to such questions, only approaches. Forming the question begins the process. Exploring my life, my being, my body, asking always, opens the way to the holographic field where knowing is eternally present. Opening ancient paths which have been long closed, entering into the maze where wisdom is hidden in each turn of the pattern, celebrating and affirming the reality of that which has been hidden, releases the *geas*, the spell, and bits of truth begin to seep through the fog, slowly at first, testing for safety, then more quickly, leaping into the mind and heart with delight, eager to entwine themselves with each other and with those who welcome the deep inner knowing.

Then we discover that we have always known certain things but we have named them something else. Truth has lain, hidden, in plain sight. Discreditation of individual knowledge of truth is an incredibly powerful tool, used to gain control over another person, which has been skillfully wielded for centuries. When we reclaim our knowing, affirming its truth in spite of opposition, we find ourselves believing we can truly sense people's thoughts, listen to the angels and nature spirits, find the patterns which flow between friends and perhaps, one day, fly. Imagination allows our minds to leap beyond the imposed boundaries into truth.   We might consider expanding our numbering of the senses to include a sixth, which we already have named to include those things we know but don't understand.   We need to recognize the importance of imagination, for it is through that "sixth sense" that we gain information about the Unseen World, the things science tried to say did not exist.[9] Restoring imagination to its rightful place as a means of receiving information, as surely as our nose gives us identifying nuances of smell, would infinitely expand our knowledge of the world around us.

Perhaps this is, finally, the opening key. Begin with the things you know are true, your memories of childhood abilities, insights, intuitions. Add adult awareness of injustice, mix in the longings of your soul. Ground yourself in the Presence of the eternal spirit, however you choose to name it. Fix your intention on your connection with the true knowing and give yourself over to your imagination, trusting it will lead you home.

*   *   *

The night was cool and clear, the only light came from the stars, for the moon was in her dark phase. The women gathered in a clearing among thick fir trees, deep within the farm belonging to Sally and Colin. The lanterns and lights they carried were set on old stumps at the edge of the clearing. Three paths led to this place, and each was guarded by partners, husbands, and family. Colin and the two dogs were at the southern entrance where the path branched off from the river. Sarah's husband, Frank, kept the northern quadrant, while their sons fed a bonfire with gathered cones and branches. To the east a huge thicket of blueberry and olive bushes made an impenetrable wall. In the west, where a small path led from the main road, Joe and Howard, Tara's father, sang songs with Daphne's daughters. Nora and Catherine had beautiful voices, and Nora had brought her guitar. Still teenagers, they looked forward to the time when they would be able to participate in the mysteries. For now, they were happy to help secure the privacy of the women, understanding through their own experience the power these activities had on all of their lives.

Laura was thinking a similar thought as she approached the clearing. It was tremendously exciting to realize they had, by following their intuitions, stepped across ancient boundaries into the deep mysteries of women. Books and research had taken them part of the way, but the final insights, the last pieces of forgotten memories had come from their own explorations, individually and together. The most exciting thing about it all was the knowledge this was women's work, women's privilege, women's sacred honor. They had understood, finally, and the men had helped, that the role of the male in the mysteries was to guard the portals, for by doing so he gave support and structure, defined the perimeter, and deeply affirmed the importance of the mystical connection for the community.

A slight breeze stirred the flames, sending shadows dancing among the trees. The women sat, holding hands in a circle. Each said her name, affirming her presence.

"Daphne, daughter of Moira, present."

"Jennifer from the forest, present."

"Celeste, maker of pots, present."

"I am Sally, lover and friend, I am present."

"Sarah, granddaughter of Lucia, daughter of Lillian, I am present."

"I am called Elanor, of the bright moon. I am present."

"Alice, I am, sister to the birds. Present."

"Tara, the weaver, present."

"Laura, wind woman, present."

Their voices wove into the darkness, blending, creating. They turned, each to another, affirming the name, raising each other from the ground. When they were all standing they unfolded the dark cloaks they had brought and wrapped them around their shoulders.

Silence now. Heeding the call from within, each woman turns to the pattern unfolding within her mind. One draws her hood over her head in silent contemplation. One lifts her face to the dark air, tracing the flight of the night birds. Two join with three to tread the points of a star. One gathers the earth in her hand, one hears the music of the trees. Excitement rises as they sense the patterns overlapping, joining. Indigo shadows traced with silver flow smoothly through their minds, trailing sparkles of gold. The patterns turn, the curves echoed by their bodies, dancing now, shaping and treading the intertwining shapes, each following into another, meeting and parting, until the lines are clear and harmony of purpose is tangibly present.

They circle. Fragments of time fall from their shoulders. Their bodies meet and part, meet and part, curving round each other around the circle, into the center. Hair falls softly on faces as the wind stirs. Light grows luminous within the bones.

Feel now the inner magic begin. It rises like a tide, spreading warmth and softness through the bodies of women. Surging forth, demanding expression, it links arms, legs, breasts, thighs. Skin thins, the golden power flows from cell to cell, filling all the crevices, vibrating the roots of hair, the deep nerves behind the eyes. Fingers trace lines of softly glowing light which reach deeply into tissue and blood. Limbs tremble, shake, writhe and tangle. The power flows into the earth, through the grasses, down the roots of trees, deeply through rock and soil till the answering throb begins. Earth responds to the call of women, the rich dark rhythm expands, contracts, breathing itself, breathing the night, breathing the bodies which lie, now, spread face down upon it, dark cloaks flowing into the dark ground. Deep rhythms exchange, throb, merge, separate. Faces rise, glowing with fullness of the earth.

Mysteries must remain mysterious, yet may trace a path for those who search. Each woman makes a mask to wear, rich with clues and symbols. It is a reminder, a protection, a secret retreat, a guide. Now, as the power swells, hands bring the mask close to woman's face. And the mask becomes a living thing, imbued with power, radiating light and shadow, trembling with the force of becoming. Each to each, the woman fits the mask to lie close, feeling nose, eyebrows, chin, slide into familiar spaces. It becomes skin, light flashes from eyes, mouths open, tongues protrude, tasting the air.

Dance now. Cloaks swirl outward, bodies sway, feet repeat the rhythm of the earth. Masked faces shine with the reflected light of lanterns. Through the trees, around rocks and bushes, weaving lines of energy, shaping form in the dark air, the dance continues, building power. The wind rises. Stars echo the song. A dark bird flies through the air, sounding a single note. All motion stops. Silence. Power, contained, expands to the fullest. The bird cries once again. The Power shatters, spreading, spreading, flowing and sparking, surging through the air, the ground, the trees, returning through the roots, leaping up mountains. It flashes down the paths, the watching families feel it burst among them. "It is done!" they cry with delight, and run towards the clearing.

Laura's knees were weak as she staggered to the nearest log. As she sank to the ground, slipping off her mask, she felt Joe supporting her, easing her body to a comfortable position, wrapping her cloak about her. Murmuring a grateful blessing, he was off to tend to Jennifer. Soon they were all sitting, sipping hot tea from a big thermos. Frank passed around a basket of scones, Nora brought the grapes. They all sat for a while, companionably silent, sensing the heightened energy.

Before leaving, they all stood in a circle, hands joined, hearts full of gratitude for the earth, for themselves, for the power, for the mystery. And the old song came to their lips and voices:

As it was in the Beginning
Is now and ever shall be
World without end. Amen. Amen.

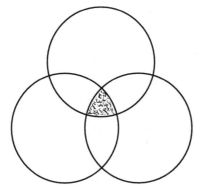

∞ Appendix ∞

Research: Methodology and Participants

The heuristic method of research demands that inquiry be rooted in the personal experience of the researcher. The initial stage of such research requires an immersion in the question, an identification with it, a trust in the process of self-examination, and a willingness for complete involvement. Intuition and inner knowing are essential as the focus of attention moves inward. This is a clear departure from the traditional scholarly methods of research which require that the researcher be separated from any emotional involvement with the inquiry.

It was evident from the beginning that the heuristic form of inquiry was not only appropriate for my quest, but was indeed the only possible way for me to approach something as ephemeral and personal as memories of flying. Childhood experiences which do not fit into the acceptable pattern of society are generally discounted, suppressed, or explained away, and retrieval is often difficult. In such cases, personal revelation offers the easiest access. Often a woman would initially say she didn't think she had anything to offer. Then my recounting of a few experiences would give validation to secrets hidden away, freeing her memory.

The question of choice of participants in the inquiry was discussed at length, but the final decision was to trust that those who were interested would be drawn to me. This decision was consistent with the trust in the process of unfoldment inherent in the heuristic process. It was also consistent with my desire to center my work within the context of women's knowing, seeking always to return to that deep awareness of the rhythms of life, letting form follow the need. I found respondents in unexpected places and casual conversations turned into inquiry questions.

There were also continued questions concerning the

involvement of men, who certainly have these memories.   I was always clear that this was a women's inquiry, an exploration of the particular way women access the inner knowing.   I approach the question as a woman.   Heuristically, the integrity of the research demands that it remain within the circle of women.

I had two stated purposes for this inquiry.   The first was to gather memories; not to prove women had the experiences, for I already knew this was true, but to let them collect together, validating and appreciating the secrets.   The second was to create an awareness that such experiences are to be treasured, that they have reality, and that they have a place in our lives.   This is a ripple effect which I hope will continue for those who have learned of my interest.

My research request included these questions:

What do you know that you don't know you know?

When you were little, was there something you knew or could do that was special?

For Example:

Do you remember learning how to fly?

Did you understand what animals were telling you?

Could you see auras around people?

Did you talk with trees and flowers?

Did you see fairies, elves, little people?

Did you see or hear angels?

Do you remember knowing things other people didn't
seem to know?

Could you understand what people were thinking?

Did you have a playmate, a friend, that you called
imaginary? Did you talk with this friend?
Could you see her or him?

Did you know what was going to happen before other
people did?

Did you ever know where to find something that was
lost?

The women who responded to my inquiry have allowed me to use their first names, or have provided me with another name.

I would like to be able to tell each story fully, but space does not permit. Many of the experiences appear in the body of this work. 40 women have responded. Most of them remember more than one ability. Some of these continue into adulthood, notably the ability to know what others are thinking.

I list sixteen areas of abilities. Each woman's experience is different, and their stories are fascinating. Within each area are variations: the following explanation gives a sampling of some of the specifics.

1. *Flying*. This category includes a number of women whose experience is similar to mine, flying down stairs. Others, such as Kathleen and Marian, and Pam, flew horizontally or up. Heather remembers sitting beside her bed and levitating.

2. *Playmates*. "Imaginary playmates" were generally accepted by parents with amused tolerance. It was clear from the stories, however, that these playmates were not made up by the children but rather came of their own volition. Bettie, for instance, had a "friend" from Salem, Massachusetts who lived in the 16th century, and the two told each other of their very different lives.

3. *Angels*. Connection with angels was fairly widespread: these respondents mentioned particular experiences.

4. *Healing*. Larissa continues her healing into adulthood.

5. *Moved Objects*. Ashley could move rocks—her dogs helped her.

6. *Trees/flowers*. These are women who remember close connections with the nature. Some of them felt they were not understood by their families and found solace in their friendship with the trees.

7. *Knew thoughts*. Knowing what others were thinking is a useful ability which most of the respondents still have. Jill said she didn't even know she did it till she married, and her husband objected. Kathi's mother could do it too, and encouraged her daughter—one of the few instances where a gift was recognized and celebrated.

8. *Knew things*. This is a broad category: Pam knew she was her grandmother. Carlin tells of a vision she had of a place that sounds like Utopia. Patricia knew her imagination was

special and different. Joan knew when someone was lying.

9. *Don't belong here.* These women felt they should have been somewhere else, another world or another time.

10. *Animals.* Connections with animals are common for many people, but the women who listed this category speak of knowing what their pets were thinking and having communication with them.

11. *Breathe underwater.* This was mentioned as an afterthought. Jeanne didn't want to come up, she was playing with her little friends and perfectly comfortable.

12. *Premonitions.* This includes dreams coming true and knowing things were going to happen, like someone dying.

13. *Saw little people.* This varied from fairies to Lee's workman people.

14. *Auras.* This ability continues into adulthood.

15. *Saw "others".* Kris saw a cat that had died. Ruth had visits from E.T.s. Some saw people who had died.

16. *Out of body.* Pamela had this experience when very young.

The following compilation provides a summary of the various areas of ability which were mentioned by the respondents and the women who have memories of these activities. The fact that some areas have few names does not necessarily indicate a lack of that ability within the group. My initial inquiry listed some possible areas of memory and respondents added things they remembered. If I wrote again to everyone with the entire list, I expect there would be additional names in some categories. Some of these secrets lie very deeply hidden and the question must be asked directly before memory reveals itself.

INQUIRY RESPONDENTS

Flying
Nancy
Diane
Kathleen
Patty
Heather
Lee
Pam
June
Sheila
Lori
Joan
Pamela
Ashley
Marian

Playmates
Jeanne
Heather
Bronwyn
Kim
Cathy
Jane
Bettie
Pamela
Linda

Angels
Nancy
Jeanne
Kathy
Lee
Pam
Karen
Joan
Jill

Healing
Sage
Larissa

Moved objects
Ashley

Trees/flowers
Marian
Joey
Carol
Brenda
Lee
Jennifer
Pam
Karen
Sage
Cathy
Larissa

Knew thoughts
Kathi
Amy
Carol
Anne
Pam
Kim
Jennifer
Sage
Jill

Knew things
Anne
Carol
Lee
Pam
Carlin
Sage
Joan
Kris
Patricia

Don't belong here
Lucy
Nancy
Linda
Kathi
Amy

Animals
Marian
Joey
Carol
Lee
Sage
Cathy
Mary Jo
Larissa
Eva

Breathe underwater
Jeanne

Premonitions
Brenda
Kathi
Amy
Jill
Jennifer
Sage
Eva

Saw little people
Jeanne
Lee
Jennifer

Auras
Marian
Brenda
Larissa

Saw "others"
Nancy
Kris
Joan
Larissa
Eva
Ruth

Out of body
Pamela

∞ Endnotes ∞

∞ Preface ∞

[1] "Western life seems to be drifting toward increasing entropy, economic and technological chaos, ecological disaster, and ultimately, psychic dismemberment and disintegration..." Morris Berman, *The Reenchantment of the World* (Ithica: Cornell University , 1981), 15.

[2] See T.S. Eliot, *Four Quartets* (New York: Harcourt, Brace, 1943)

∞ A ∞ Overview

[1] My friend, Myles Laffey, who read this in manuscript, remarked that I must have a Celtic background, for in Ireland there is much more acceptance of the "little people" and of magical happenings. I am a mix of many nationalities, Irish among them, but my ancestors were early settlers in America and thoroughly incorporated. Myles brings me the quote from Thomas Merton: "For the Celt...the true reality is that which is manifested obscurely and sacramentally in symbol, sacrament, and myth." *Ways of the Christian Mystics* (Boston:Shambala, 1994), 15. Deep within me a figure raises her head - she is a gypsy, dark, hair matted with twigs, earth on her hands and face. I have kept her hidden as long as I can remember.

[2] Morris Berman, *The Reenchantment of the World* ,15.

[3] James Hillman, in *We've Had a Hundred Years of Psychotherapy - And the World's Getting Worse* with Michael Ventura (New York: HarperSanFrancisco, 1992), 45, says: "The depression we're all trying to avoid could very well be a prolonged chronic reaction to what we've been doing to the world, a mourning and grieving for what we're doing to nature and to cities and to whole peoples—the destruction of a lot of our

world. We may be depressed partly because this is the soul's reaction to the mourning and grieving that we're not consciously doing."

[4] Among the writers who have researched and presented the historical progress of the subjugation of the matriarchal era are:

Riane Eisler, *The Chalice and the Blade: Our History Our Future* (New York: Harper & Row, 1988).

Elinor W. Gadon, *The Once and Future Goddess: A Sweeping Visual Chronicle of the Sacred Female and Her Reemergence in the Cultural Mythology of Our Time* (New York: Harper & Row, 1989).

Monica Sjoo & Barbara Mor, *The Great Cosmic Mother: Rediscovering the Religion of the Earth*, 2nd Edition (New York: HarperSanFrancisco, 1991).

Merlin Stone, *When God Was A Woman* (New York: Harcourt Brace Jovanovich, 1976).

[5] For a woman's perspective on the takeover of women's bodies and minds by the patriarchy, see Barbara Ehrenriech and Deirdre English, *For Her Own Good: 150 Years of the Experts' Advice to Women* (New York: Anchor, Doubleday, 1978).

[6] Paisley Dodds, " 'Witches' burned in the new South Africa,"*The New London Day*, 13 June, 1994. A shocking article about a 12-year-old girl who was "forced to douse her mother with gasoline and set her ablaze" for the "crime" of being a witch. The article further states "at least 65 people accused of witchcraft have been burned to death since January in Lebowa."

[7] Jungians use the term *The Feminine* when speaking of the feminine part of self. This is the archetypal quality which is more readily available to women, as their ego-self is female. When men are able to access their feminine aspect, a difficult task because of society's definition of male, they begin to connect with the deep knowing. This is not to say that women and men will experience the Feminine in the same way, for we remain, fortunately, female and male, but understanding and tolerance can be much improved. Many Jungian authors have discussed this. See, for example,

June Singer, *Boundaries of the Soul, The Practice of Jung's Psychology* (Garden City: Anchor /Doubleday, 1973).

Francis G. Wickes, *The Inner World of Man* (New York: Farrar & Rinehart, 1938).

[8] "I do not condemn male-imagined culture. Rather, I grieve the lack, the loss, the absence of a concomitant female-imagined culture which could flourish side-by-side, if only there were breathing room. I grieve the stunted and distorted lives of women who, shaped by the imperatives of the masculine imagination, abort the embryos of their own creativity long before gestation has completed its natural cycle." Betty DeShong Meador, *Uncursing the Dark: Treasures from the Underworld* (Wilmette: Chiron, 1992), 15.

[9] C.G. Jung, H.G. Baynes, trans., revision R.F.C.Hull, *Collected Works*, Vol. 6 *Psychological Types*, Bollingen Series XX (Princeton: Princeton University, 1971), 542.

See also David Keirsey and Marilyn Bates, *Please Understand Me* (Del Mar, CA: Prometheus Nemesis, 1978), for a clear description and a simple test to determine type.

The Myers-Briggs Personality Index is the in-depth test developed along the lines of Jung's theory of types.

[10] Many poets write of intimations, insights, comprehensions. Adrienne Rich, Olga Broumas, Audre Lorde, Anne Cameron: these are some of the women whose voices tell of possibilities. Their words sing in the heart:

> I am the one
> whose voice you hear
> in the untamed night wind
> I am the one
> lurking
> just beyond the edge
> of the clearing
> staring
> from the rain forest
> face hidden
> in moss and fog

Anne Cameron, "I Am the One They Warn Of" *The Annie Poems*, (Madeira Park, BC: Harbour , 1987), 23.

[11] Three I use regularly are:

J.C. Cooper, *An Illustrated Encyclopedia of Traditional Symbols* (London: Thames and Hudson, 1978).

The Herder Symbol Dictionary, Boris Matthews , trans., (Wilmette: Chiron, 1986).

Barbara Walker, *The Woman's Dictionary of Symbols and Sacred Objects* (New York: Harper & Row, 1988).

[12] See references above.

[13] Grahn, Judy. *Blood, Bread, and Rose*, (Boston: Beacon, 1993), xxii.

[14] David Bohm, speaking of world view, says a person's way of thinking about this "...is crucial for overall order of the human mind itself. If he thinks of the totality as constituted of independent fragments, then that is how his mind will tend to operate, but if he can include everything coherently and harmoniously in an overall whole that is undivided, unbroken, and without a border (for every border is a division or break) then his mind will tend to move in a similar way, and from this will flow an orderly action within the whole."

David Bohm, *Wholeness and the Implicate Order* (London: Ark, 1983),xi.

[15] As discussed by Larry Dossey, *Recovering the Soul: A Scientific and Spiritual Search* (New York: Bantam, 1989), 27-8.

[16] "A *field* is a continuum of energy that has no localization, no place. To be localized or placed, the energy must manifest as a thing, a specific, singular event. The field embraces the range of possibilities for *thingness* or manifestation which that expression of energy contains within it. In order to manifest as a thing or event, all those variables appropriate to that field are eliminated, and the field is said to 'collapse' to the particle event then expressed." Joseph Chilton Pearce, *Magical Child Matures* (New York: Dutton, 1985), 94.

[17] Jung, *Collected Works*, Vol.9,1 *The Archetypes and the Collective Unconscious*, 3-53.

[18] "Just as every portion of a hologram contains the image of the whole, every portion of the universe enfolds the whole. This means that if we knew how to access it we could find the andromeda galaxy in the thumbnail of our left hand....Every cell in our body enfolds the entire cosmos." Michael Talbot, *The Holographic Universe* (New York: HarperCollins, 1991), 50.

[19] "Could simultaneous discovery be due to the absorption of individual minds in the Universal Mind, whereby information could conceivable be shared by everyone?" Dossey, *Recovering the Soul*, 37.

[20] Cooper explains that for the Taoist the ox depicts the animal nature in humans (124) while Walker tells us it relates to the earth element (385). Herder links the ox with the water buffalo, and relates it from there to White Buffalo Woman who brought to the Sioux the Sacred Pipe which linked heaven and earth (144). All these references bring the ox and earth into close connection. It is the wisdom of the earth and of woman for which I seek.

[21] Kim Chernin, in her creative examination of the story of Eve, says "I could talk about Eve eating the apple becasue she knew perfectly well it was the flesh and fluid of the Goddess." She continues,

"Perhaps Eve gave in to the snake because she had figured out the snake would take her back to the Mother Tree? Eve has been so many things to so many people. Why shouldn't she come to be for us, who are hungering for the Woman Who Is Not Yet, a rebel who put the apple in her mouth because she yearned to be reunited with the Goddess through a sacred feast that would restore to her the knowledge that, long before she awoke in the house of the Father, she had been, from the very beginning, her Mother's daughter?" *Reinventing Eve: Modern Woman in Search of Herself* (New York: Times, 1987).

[22] See James Gleick, *Chaos, Making a New Science* (New York: Penguin, 1987), and M. Mitchell Waldrop, *Complexity, The Emerging Science at the Edge of Order and Chaos* (New York: Simon & Schuster, 1992).

[23] Stephen Jay Gould. *Wonderful Life, The Burgess Shale and the*

Nature of History (New York: Norton, 1989). A clearly written explanation of the fossil discoveries which challenge the accepted theories of evolution.

²⁵. Lilith appears in the Gnostic Gospels as the first wife of Adam.

²⁵ Among Quakers, when conflicts arise, a moment of silence is requested. Dropping all arguments, the group slips instantly into the familiar peace of attending on the will of the Spirit. With this silent attending, the saying is: "Way will open."

∞ **B** ∞   **The Process**

¹ These are alternate spellings sometimes used in women centered literature. They were developed to avoid the use of the word "men", so that women are not identified as an appendage to the male but rather as separate individuals.

² Marion Weinstein, *Positive Magic: Occult Self-Help* (Surrey, BC: Phoenix, 1978).

³ See Adam McLean, *The Triple Goddesses: An Exploration of the Archetypal Feminine*, Hermetic Research Series Number 1 (Grand Rapids, MI: Phanes, 1989).

⁴. Barbara G. Walker, *The Woman's Encyclopedia of Myths and Secrets* (New York: Harper & Row, 1983), 1018-1020.

⁵ C.G. Jung, *Collected Works*, Vol. 6, *Psychological Types*, 480.

⁶ Carol Bigwood, *Earth Muse, Feminism, Nature, and Art* (Philadelphia: Temple University, 1993), has woven several themes together in a unique blend which attempts this same task. On the base of her philosophical expertise she layers experiential encounters with the sculpture of Brancusi, the Minoan Snake Goddess, and a cycladic figurine. Interspersed with the writing about Heidegger, Merleau-Ponty, and Aristotle are intensely personal paragraphs about her swelling body, pregnant with her son, the difficult birth, her life in a wilderness log cabin. Phrases from a wide variety of sources punctuate the sections of the book which circles through feminism, woman, ecology, earth, and being. She says: "Art can help philosophy

because art holds in place the very phenomena that philosophy attempts to describe." "Thinking through art allows me to do philosophy in a way that lets in my body and desire, as long as I take care not to translate or explain away the art's sensuous presence." "While the chapters lay out and gather thoughts surrounding philosophical, feminist, and ecological problems, these art essays are the ruptures and well-springs of thought." 8

⁷ Jean Troy-Smith tells me there are cultures whose languages allow for overlap and circling. Since I am not a linguist, I am appreciative of her pointing out that some American Indian languages, Gaelic, some African dialects and Spanish are more flexible in this way.

⁸ J.R.R. Tolkien, *The Hobbit* (Boston: Houghton Mifflin 1938), 64.

⁹ Ibid, 214-17.

∞ C ∞   Beginning

¹ Dylan Thomas, "Fern Hill", *Dylan Thomas: The Poems* (London: J.M. Dent), 195.

² Joseph Chilton Pearce, *Evolution's End: Claiming the Potential of our Intelligence* (New York: HarperSanFrancisco, 1992), 110-115.

³ Joseph Chilton Pearce, *Magical Child* (New York: Plume, Penguin, 1977), 45.

⁴ Pearce, *Evolution's End*, 116.

⁵ Rupert Sheldrake, "Seven Experiments That Could Change The World" *Noetic Sciences Review* 31 (Autumn 1994): 20,21.

⁶ Ibid, 20.

⁷ Pearce, *Evolution's End*, 130-134.

⁸ P.L. Travers, *Mary Poppins and Mary Poppins Comes Back* (New York: Harcourt Brace & World, 1934). In chapter nine, "John and Barbara's Story", the twins are wondering why their older sister and brother cannot hear the Starling talk:

"They did once," said Mary Poppins, folding up one of Jane's nightgowns.

"What?" said John and Barbara together in very surprised

voices. "Really? You mean they understood the Starling and the Wind and—?"

"And what the trees say and the language of the sunlight and the stars—of course they did! *Once,*" said Mary Poppins. 92.

In the obituary for P.L.Travers, who died April 25, 1996, Sue Leeman, Associated Press Writer, quotes Travers from a 1988 article for The Sunday Times, London: "There are worlds beyond worlds and times beyond times, all of them true, all of them real, and all of them (as children know) penetrating each other."

∞ D ∞   Holding the Wonder

[1] J.E. Cirlot, trans. Jack Sage, *A Dictionary of Symbols* (New York: Philosophical Library, 1962), 203.

[2] Weaving is a metaphor used by many women to describe the work of finding relationships between the varied aspects of life. The woven cloth is sometimes called a web, another word which calls to mind organic interconnectedness and is used by those concerned with Nature. Recent book titles attest to the appropriateness of these terms: Peter Marshall, *Nature's Web* (New York: Paragon, 1994), Irene Diamond and Gloria Feman Orenstein, *Reweaving the World* (San Francisco: Sierra Club, 1990), Judith Plaskow and Carol P. Christ, *Weaving the Visions* (New York: HarperSanFrancisco, 1989), and Barbara Black Koltuv, *Weaving Woman* (York Beach: Nicolas-Hays, 1990). When I plan a weave, I gather together cones of yarn, sorting and assembling colors until I have the combination which best matches the images in my head. The weaving, carefully laying one thread next to another, watching the pattern grow as the shuttle flies back and forth, is deeply satisfying. While it is not an activity exclusively in the province of women, it belongs in the realm of the Feminine with its gathering, sorting, winding, treadling the pattern; a multitude of tasks to produce the finished cloth. Koltuv, a Jungian analyst, says: "There is no such thing as a completed definition of woman. A woman is a weaving, woven, unravelling, *moving* female energy and experience." 114.

[3] Carol Christ, *Diving Deep and Surfacing* (Boston: Beacon, 1980), in the preface to the second edition (1986) looks back on herself as the author and writes:"Somehow she held tight to her intuition,...that if she was feeling something deeply in that growing place within herself, then others must be feeling it too, because others are products of the same times, the same historical and cultural forces." x.

[4] Kay Boyle, *The Youngest Camel* (Boston: Little, Brown, 1939).

Susan Cooper, *The Dark is Rising*, (Atheneum, 1973).

Diane Duane, *The Door into Shadow* (New York: Tom Doherty, 1984).

Patricia A. McKillip, *The Riddle Master of Hed* (New York: Ballantine, 1976).

George Macdonald, *The Princess and the Goblin* (New York: Grosset & Dunlap, 1907).

[5] Brian Attebery, *State of the Fantastic*, ed. Nicholas Ruddick: "Fantasy and the Narrative Transaction"(Westport, CT: Greenwood, 1992), 15.

[6] Zenna Henderson's works are now collected in a single volume, *Ingathering, The Complete People Stories*, Mark and Priscilla Olson, eds.(Framingham, MA: NESFA, 1995).

[7] This poem was brought to me years ago, copied from a poster. It is attributed to Teller.

[8] Anne McCaffrey, *To Ride Pegasus* (New York: Ballantine, 1973).

_____ *Get Off The Unicorn* (New York: Ballantine, 1977).

McCaffrey says, of these stories: "I'm a practical sort and thought that the various areas of ESP *could* actually be useful commercially - like the man with the fire affinity, or the 'finder' or even the lady who kept hearing voices. So I applied some common sense and came up with useful professional services." (personal correspondence, 1995.)

[9] Brooke Medicine Eagle, *White Buffalo Woman Comes Singing* (New York: Ballantine, 1991), 44-5.

[10] See Appendix for listing of these women.

[11]. *Collected Works*, 9ii, 14. See also:

Ann Bedford Ulanov, *The Feminine in Jungian Psychology and in Christian Theology* (Evanston: Northwestern University, 1971), says, "There is no access to full conscious and unconscious life without the feminine modality. The feminine must be worked on, probed, examined, meditated upon, conjectured about, and contemplated, for the feminine is the completing element in every effort we can make to become a fully human person." 134.

[12] Brown and Gilligan, *Meeting at the Crossroads: Women's Psychology and Girls' Development* (New York: Ballantine,1992), 15.

[13] Ibid. 16.

[14] See also: Shulamit Reinharz, *Feminist Methods in Social Research* (New York: Oxford University, 1992).

Joan C, Chrisler, Doris Howard, ed., *New Directions in Feminist Psychology: Practice, Theory, and Research* (New York: Springer, 1992).

[15] Christ, *Diving Deep and Surfacing*, points out: "We understand that even the most seemingly objective scholarship in every field reflects an implicit interest in preserving the patriarchal status quo, including certain notions of canon, authority, and tradition from which the contributions of women and others have been excluded....But when feminist scholars discuss the interests which inspire our work, such as understanding our own lives and the lives of other women and transforming scholarship and the social world in which it is embedded, our work is often dismissed as being merely personal or polemical." xi.

Whether consciously or unconsciously, the system has worked hard to prevent women from coming into awareness of the deep personal body power and wisdom, seeming to fear this true knowing.

[16] Clark Moustakas, *Heuristic Research: Design, Methodology, and Applications* (Newbury Park,CA: Sage, 1990), 9.

[17] Ibid, 10

[18] Ibid, 24.

[19] Ibid, 27-32

∞ E ∞   **What is a Woman?**

[1] Faludi, Susan, *Backlash: The Undeclared War Against American Women* (New York: Crown, 1991), xxii.

[2] An extensive survey of the multiple abuses perpetrated against women is not my intent here. For those who wish further reading in this field, some possible sources are:

Mary Daly, *Gyn/Ecology* (Boston: Beacon, 1978)

Barbara Ehrenreich and Deirdre English, *For Her Own Good* (New York: Doubleday, 1978).

Susan Griffin, *Pornography and Silence* (New York: Harper & Row, 1981).

Gerda Lerner, *The Creation of Feminist Consciousness* (New York: Oxford University, 1993).

Harriet G. Lerner, *The Dance of Deception* (New York:Harper Collins, 1993).

Alice Walker, *Possessing the Secret of Joy* (New York:Harcourt Brace Jovanovich, 1992).

[3] See Jung, *Collected Works*, Vol 8, 200-216.

[4] M. Esther Harding, *Woman's Mysteries: Ancient and Modern* (New York: Harper & Row, 1971), 10.

[5] Irene Claremont deCastillego, *Knowing Woman, a Feminine Psychology* (New York: G.P. Putnam's Sons, 1973).

Ann Bedford Ulanov, *The Feminine*.

Edward C. Whitmont, *The Symbolic Quest: Basic Concepts of Analytical Psychology* (Princeton: Princeton University, 1969).

[6] Two books which address this dark journey downward are:

Betty DeShong Meador, *Uncursing The Dark: Treasures from the Underworld* (Wilmette, IL: Chiron, 1994).

Sylvia Brinton Perera, *Descent to the Goddess, A Way of Initiation for Women* (Toronto: Inner City, 1981).

[7] Carol P. Christ and Judith Plaskow, eds. *Womanspirit Rising, A Feminist Reader in Religion* (New York: HarperSanFrancisco, 1992), 228.

⁸ In the ancient myths there are a number of references to the journey into the Underworld. The most ancient, that of Innana, Queen of Heaven is a Sumerian tale. Innana descends to the realm of Ereshkegal, her sister, where she is stripped of all her worldly power and reduced to a piece of rotting meat, hung on a hook. She has, fortunately, told a trusted friend to get help if she does not return in three days. The story ends happily and Innana is rescued, but the image of hanging, rotting, on a hook deep in the darkness is a powerful image for many women who have endured depression.

The mortal woman, Psyche, was married to the Greek god Eros. Through a mistaken act urged on her by her jealous sisters, Eros was taken from her. In her grief, Psyche beseeched his mother, Aphrodite, for his return and was given four tasks, the last of which was to enter the underworld and obtain a box of Persephone's beauty ointment. Her venture across the river Styx which flows at the boundary between the upper world and Hades, and the temptations she resisted to win through to her goal are a metaphor for survival of the downward journey.

Persephone, daughter of Demeter who was the Greek goddess of harvest and grain, was abducted by Pluto, lord of the Underworld. Her cries echoed through the land, but her sorrowing mother could not find her. At last, as the desperate Demeter forbade all plants to grow, Zeus prevailed upon Pluto to release Persephone. As the young woman was leaving Hades, she consented to eat four seeds of the pomegranate, although she knew no food nor drink should pass her lips in that place. Because of this mistake we have the seasons, for Persephone must return to the land of Hades for four months of the year, during which Demeter grieves and the land lies fallow. In the spring, when Persephone returns, flowers spring from the land at her step.

An enlightening exploration of the Innana myth can be found in Sylvia Brinton Perera, *Descent to the Goddess: A Way of Initiation for Women* (Toronto: Inner City, 1981).

⁹ Linda Fierz-David, quoted by Edward C. Whitmont in *The*

Symbolic Quest, 173.

[10] For an excellent history of this, see Barbara Ehrenreich and Deirdre English, *For Her Own Good*.

[11] Christine Northrup, *Women's Bodies, Woman's Wisdom* (New York: Bantam, 1944). See also her newsletter, "Health Wisdom for Women," (Phillips, 7811 Montrose Road, Potomac, MD, 20854).

[12] As I previously pointed out in this chapter, women participate in the imbalance of relationships. It is a touchy subject, and leads us back to origins, for would women want to be subjugated if the idea had not been introduced by men and become the "normal" way of being? It is difficult to discuss it today without some sort of blame being felt by someone. I know a number of men who feel they sincerely want to be with women in equality, yet discover the women desire the traditional unequal pattern. Myles says "The greatest frustration of being attuned to, and empathetic to women, is women." Women could say the same thing about men. We are in need of real transformation.

[13] Gerda Lerner, *The Creation of Feminist Consciousness*, vii.

[14] Carol Lee Flinders, *Enduring Grace: Living Portraits of Seven Women Mystics* (New York: HarperSanFrancisco, 1993). See also the audio tapes of the same title from Sounds True, Boulder, Co.

[15] J. Giles Milhaven, "A Medieval Lesson on Bodily Knowing: Women's Experience and Men's Thought" *Journal of the American Academy of Religion*, LVII/2, 350

[16] Heinrich Kramer and Jacob Sprenger, *Malleus Maleficarum: The Hammer of Witches*, Pennethorne Hughes (ed.), Montague Summers (trans.) (London: Folio, 1968), 218.

[17] Mary Daly, *Gyn/Ecology*, 184.

∞ F ∞ **Unwinding the Spell**

[1] Margaret Atwood, *The Handmaid's Tale* (New York: Fawcett, 1985).

[2] The development of archetypes as a psychological

component is credited to Jung. (*Collected Works*, vol. 9:1, 160). Recognizing their universal and widespread qualities, he noted that by definition an archetype is more than we can know; the edges remain obscure. I find it useful to have a metaphor available when trying to explain something that is not apparent to our five senses, so when talking about, for example, the archetype of despair, I say, "Imagine that the archetype is like a cloud hovering over you in the sky. From this cloud to you there is a long tube, like an umbilical cord, and you are connected. The cloud has all the emotions people have felt about despair, and it is only despair. It is huge, larger than you can imagine, and it possesses you. It will not let you go, and it has some curious characteristics. When it possesses you, it makes you feel as though you must resolve the situation yourself, that no one else can help you."

The best way I know to change the situation and be released from the archetypal possession is through consciousness, and the first act of consciousness is to realize that it is, indeed, an archetype which creates the feeling of despair, and that this archetype is far greater than anything one person could ever experience. It contains all the   possibilities of despair, and is a universal energy. It is important to realize this, and to name the archetype Despair.

The next step is to separate out the personal experience of despair, the individual connections and feelings that make one susceptible to the archetypal possession. And then the final step.

"Remember the connecting tube between you and the archetype through which Despair can draw all your energy up to feed itself. Now imagine that on that tube is a valve, a shut off valve, like the one on water pipes in the basement, or a check valve on an IV bag. Now, recognizing that you have your own personal despair, and that you do not need to be available to the archetypal Despair, turn the valve to shut off the flow, thus separating yourself from the universal experience."

Shutting off the valve allows one to deal clearly with personal despair, which is possible, and frees one from the futile attempt to affect the archetypal energy.

[3] Jung, *Collected Works*, vol.10, 179-193.

[4] "The New London Day," 8/1/94, page 1.

[5] Wolfgang Lederer, *The Fear of Women* (New York: Grune & Stratton, 1968), vii.

[6] "All wickedness is but little to the wickedness of a woman ....When a woman thinks alone, she thinks evil." "...that since they are feebler both in mind and body, it is not surprising that they should come more under the spell of witchcraft." *Malleus Maleficarum* (part I question 6.)

[7] For one such account, see Cerridwen Fallingstar, *The Heart of the Fire* (San Geronimo, CA: Cauldron, 1990).

[8] For an excellent account of the centuries of the persecution of witches, see the video, *The Burning Times*, Directed by Donna Reed, Direct Cinema, Santa Monica, CA.

[9] Louis Horst was a composer, a musician, for years a close associate of modern dancer, Martha Graham. In his classes in Pre-Classic Dance Forms and Modern Forms, he taught choreography with the discipline of musical forms of composition. He was an amazing teacher, absolute in his demand for perfection, giving of his time, unswerving in his commitment to truth. The lessons I learned from him have translated into most of my other endeavors.

G. I. Gurdjieff was a teacher of the Fourth Way, a complex combination of Eastern self-development made comprehensible to Westerners. He developed his system in collaboration with P. D. Ouspensky. Maurice Nicoll was one of his students who went on to form his own groups. His *Commentaries on the Teachings of Gurdjieff and Ouspensky* (London: Stuart & Watkins, 1970), span five volumes and make the Work, as it is called, far more accessible than Gurdjieff's own *All and Everything* (New York: Harcourt, Brace, 1950).

[10] Starhawk, *Truth or Dare: Encounters with Power, Authority, and Mystery* (New York: HarperSanFrancisco, 1987), 177.

[11] In the realm of fantasy and tales, *geas* is a spell laid on a person, which then must be lived out until it is broken; or

completed.

∞ **G** ∞   **Remembering Wisdom**

[1] Sophia is the embodiment of feminine wisdom, often considered the female aspect of God.
"Sophia appears in nearly every culture and society. She is clearly distinguished by unique qualities and symbolic representations: she is concerned with the survival and maturation of all creation. She is the leavening influence of life." Caitlin Matthews, *Sophia Goddess of Wisdom: The Divine Feminine from Black Goddess to World-Soul* (London: Aquarian/Thorsons, 1992), 11.

[2] Barbara Walker, *The Crone: Woman of Age, Wisdom, and Power* (New York: Harper & Row, 1985), 54.

[3] Antiga. *Crone and Crony,* "Crone Chronicles," #23, Summer, 1995.

[4] Esther Harding, *Women's Mysteries*, 103.

[5] Henny Carioba, Dorothea Blum, Eugenia Friedman; Laura Payson, Lily Payson, Anna Brinton. Winifred Rawlins, Bettie Chu, Eleanor Perry; Margaret Stannicci, Edith Sullwold, Olga Reigeluth.

[6] Winifred Rawlins, "Anna Cox Brinton," *Roots of Happiness and Other Poems* (Moylan, PA: Whimsie, 1977), 12.

[7] Pendle Hill is a Center for Study and Contemplation, based on Quaker principles, in Wallingford, Pennsylvania. For a catalog and information, write to: Pendle Hill, 338 Plush Mill Road, Wallingford, PA, 19086.

[8] Friends Conference on Religion and Psychology was begun over forty years ago as a place where Quakers and Jungians could share their similar interests and points of view. It has continued in an unbroken line up to the present day. It meets on the Memorial Day Weekend.

[9] Anne Cameron, *Daughters of Copper Woman* (Vancouver: Press Gang, 1981), 149.

[10]In a wonderful gathering of women, Sherry Ruth Anderson

and Patricia Hopkins have written *The Feminine Face of God, The Unfolding of the Sacred in Women* (New York: Bantam, 1991). In the preface, Sherry recounts a powerful dream, at the end of which a group of patriarchs dance around her and tell her "We are celebrating because you, a woman, have consented to accept full spiritual responsibility in your life....And you are not the only one. Many, many women are coming forward now, to lead the way...We have initiated you and we give you our wholehearted blessings. But we no longer know the way.   Our ways do not work anymore. You women must find a new way." 3-4.

[11] Helen Kimberly McElhone, *The Secrets of the Elves* (New York: Devin-Adair, 1913).

[12] I am endlessly amazed at the ways the mind protects and shutters off information and connections.   When Jean Troy-Smith read this manuscript she noted "and your Mother?" at this point. Suddenly I realized I had never considered the possibility that my mother also, in some long-ago era, might have been heavily persecuted for her beliefs and practices.   Even when writing the *"Geas"* in the last chapter, it did not occur to me to think of my own mother, or that I might have been voicing my own personal ancestral spell.

∞ H ∞   Tell Me a Story

[1] Joseph Chilton Pearce, *Evolution's End*, 21-22.

[2] Diane Duane, *The Door into Shadow* (New York: Tom Doherty, 1984). The part about the dragon begins on page 38 and continues throughout the book.

[3] Pearce, *Evolution's End*, 130-134.

[4] *The Findhorn Garden*, by Findhorn Community (New York: Harper & Row, 1968), 24.

[5] Ibid, 79-94.

[6] Ibid, 101.

[7] Ibid. p.125.

[8] There is a lovely little book of photographs of fairies, taken

by two little girls in England. There are letters attesting to the fact that the photographs were not altered in any way. Edward L. Gardner, *Fairies (The Cottingley photographs)* (London: Theosophical, 1966.) There is also the work by Brian Froud and Alan Lee, *Faeries* (New York: Peacock /Bantam, 1978) which depicts in wonderful drawings and text the wide variety of the world of Faerie. They say, in the introduction, "Faerie represents Power, magical power, incomprehensible to humans and hence, inimical."

[9] *The Boy Who Saw True* (Essex, GB: C.W.Daniel 1953).

[10]Diane Stein, *The Women's Book of Healing* (Llewellyn, 1987) has some information on how to see auras.

[11] Pearce, speaking of examples where young children had telepathic and clairvoyant experiences and citing a study in which "virtually all normally hearing children had perfect pitch, but almost all lost it at around age seven," concludes: "The reason for the loss seems to be lack of development and stabilization of such intuitive ability during its specific time for development. If no model is given to stimulate and stabilize the capacity, it atrophies." *Magical Child Matures* (New York: E.P. Dutton, 1985), 68.

[12] Zenna Henderson. *Ingathering*.

∞ I ∞   **Into the Eye**

[1] Barbara G. Walker, *The Woman's Dictionary of Symbols & Sacred Objects* (San Francisco: Harper & Row, 1988) says this symbol is an old one for the dragon's eye. A shape used in the cutting of magical stones and crystals, it "...has an illusory quality. Steady gazing at its center can develop the illusion of three dimensions, so that it appears to be a tetrahedron seen from above or from one corner....The Dragon's Eye also forms a triple triangle, sacred to the ancient Goddess in some of her ninefold forms...this figure and certain of its variations appeared often in medieval books of magic, to invoke the protection of female spirits." 35.

[2] Smaug is the guardian of the treasure in *The Hobbit* by J.R.R. Tolkien. Kalessin is the ancient dragon in Ursula LeGuin's *The Farthest Shore*. Anne McCaffrey writes of the land of Pern where dragons choose their human for life. One of the main characters in Diane Duane's *The Door Into Shadow* is the dragon Hasai.

Years ago I dreamed of a dragon who came flying out of the north, swooping down to me as I stood under the night sky. I wrote of this in "In Praise of Dragons," *Inward Light*, Vol XLIV No.96.

[3] Some stories appear as I read. Edith Wharton, from "Life and I", *Writing Women's Lives* edited by Susan Cahill (New York: HarperPerennial, 1994) recounts a feeling of being "..,myself, an intermediate creature between human beings & animals, & nearer, on the whole to the furry tribes than to homo sapiens. I felt that I *knew things about them*—their sensations, desires & sensibilities—that other bipeds could not guess." 13. Felicitas Goodman remembers the time she began to menstruate was a point of departure from the magical world she previously inhabited. "I noticed the curious impediment first with the fresh, crunchy snow which fell right after my birthday. It was nice, but I could not make it glow. Bewildered, I began paying more attention to my seeming disability. The orange glow of dawn streaming through the bedroom window was the same as before: so was the smell of the horses on the market. But I had changed." *Where the Spirits Ride the Wind, Trance Journeys and Other Ecstatic Experiences*, (Bloomington: Indiana University, 1990), 3. And June Singer tells a wonderful story: "I also remembered that at an early age I knew I was a tiger, but I somehow sensed that this information would not be properly appreciated by my parents." She goes on to recount how one evening when her parents were giving a dinner party, she crept under the table and bit one of the ladies on her ankle. The psychoanalyst to whom she was sent was understanding, and recommended art lessons to give her "imagination" room to roam. "So I was saved from the necessity of abandoning my

secret world, and I had the privilege of keeping to myself the secret knowledge I had concerning my tiger while at the same time bringing forth what lurked inside of me." Fortunate child! *Seeing Through the Visible World: Jung, Gnosis, and Chaos* (New York: HarperSanFrancisco, 1990) ,9-11.

[4] Shepherd, Linda Jean, *Lifting the Veil: The Feminine Face of Science* (Boston: Shambhala, 1993), 19.

[5] Talbot, Michael, *The Holographic Universe* (New York: HarperCollins, 1991), 2.

[6] Bohm, David, *Wholeness and the Implicate Order* (London: Ark, 1980), 156.

[7] T.S. Eliot, *Four Quartets* (New York: Harcourt, Brace, 1943), 3.

[8] Talbot, *The Holographic Universe*, 48.

[9] B.O.T.A, The Builders of the Adytum, provides an in-depth course of study of the Tarot. It is available by mail. Write to B.O.T.A., 5105 North Figueroa Street, Los Angeles, CA, 90042.

[10] Pearce, *Evolution's End*, 3-14.

[11] Pearce. p.10.

[12] Bohm, 6.

[13] A fascinating study of the subject is Sig Lonegren, *Labyrinths: Ancient Myths & Modern Uses* (Somerset, GB: Gothic Image, 1991)."

[14] "Sacred space is a place where one can go to get help in contacting non-physical realms." Ibid, 19. Lonegren has provided an explicit, informative, and interactive book, rich with drawings and exercises.   He says: "Like their other sacred space counterparts, ancient labyrinths were located on power centers...The purpose of sacred space is to enhance the possibility that the supplicant will contact the non-physical, the non-rational. Labyrinths are excellent tools to aid the seeker not only in contacting the numinous, but also in helping the intuitive side of the seeker's being to come to the fore." 22.

[15] Many journeys of this sort are undertaken.   Some find a mountain to climb, as Rene Dumal did in *Mount Analogue* (New York: Pantheon, 1952).   Irene went deep under the mountain in

The Princess and the Goblin. Alberto Manguel & Gianni Guadalupi, *The Dictionary of Imaginary Places* (New York: Harcourt Brace Jovanovich, 1987), lists hundreds of journeys to mystical lands and fabled isles. They are all real; our inner journeys change us irrevocably, we discover new connections, meet strange guides, set out on new paths of life when we return. We are always changed.

[16] The Serenity Prayer, widely used, is a foundation of Alcoholics Anonymous:

> God/Goddess, grant me the Serenity to accept the things
> I cannot change;
> Courage to change the things I can;
> And the wisdom to know the difference.

[17] I find myself repeatedly using computer terminology to describe the processes of the psyche. It always delights and astounds me, how closely they match.

[18] Caryl Churchill, *Vinegar Tom*, music by Helen Glavin (New York: Samuel French, 1978), 38.

[19]These men, among others, have been exploring and writing about the joys and difficulties of being male in our society. They bring a wonderful perspective to the struggle. Some of their books are:

James Hillman, *Puer Papers* (Dallas:Spring, 1994).

Sam Keen, *Fire in the Belly: On Being a Man* (New York: Bantam, 1991).

Michael Meade, *Men and The Water of Life: Initiation and the Tempering of Men* (New York: HarperSanFrancisco, 1993).

[20] Duncan was the originator of Modern Dance. In the 1920's her free style, unencumbered by the formal stiffness of balletic costume, grew popular and had many followers, some of whom went on to develop the techniques used by modern dancers today.

∞ J ∞   Medusa, The Myth Unfolded

[1]See Barbara G. Walker, *The Woman's Encyclopedia of Myths*

and Secrets (New York: Harper & Row, 1983), 629.

² Adam McLean, *The Triple Goddess: An Exploration of the Archetypal Feminine* (Grand Rapids, MI: Phanes Press, 1989), 39.

³See Walker, 629.

⁴See Walker, 721.

⁵ Demetra George, *Mysteries of the Dark Moon: The Healing Power of the Dark Goddess* (New York: HarperSanFrancisco, 1992), 159.

⁶ Walker, (gorgon),349, (menstrual blood), 635;   George, (menstrual blood and the Gorgon Head), 159,

⁷ George, 159-60.

⁸ See Elinor W. Gadon, *The Once and Future Goddess*; Demetra George, *Mysteries of the Dark Moon*; Donna Wilshire, *Virgin, Mother, Crone, Myths & Mysteries of the Triple Goddess* (Rochester, VT: Inner Traditions, 1994), among others.

⁹ "Memory sleeps coiled
    like a snake in a basket
    of grain
    deep in the storehouse
  Breathe deep
  Let your breath take you down

    Find the way there
    And you will find the way out
Starhawk, *Truth or Dare*, 70.

¹⁰ Adam McLean, *The Triple Goddess*, 110.

¹¹ Jean Houston "Calling Our Spirits Home", *Noetic Sciences Review* 32 (Winter, 1994): 11.

¹² The cards I use here are *Motherpeace Round Tarot* by Vicki Noble and Karen Vogel.   The accompanying book is by Vicki Nobel, *Motherpeace: A Way to the Goddess through Myth, Art, and Tarot* (New York: Harper & Row, 1983), 171.

¹³ Ibid, 168.

¹⁴ Ibid, 171-2.

¹⁵ D.H.Lawrence, "Making Pictures", *The Creative Process: A Symposium*, Brewster Gheselin, ed. (Berkeley: New American

Library, 1952), 69.

∞ **K** ∞   **Wise Body**

[1] Christine Downing, *The Goddess: Mythological Images of the Feminine* (New York: Crossroad, 1981).

Stephanie Demetrakopoulos, *Listening to our Bodies: The Rebirth of Feminine Wisdom* (Boston: Beacon, 1983).

ChristineNorthrup.*Women'sBodies, Women's Wisdom*, (New York: Bantam, 1984).

[2] Cerridwen Fallingstar, *The Heart of the Fire.*

Elizabeth Cunningham, *The Return of the Goddess: A Divine Comedy* (Barrytown, NY: Station Hill, 1992).

[3] Among the many slang words for vagina is "box".

[4] For an excellent source of information about exceptional experiences, see Rhea White's journal, *Exceptional Human Experience* and newsletter, *Exceptional Human Experience News.* Write to: The Exceptional Human Experience Network, 414 Rockledge Rd., New Bern, NC, 28562.

[5] In this place, images flow freely as in dreams, leaving their associations to be explained later. Mary is the Virgin Mother who is so often depicted enclosed in the almond shaped *vesica piscis* (ancient symbol for the vulva) or mandorla. Georgia O'Keeffe painted from nature, frequently entering into the heart of flowers. Although she never acknowledged that her paintings were anything other than the form she was painting, countless women have enjoyed the sensuality and intimacy connecting them with their own bodily experiences which her images arouse. Judy Chicago has been openly graphic about her desire to portray the female body as generative and sensual. Her major work, *The Dinner Table*, is a series of place settings, each one depicting scenes from the life of an important woman, from Gaia to O'Keeffe. The large ceramic plates are designed with the *vesica piscis* as the central shape, each one embellished and varied depending on the woman it is reflecting.

[6] Erishkegal, the sister of Inanna, Ruler of the Underworld.

[7] The American College Dictionary.

∞ L ∞   **Magical Woman**

[1] May Sarton writes of her daily life in her wonderful journals. Through her words we are privileged to have a window into the world of a woman who has travelled widely in body, soul, and imagination. She writes of her pleasure in her garden, of her dear friends, of her houses. Simple things, like the fall of sun on a polished floor on a summer morning remind us of the value of living within the moment, of treasuring the present, of finding truth in a single flower. "The early morning walk around the garden is contemplative. It is not a time to work but rather a time to taste the air, and not only to look at the flowers but to look out beyond the tamed world to the long meadow and the great trees beyond it, for they too are always changing. A most delightful thing about this garden is the wilderness it lies in, a small orderly pocket in a vast natural world." *Plant Dreaming Deep* (New York: Norton, 1968), 123.

[2] In an article on psychedelics, the following comment provides an interesting perspective. "Hallucinogenic plants with magical as well as healing properties were essential elements of this indigenous pharmacopeia. In taking action against the indigenous use of psychotropic plants, the Church of that period sought to eliminate a perceived threat to its oligarchic powers and reassert its monopoly on legitimate access to the supernatural. By casting the healer as a witch and the hallucinogenic plants as tools of Satan, the Church succeeded not only in eliminating competition with the elite physician class but also in virtually eradicating knowledge of these vestiges of pagan and shamanic consciousness."

Charles Grob and Willis Harmon, "Making Sense of the Psychedelic Issue", *Noetic Sciences Review* 35 (Autumn 1995): 9.

[3] This fear has become so widespread that it has become its own archetype, resulting in Black magic which is used for personal power and which contains strange distortions.

[4] Doreen Valiente, *Natural Magic* (Custer, WA: Phoenix, 1975), 9.

[5] Starhawk tells us: "Magic teaches that living beings are beings of energy and spirit as well as matter, that energy—what the Chinese call *chi*—flows in certain patterns throughout the human body, and can be raised, stored, shaped, and sent." *Truth or Dare*, 24.

[6] One of the lovelier and more educated works which address this subject is Annie Dillard's *Pilgrim at Tinker Creek* (New York: Bantam, 1974). "What I aim to do is not so much learn the names of the shreds of creation that flourish in this valley, but to keep myself open to their meanings, which is to try to impress myself at all times with the fullest possible force of their very reality. I want to have things as multiply and intricately as possible present and visible in my mind." 140.

[7] Cameron, *Copper Woman*, 147.

[8] *Context* — derived from the Latin *contexere*, meaning to weave or braid together (American College Dictionary). Weaving all the parts into a sense of self, free from repression, brings the inconsistencies into view.

[9] "*Omphalos*, Greek transliteration of Latin *umbilicus*, the navel or hub of the world, center of the Goddess's body, source of all things. As every ancient nation regarded its own version of the Great Mother as the cosmic spirit, so its own capital or chief temple was located at the center of the earth, marked by the stone*omphalos* that concentrated the Mother's essence." Walker, *Women's Encyclopedia of Myths and Secrets*, 740.

[10] T.S.Eliot, *Four Quartets*.

[11] Mary Field Belenky, Blythe McVicker Clinchy, Nancy Rule Goldberger, Jill Mattuck Tarule, *Women's Ways of Knowing; The Development of Self, Voice, and Mind* (New York: Basic, HarperCollins, 1986), 141.

[12] Joseph Chilton Pearce, "The Roots of Intelligence", Sounds True.

[13] For good references to the various aspects of the Women's Spirituality movement see:

Margot Adler, *Drawing Down the Moon* (Boston: Beacon, 1979). Cynthia Eller, *Living in the Lap of the Goddess: The Feminist Spirituality Movement in America* (New York: Crossroad, 1993).

[14] There are many resources for Wicca. Starhawk, *The Spiral Dance, A Rebirth of the Ancient Religion of the Great Goddess* (New York:Harper & Row, 1979), is a good place to begin. There are also many newsletters. Two are "Circle Network News", Box 219, Mt. Horeb, WI.,53572, and "Of a Like Mind", Box 6677, Madison, WI, 53716.

[15] Ellen Goodman. "Barbarism reaches our shores." (CT: "The New London Day," October 20, 1995), an article about female genital mutilation and its increasing occurrence in America. She notes "It happens among people who regard a women's sexuality as so dangerous that it must be eliminated."

[16] Again I want to emphasize that both men and women have access to the Feminine. The way women experience it is different, by nature, from that of men. I am weaving the awareness of women's reality and therefore do not always make the reference to men who are sensitive to, honor, and incorporate the Feminine. I do not mean to be exclusionary.

∞ M ∞   Can You Imagine...

[1] Margaret Ball, *Changeweaver* (Riverdale, NY: Baen, 1993).

[2] See Rix Weaver *The Old Wise Woman: A Study of Active Imagination* (New York: G.P.Putnam's Sons, 1973), for a good description of this technique.

[3] For an extensive listing of many of these abilities, see Michael Talbot, *Holographic Universe.*

Also, Rhea White, *Exceptional Human Experience.*

[4] "If we strive to function as fully ensouled beings, we must expand our understanding of nature in order to obtain the physical vehicle capable of operating within the full light of the soul." Machaelle Small Wright, *Behaving as if the God in All Life Mattered* (Jefferson, VA: Perelandra, 1987), 176.

∞ **N** ∞   **Ancient Connections**

¹ It is time. Our world is in crisis on every front, and we can no longer wait. Change happens whether we want it or not, and there are major shifts taking place. Some say there will be cataclysmic earth changes which will eliminate part of the seacoasts, rearranging the geography of the earth. Others feel there is an evolutionary shift occurring which will result in the transformation of humans into the next phase of our development. It is evident that the former is already in process as we note an increase in earthquake activity, major flooding, fires, and hurricanes. The evolutionary activity is not so noticeable and does not make the front page headlines nor the top spot on the evening news. It manifests in the quiet decisions of individuals to not participate in certain activities and attitudes. There is a growing understanding about the limitations which our addictions place upon our lives, and men and women are learning to shed their dependence upon alcohol, drugs, food, and other addictive behaviors. There is an interest in healthy eating, in exercise, in meditation. People who are making these changes are able to see themselves and others more clearly and participate more fully in their lives. I believe there are cellular changes occurring which will, in time, shift the way our brains and bodies operate and these changes will have better opportunity to occur in a system which is functioning more clearly.

². Linda Jean Shepherd, *Lifting The Veil*, 94.

³. Olga Broumas, "Artemis," *Beginning with O* (New Haven: Yale University, 1977), 24.

⁴ Jean Houston, Mystery school tapes, January (Boulder: Wind Over The Earth, 1995), Tape 1, side one.

⁵ Duane Elgin, *Awakening Earth: Exploring the Evolution of Human Culture and Consciousness* (New York: William Morrow, 1993), 303.

⁶ When an apple is split in half across, the seeds form the

pattern of the pentagram.

∞ O ∞   **In My End is My Beginning**

[1] T.S. Eliot, *Four Quartets*, 4.

[2] *The Hundredth Monkey*, a story popular in the 1960's.

[3] Jean Houston, speaking about the ancient Sumerian understanding of the universe:
"The cycles of heavenly time were minutely aligned with the passage of time on earth, even with the pulse rate in the human body. And that humanity, by attuning the cycles of its own life with the life of the earth to the immensly greater cycles of the cosmic time to the life of the blood flow in their body could not only discover their place and role in the universe but could cooperate with unseen powers of nature that ordered this hidden relationship." Mystery School, First session, 1995, tape 2, side A.

[4] Morris Berman, *The Reenchantment of the World*, 16.

[5] Philip Slater, *Earthwalk* (New York: Bantam, 1975), 233.

[6] "...for they had connected directly with life and not with its reflection; the mysteries they found themselves involved in, simply by being alive and knowing each other, carried them much deeper into reality than 'society' often permits people to get." Alice Walker, *The Temple of My Familiar* (Simon & Schuster, 1989), 192.

[7] Peter Marshall, *Nature's Web*, 390.

[8] This term is proposed by Morris Berman.

[9] In a wonderful reversal of opinions which had been held for years, physicists discovered there was order in the seemingly inconsequential small anomalies they had been ignoring, thus giving rise to the theory of Chaos. This is intelligently and clearly set forth by James Gleick in *Chaos: Making a New Science*.

∞ Selected Bibliography ∞

Adler, Margot. *Drawing Down the Moon.* Boston: Beacon, 1986.

Anderson, Sherry Ruth and Patricia Hopkins. *The Feminine Face of God: The Unfolding of the Sacred in Women.* New York: Bantam, 1991.

Anonymous. *The Boy who Saw True.* Essex, GB: The C.W. Daniel Company, 1953.

American College Dictionary. New York: Random House, 1968.

Atwood, Margaret. *The Handmaid's Tale.* New York: Fawcett, 1985.

Ball, Margaret. *Changeweaver.* New York: Baen, 1993.

Belenky, Mary Field, Blythe McVicker Clinchy, Nancy Rule Goldberger, Jill Mattuck Tarule. *Women's Ways of Knowing: The Development of Self, Voice, and Mind.* New York: HarperCollins, 1986.

Berman, Morris. *The Reenchantment of the World.* Ithaca: Cornell University, 1981.

Bigwood, Carol. *Earth Muse: Feminism. Nature, and Art.* Philadelphia: Temple University, 1993.

Bohm, David. *Wholeness and the Implicate Order.* New York: Ark, 1980.

Boyle, Kay. *The Youngest Camel.* Boston: Little, Brown, 1939.

Brooke Medicine Eagle. *White Buffalo Woman Comes Singing.* New York: Ballantine, 1991.

Broumas, Olga. *Beginning With O.* New Haven: Yale University, 1977.

Brown, Lyn Mikel and Carol Gilligan. *Meeting at the Crossroads: Women's Psychology and Girl's Development.* New York: Ballantine, 1992.

Cameron, Anne. *Daughters of Copper Woman.* Vancouver: Press Gang, 1981.

_____ *The Annie Poems.* Madeira Park, BC: Harbour, 1987.

Chernin, Kim. *The Flame Bearers.* New York: Harper & Row, 1986.

_____ *Reinventing Eve: Modern Woman in Search of Herself.* New York: Times, 1987.

Chicago, Judy. *The Dinner Party: A Symbol of Our Heritage.* Garden City: Doubleday, 1979.

Chrisler, Joan C. and Doris Howard, eds. *New Directions in Feminist Psychology: Practice, Theory, and Research.* New York: Springer, 1992.

Christ, Carol P. *Diving Deep and Surfacing: Women Writers on Spiritual Quest.* Boston: Beacon, 1980.

Christ, Carol P. and Judith Plaskow, ed. *Womanspirit Rising: A Feminist Reader in Religion.* New York: HarperSanFrancisco, 1992.

Churchill, Caryl. *Vinegar Tom.* New York: Samuel French, 1978.

Cirlot, J.E. *An Illustrated Encyclopedia of Traditional Symbols.* London: Thames and Hudson, 1978.

Clarke, Arthur C. *Childhood's End.* New York: Ballentine.

Cooper, J.C. *An Illustrated Encyclopedia of Traditional Symbols.* London: Thames and Hudson,1978.

Cooper, Susan. *The Dark is Rising.* New York: Atheneum, 1973.

Cunningham, Elizabeth. *The Return of the Goddess, A Divine Comedy.* New York: Station Hill, 1992.

Daly, Mary. *Gyn/Ecology.* Boston: Beacon, 1978.

DeCastillego, Irene Claremont. *Knowing Woman, a Feminine Psychology.* New York: G.P Putnam's Sons, 1973.

Demetrakopoulos, Stephanie. *Listening to our Bodies: The Rebirth of Feminine Wisdom.* Boston: Beacon, 1983.

Diamond, Irene and Gloria Feman Orenstein, eds. *Reweaving the World: The Emergence of Ecofeminism.* San Francisco: Sierra Club, 1990 .

Dillard, Annie. *Pilgrim at Tinker Creek: A Mystical Excursion Into the Natural World.* New York: Bantam, 1974.

Dossey, Larry. *Recovering the Soul: A Scientific and Spiritual Search.* New York: Bantam, 1989.

Downing, Christine. *The Goddess: Mythological Images of the Feminine.* New York: Crossroad, 1981.

_____, ed. *Mirrors of the Self: Archetypal Images That Shape Your Life.* Los Angeles: Jeremy P. Tarcher, 1991.

Duane, Diane. *The Door Into Shadow.* New York: Tom Doherty, 1984.

Dumal, René. *Mount Analogue.* New York: Pantheon, 1952.

Ehrenriech, Barbara and Deirdre English. *For Her Own Good: 150 Years of the Experts' Advice to Women.* New York: Doubleday, Anchor, 1978.

Eisler, Riane. *The Chalice and the Blade: Our History Our Future.* New York: Harper & Row, 1988.

Elgin, Duane. *Awakening Earth: Exploring the Evolution of Human Culture and Consciousness.* New York: William Morrow, 1993.

Eliot, T.S. *Four Quartets.* New York: Harcourt, Brace, 1943.

Eller, Cynthia. *Living in the Lap of the Goddesss.* New York: Crossroad, 1993.

Fallingstar, Cerridwen. *The Heart of the Fire.* San Geronimo, CA: Cauldron, 1990.

Faludi, Susan. *Backlash: The Undeclared War Against American Women.* New York: Crown, 1991.

Findhorn Community. *The Findhorn Garden.* New York: Harper & Row, 1975.

Flinders, Carol Lee. *Enduring Grace: Living Portraits of Seven Women Mystics.* New York: HarperSanFrancisco, 1993.

_____ *Enduring Grace.* Audio tapes. Boulder, CO: Sounds True.

Froud, Brian and Alan Lee. *Faeries.* New York: Peacock/Bantam, 1978.

Gardner, Edward L. *Fairies (The Cottingley photographs)* London:Theosophical, 1966.

Gadon, Elinor W. *The Once and Future Goddess: A Sweeping Visual Chronicle of the Sacred Female and Her Reemergence in the Cultural Mythology of Our Time.* New York: Harper & Row, 1989.

George, Demetra. *Mysteries of the Dark Moon: The Healing Power of the Dark Goddess.* New York: HarperSanFrancisco, 1992.

Gilman, Greer Ilene. *Moonwise.* New York: Penguin, 1991.

Gimbutas, Marija. *The Language of the Goddess.* New York: HarperSanFrancisco, 1991.

Gleick, James. *Chaos, Making a New Science.* New York: Penguin, 1987.

Goodman, Felicitas D. *Where the Spirits Ride the Wind: Trance Journeys and Other Ecstatic Experiences.* Bloomington: Indiana University, 1990.

Gould, Stephen Jay. *Wonderful Life, The Burgess Shale and the Nature of History.* New York: W.W. Norton, 1989.

Grahn, Judy. *Blood, Bread, and Roses.* Boston: Beacon, 1993.

Griffin, Susan. *Pornography and Silence.* New York: Harper & Row, 1981.

Hall, Nor. *The Moon and the Virgin: Reflections on the Archetypal Feminine*: New York: Harper & Row, 1980

Hamilton, Edith. *Mythology: Timeless Tales of Gods and Heroes.* New York: New American, 1940.

Harding, M. Esther. *Woman's Mysteries: Ancient and Modern.* New York: Harper & Row, 1971.

Henderson, Zenna. *Ingathering, The Complete People Stories.* Mark and Priscilla Olson, eds. Framingham, MA: NESFA, 1995.

Herder Symbol Dictionary. Trans. Boris Matthews. Wilmette, IL: Chiron, 1986.

Hillman, James and Michael Ventura. *We've Had a Hundred Years of Psychotherapy—And the World's Getting Worse.* New York: HarperSanFrancisco, 1992.

Houston, Jean. "Mystery School" tapes. Boulder: Wind Over The Earth, 1995.

Jung, C.G. H.G. Baynes, trans., revision R.F.C. Hull. *Collected Works,* Vol. 6, 8, 9i, 9ii, 10. Bollingen Series XX, Princeton: Princeton University, 1971.

Kiersey, David and Marilyn Bates. *Please Understand Me.* Del Mar, CA: Prometheus Nemesis, 1978.

Koltov, Barbara Black. *Weaving Woman: Essays in Feminine Psychology from the Notebooks of a Jungian Analyst.* York Beach, ME: Nicolas-Hays, 1990.

Kramer, Heinrich and Jacob Sprenger. *Malleus Maleficarum: The Hammer of Witches.* Pennethorne Huges, ed., Montague Summers, trans. London: Folio Society, 1968.

Lawrence, D.H. "Making Pictures", *The Creative Process: A Symposium.* Brewster Gheselin, ed. Berkeley: New American, 1952.

Lederer, Wolfgang. *The Fear of Women.* New York: Grune & Stratton, 1968.

LeGuin, Ursula K. *The Farthest Shore.* New York: Bantam, 1972.

Lerner, Gerda. *The Creation of Feminist Consciousness.* New York: Oxford University, 1993.

Lerner, Harriet G. *The Dance of Deception.* New York: HarperCollins, 1993.

Lonegren, Sig. *Labyrinths: Ancient Myths & Modern Uses.* Somerset, GB: Gothic Image, 1991.

Lorde, Audre. *The Black Unicorn.* New York: Norton, 1978.

Macdonald, George. *The Princess and the Goblin.* New York: Grosset & Dunlap, 1907.

Manguel, Alberto and Gianni Guadalupi. *Dictionary of Imaginary Places.* New York: Harcourt Brace Jovanovich, 1987.

Marshall, Peter. *Nature's Web: Rethinking Our Place on Earth.* New York: Paragon, 1994.

Matthews, Caitlin. *Sophia Goddess of Wisdom: The Divine Feminine from Black Goddess to World-Soul.* New York: HarperCollins, 1992

McCaffrey, Anne. *To Ride Pegasus.* New York: Ballantine, 1973.

_____ *Get Off the Unicorn.* New York: Ballantine, 1977.

McElhone, Helen Kimberly. *The Secrets of the Elves.* Devin-Adair, 1913.

McKillip, Patricia A. *The Riddle Master of Hed.* New York: Ballantine, 1976.

McLean, Adam. *The Triple Goddesses: An Exploration of the Archetypal Feminine.* Hermetic Research Series Number 1. Grand Rapids, MI: Phanes, 1989.

Meador, Betty DeShong. *Uncursing the Dark: Treasures from the Underworld.* Wilmette, IL: Chiron, 1994.

Moustakas, Clark. *Heuristic Research: Design, Methodology, and Applications.* Newbury Park, CA: Sage, 1990.

Nicoll, Maurice. *Commentaries on the Teachings of Gurdjieff and Ouspensky.* Five vols. London: Stuart & Watkins, 1970.

Noble, Vicki and Karen Vogel. *Motherpeace Round Tarot.*

Noble, Vicki. *Motherpeace: A Way to the Goddess through Myth, Art, and Tarot.* New York: Harper & Row, 1983.

Noddings, Nel. *Women and Evil.* Berkeley: University of California, 1989.

Northrup, Christine. *Women's Bodies, Women's Wisdom.* New York: Bantam, 1994.

Parabola XVII #2 (Summer 1992) "Labyrinth".

Pearce, Joseph Chilton. *Evolution's End: Claiming the Potential of Our Intelligence.* New York: HarperSanFrancisco, 1992.

_____ *Magical Child.* New York: Plume, 1977.

_____ *Magical Child Matures.* New York: E.P. Dutton, 1958.

_____ *The Roots of Intelligence.* Audio tape. Sounds True.

Perera, Sylvia Brinton. *Descent to the Goddess, A Way of Initiation for Women.* Toronto: Inner City, 1981.

Rawlins, Winifred. *Roots of Happiness and Other Poems.* Moylan, PA: Whimsie, 1977.

Reed, Donna, director. *The Burning Times.* Video. Santa Monica, CA: Direct Cinema.

Reinharz, Shulamit. *Feminist Methods in Social Research.* New York: Oxford University, 1992.

Rich, Adrienne. *A Wild Patience Has Taken Me This Far.* NY: W.W. Norton, 1981.

Ruddick, Nicholas. *State of the Fantastic; Studies in the Theory and Practice of Fantastic Literature and Film.* Ed. Brien Attebery. Westport, CT: Greenwood, 1990.

Sarton, May. *Plant Dreaming Deep.* New York: W.W. Norton, 1968.

Shepherd, Linda Jean. *Lifting the Veil; The Feminine Face of Science.* Boston: Shambhala, 1993.

Singer, June. *Seeing Through the Visible World: Jung, Gnosis, and Chaos.* New York: HarperSanFrancisco, 1990.

_____, *Boundaries of the Soul,The Practice of Jung's Psychology* . Garden City: Doubleday, 1973.

Slater, Philip. *Earthwalk.* New York: Bantam, 1975.

Sjoo, Monica and Barbara Mor, *The Great Cosmic Mother: Rediscovering the Religion of the Earth,* 2nd Edition. New York: HarperSanFrancisco, 1991.

Starhawk. *The Spiral Dance: A Rebirth of the Ancient Religion of the Great Goddess.* New York: Harper & Row, 1979.

_____ *Truth or Dare: Encounters with Power , Authority and Mystery.* New York: HarperSanFrancisco, 1987.

Stein, Diane. *The Women's Book of Healing.* St.Paul: Llewellyn, 1987.

Stone, Merlin. *When God Was A Woman.* New York: A Harvest/HBJ Book, Harcourt Brace Jovanovich, 1976.

Talbot, Michael. *The Holographic Universe. New York: Harper Collins, 1991.*

Thomas, Dylan. *Dylan Thomas: The Poems.* London: J.M. Dent, 1971.

Tolkien, J.R.R. *The Hobbit.* Boston: Houghton Mifflin, 1938.

Travers, P.L. *Mary Poppins and Mary Poppins Comes Back.* New York: Harcourt Brace & World, 1934.

Ulanov, Anne Bedford. *The Feminine in Jungian Psychology and in Christian Theology.* Evanston: Northwestern University, 1971.

Valiente, Doreen. *Natural Magic.* Custer, WA: Phoenix, 1975.

Waldrop, M. Mitchell. *Complexity, The Emerging Science at the Edge of Order and Chaos.* New York: Simon & Schuster, 1992.

Walker, Alice. *Possessing the Secret of Joy.* New York: Harcourt Brace Jovanovich, 1992.

_____ *The Temple of My Familiar.* New York: Simon & Schuster, 1989.

Walker, Barbara. *The Crone: Woman of Age, Wisdom, and Power.* New York: Harper & Row, 1985.

_____ *The Woman's Dictionary of Symbols and Sacred Objects.* New York: Harper & Row, 1988.

_____ *The Woman's Encyclopedia of Myths and Secrets*. New York: Harper &Row, 1983.

Weaver, Rix. *The Old Wise Woman: A Study of Active Imagination*. New York: Putnam, 1973.

Weinstein, Marion. *Positive Magic: Occult Seld-Help*. Canada: Phoenix, 1978.

White, Rhea A. *Exceptional Human Experience: Studies of the Psychic, Spontaneous, Intangible*. Vols. 8,9. Dix Hills, NY: Parapsychology Sources of Information Center, 1990, 1991.

Whitmont, Edward C. *The Symbolic Quest: Basic Concepts of Analytical Psychology*. Princeton: Princeton University, 1969.

Wickes, Francis G. *The Inner World of Man*. New York: Farrar & Rinehart, 1938.

Williams, Selma R. and Pamela Williams Adelman. *Riding the Nightmare: Woman & Witchcraft from the Old World to Colonial Salem*. New York: Harper, 1978.

Wilshire, Donna. *Virgin, Mother, Crone, Myths & Mysteries of the Triple Goddess*. Rochester, VT: Inner Traditions, 1994.

Woodman, Marion. *Conscious Femininity: Interviews with Marion Woodman*. Toronto: Inner City, 1993.

Wright, Machaelle Small. *Behaving as if the God in All Life Mattered: A New Age Ecology*. Jeffersonton, VA: Perelandra, 1987.

Zwinger, Susan and Ann Zwinger. *Women in Wilderness: Writings and Photographs*. New York: Harcourt Brace, 1995.

∞ Index ∞

—A—

angel, 2, 22, 38, 103, 104, 107, 166, 183
apple, 14, 15, 70, 136, 188
Aquarius, 3, 14, 142
archetype, 48, 67-70, 128, 179
Athena, 5, 123, 125, 126, 148, 149, 151
Atwood, Margaret, 67
auras, 97, 98
azalea, 30, 31

—B—

birth, 7, 21, 34, 35, 48, 137, 148
Bohm, David, 107, 108
box, 140, 141, 143, 145
brain, 2, 5, 12, 48, 93, 161, 182
Brown, Lyn Mikel, 49

—C—

Cameron, Anne, 157
candle, 66, 154
cat, 36, 37, 163
clay, 144, 199, 200, 201
crone, 82

—D—

Daughters of Copper Woman, 86

depression, 26, 54, 57, 74, 217
devil, 9, 66, 69
dragon, 43, 45, 94-5, 99, 105- 6, 111, 120, 123, 134, 203
dream, 95, 105, 121, 170, 180-182, 186

—E—

egg, 62, 144, 186, 190
Eliot, T.S., iv, 109, 160
elves, 44, 88, 97, 98, 173
Erishkegal, 145
Eve, 14, 15, 69, 70, 71, 136
evil, 9, 15, 16, 69, 70, 123-125, 127, 136

—F—

Feminine, 6, 9, 15, 16, 20, 25, 48-51, 55-58, 63, 64, 124, 161, 163, 179
Findhorn, 96
flying, 2, 11, 39, 46, 47, 94, 95, 100-102, 106, 143, 166, 168-173, 183
fog, 42-4, 60, 72- 78, 163, 203
friends, 97, 109, 116, 189, 193, 196, 197, 199, 200, 204
Friends, see also Quaker, 20, 84, 85

—G—

Geas, 77, 79, 80, 155, 203
Gilligan, Carol, 49
Goddess, 4, 9, 16, 20-4, 52, 56,
   57, 61, 70, 77, 118, 125-128,
   136, 144, 159, 161
Gorgon, 121, 123, 125, 126,
   129, 150, 151
grandmother, 60, 82, 83, 85, 86,
   89, 90, 121, 175
Greece, 148, 149
Gurdjieff, 75

—H—

Harding, M. Esther, 56
Henderson, Zenna, 45, 46, 102,
   173
heuristic, 51, 211
Hobbit, 28, 44
holographic universe, 109, 201
Houston, Jean, 128, 183, 243

—I—

infinity, 160, 162, 193

—J—

Jung, C. J., 6, 11, 12, 15, 20, 26,
   48, 56, 67, 109, 169

—L—

labyrinth, 110-113, 115, 137,
   139, 151
Lilith, 16
little people, 37, 95, 96, 97, 107,
   173, 217

—M—

magic, 3, 4, 5, 44-6, 50, 88, 100,
   131, 154-5, 158-9, 161, 163,
   167, 169, 175, 181, 185, 197,
   206
mandorla, 41, 137, 144
Mary Poppins, 38, 166
Masculine, 15, 20, 49, 124, 179,
   180
mask, 121, 127, 150, 192, 199,
   200, 206, 207
maze, 21, 43, 111-114, 133, 141,
   147, 150, 151, 157, 159, 203
McCaffrey, Anne, 47
McLean, Adam, 128
Medusa, 4, 5, 70, 121-3, 125-9,
   131, 134, 136, 141, 146, 147,
   149, 150-152, 159, 163, 183
Metis, 125, 126, 148
moon, 7, 19, 20-4, 52, 58, 59,
   99, 100, 112, 126
mother, 31, 33-5, 53, 54, 58, 60-
   64, 71, 74-5, 78, 84, 86, 89,
   90, 140, 155, 159, 165, 167-
   170, 175, 184, 202
Moustakas, Clark, 51
mysteries, 19, 50, 63, 115, 121,
   123, 126-7, 137, 141, 148-
   151, 159, 197, 198, 205, 206
myth, 123, 125, 136, 147-8,
   151, 217

—N—

nature, 9, 14, 22, 30, 33-5, 39,
   48, 87, 96, 110, 154, 161,
   178-9, 181, 183, 194-5, 197,
   201, 217

—O—

occult, 3, 154
Omphalos, 62, 159

—P—

Pendle Hill, 85, 189
penguin, 31, 32
priestess, 70

—Q—

Quaker, 20, 75, 85, 109
quantum physics, 11, 13, 108,
   201

—R—

Rawlins, Winifred, 84, 85
repression, 54, 57, 58, 67, 70,
   140-2, 158, 195

—S—

Serena, 130, 135
serpent, 16, 70, 78-9, 125-6,
   134, 136, 142, 146, 147
Sheldrake, Rupert, 12, 36
silver, 58, 59, 143, 146
snake, 121, 125, 126, 147, 150,
   151, 155
solitary, 177, 187, 189
Sophia, 52, 81, 125, 134
spell, 17, 43, 74-9, 150, 155,

203
swamp, 42, 74
Sybil, 131, 136, 137

—T—

tarot, 132, 191
terror, 19, 55, 62, 71, 89, 116,
   127, 142
Transcendent Function, 26
Triple Goddess, 24, 25, 125, 128,
   130

—U—

Unseen World, 22, 28, 204

—V—

vagina, 62, 140
Verdun, 66

—W—

weaver, 47, 158
Weinstein, Marion, 22
Wicca, 22, 161, 177
wise woman, 19, 81, 82, 85
witch, 61, 69, 71, 82, 116, 124,
   195
witchhunt, 4, 5, 72
woman's body, 42, 58, 62, 139,
   156
woman's wisdom, 82, 142
WOW, 92, 94

ORDER FORM

Please send me _____ copies of
*The Dragon's Eye: Envisioning Women's
Wisdom*

Name_____

Address_____

City/Town_____

State_____ Zip_____

Please include check or money order for $16.95
plus postage and packaging: $4.00 for first class, $2.50
for book rate.

Matrix Press
Box 119
Groton, CT, 06340